"Admittedly, in Hughes final years, with his many trials and accidents somewhat diminished his ability to utilize his time and many challenges as effectively as he had in his younger years. But even in his last days he was as sharp and as in charge of his life and his empire as he had been in his youth. Those of us who shared much of our time close to Howard Hughes can strongly testify to this to his last breath and until his allotted time and last minutes of life ran out."

—James J. Whetton, James Leo Wadsworth, and Wilbur S. Thain

We Knew HOWARD HUGHES

A Collection of Memoirs

WHETTON   WADSWORTH   THAIN

BookWise
publishing

This Howard Hughes as we remember him.

We'll never forget.

We called him our friend.

We were there.

We Knew HOWARD HUGHES

Best of Wishes for Ray [signature]

James J. Whetton

James Leo Wadsworth

Wilbur S. Thain, MD

with Ellie Pugmire and Gordon Bench

We Knew Howard Hughes: A Collection of Memoirs

James J. Whetton , James Leo Wadsworth, and Wilbur S. Thain

© Copyright 2012 by James J. Whetton , James Leo Wadsworth, and Wilbur S. Thain

All rights reserved.

BookWise Publishing

www.bookwisepublishing.com

www.weknewhowardhughes.com

Library of Congress Cataloging-in-Publication Data
Library of Congress Control Number: 2012917530
James J. Whetton , James Leo Wadsworth, and Wilbur S. Thain
We Knew Howard Hughes: A Collection of Memoirs

ISBN 978-1-60645-100-7 Soft Cover
ISBN 978-1-60645-103-8 Hard Cover
ISBN 978-1-60645-104-5 eBook

First Printing
1 2 3 4 5 6 7 8 9 10

Acknowledgements

There are so many people to whom we need to express appreciation.

Ellie Pugmire and Gordon Bench for their contributions.

Nancy Campbell Allen for her compilation of all of these stories and organizing what was an overwhelming job for a few old men.

Brian Hailes for his excellent cover illustration.

Paul Killpack for his design.

Karen Christoffersen . . . without her professional guidance and encouragement this book of remembering Howard Robard Hughes would never have come to be.

Contents

Howard Hughes

Prologue

Thirty years after the death of Howard Robard Hughes, Jr., there are dozens of accounts of his life, some told by supposed friends, gathering dust on many a bookshelf around the world. One might ask, why another book about Hughes? The answer is simple—because the truth has yet to be told.

Most of the people who actually knew and talked with Howard Hughes are dead, gone without ever writing their memories down. And many of those who published their experiences with Hughes have denigrated his memory or failed to offer anything positive about his life—so he continues to be terribly and totally misunderstood.

The fact is that Howard Hughes let very few people get close to him, therefore few people really knew him. Even as the years pass, his name and persona still carry a passionate mystique as one of the most influential entrepreneurs and industrialists of our time. But what is the true story? In previously published works concerning this great American, many "facts" have been gleaned from newspapers, gossip columns, or second- and third-hand oral reports. Very few, if any, of these authors actually knew Hughes or had any type of relationship with him. These authors and their books are mostly self-serving, and in many cases, they are dishonest and incorrect. Yes, these books cover all phases of his life—his women, airplanes, movies, friends, enemies, medical problems, and drugs—but they do not reveal the true core of the man who changed our world for the better.

The three of us (with contributors Ellie Pugmire and Gordon Bench) all worked closely with Hughes and have come together in an attempt to provide a more accurate picture of the person we knew and most loyally admired. In spite of Hughes' bad publicity as a playboy, eccentric, recluse, and someone who was continually vilified by a press with a *National Enquirer* mentality, he left an incredible legacy to mankind. Although we have been dubbed as part of the "Mormon Mafia" by the media, in this book we address Hughes' visions and accomplishments and discuss the many things he left behind for all of us to enjoy. We address the real facts relating to his medical history, mental health, and physical condition—of which we were first-hand eyewitnesses. All of us were involved with the litigated mess of the "Mormon Will" and the division of his estate after his death. We also identify many of the people that had an impact on his life as well as his impact on these same individuals.

Hughes created a huge, diversified empire through his tireless work ethic and genius. For most of his life he had successfully operated his empire on his own, but even with his exceptional abilities, he realized early on that he would not be capable of handling his vast and diversified empire without help. He began to recognize that he needed his own unique organization, based on a feudalistic platform of vassals—loyal men and women willing to be dedicated to his every need who would support him as he continued to control every facet of his realm.

The major difference between these modern and ancient feudalistic vassals was that modern-day vassals had become knowledgeable, well educated, handpicked, and well paid. One thing that did not change over the centuries was the intense loyalty and dedication, both up and down, between His Royal Highness (HRH), Howard Hughes, and his modern-day vassals.

We, a few of Hughes' vassals have finally decided to step forward and tell our personal accounts. We worked for him from 1947 in various capacities until the time of his death in 1976.

James J. Whetton worked in the Operations office directly with Mr. Hughes and later became General Manager of the Desert Inn during most of the period it was owned by Hughes.

James Leo Wadsworth, an attorney licensed in Nevada, was responsible for Hughes' legal work on land and mining claims, and was involved in Nevada's transition from mob to corporate control, thus changing the face of the State. Hughes essentially bought the mob out and brought corporate control to Nevada. He joined the Romaine Street staff in 1953 in the communications group. He was also hired at Hughes' request to handle an important personal project for Hughes concerning Hughes' wife at the time, Jean Peters.

Wilbur S. Thain, MD, a family physician, worked in operations and communications from 1948–1952, later returning as one of Hughes' rotating physicians in 1972 until after his death in 1976. Dr. Thain was the doctor who pronounced Hughes' death on a jet en route to Texas. Dr. Thain's personal journals detail medical and health aspects of the last three years of Hughes' life.

Ellie Pugmire was Hughes' only personal secretary from the day she was hired until his death. She has recorded her memoir in wonderful detail to contribute to the staging of this book. You will find many of her writings interspersed throughout *We Knew Howard Hughes*, but her memoir, in its entirety, is also located in the Appendix.

Gordon Bench's role is unique in that, in addition to working in the Operations Center, he was often called upon to work with Hughes on various sensitive and personal projects. For example, per Hughes' instructions, Gordon purchased and delivered a $10,000 fur coat to Jean Peters.

Howard Hughes (signature)

Introduction

James J. Whetton, James Leo Wadsworth, and Wilbur S. Thain, MD knew Howard Hughes. These three men worked with Hughes intimately from 1947 until his death in April 1976 and for some years beyond. As of September 2012, they and Ellie Pugmire are the last surviving members of Hughes' personal staff, and since Howard Hughes had no close, lasting friends, they became the people who knew him best.

"We spent more than six years on Howard Hughes' personal staff. He was a genius and strived relentlessly to attain his goals. His working habits were unique and unconventional, and yes, he manipulated people and made incredible demands on them. But we found Hughes to be the most fascinating and capable man we'd ever met. He lived alone most of his life, surrounded by luxury, yet he cared nothing about the everyday materialistic things that most of us are so eager to attain. We never saw him wear a new pair of pants or new shoes. He never wore a wristwatch, and he usually borrowed a jacket from someone when he needed one. He never wore a necktie and only wore white shirts that we delivered to him from the office. Nice clothing was unimportant to him, and he was labeled an eccentric as a result."

James J. Whetton, former general manager of the Desert Inn &
Ellie Pugmire, personal secretary to Howard R. Hughes, Jr.

Howard Hughes

Chronology

For those who are interested in reading the true story of the life and unparalleled accomplishments of the real Howard Hughes, this chronology of his life is fascinating. It will pique the interest of younger history buffs born since Hughes' day.

Hughes was born December 24, 1905 in Houston, Texas and, almost from birth, he began the productive life of a genius, never to be duplicated by mankind. It is interesting to note that lawsuits mentioned in this chronology that were brought about by overzealous Federal agents regarding TWA and Airwest were all settled in favor of Hughes; and in the TWA matter, the U.S. Supreme Court ruled in Hughes' favor. Likewise, the Federal case against Dr. Wilbur Thain was not only settled in Dr. Thain's favor, but also resulted in a complete revolution in the study and treatment of pain sufferers as noted in a study by Dr. Forest Tennant of Hughes' pain treatment.

Dec 24, 1905	Howard Robard Hughes is born in Houston, Texas.
Nov 10, 1908	Hughes' father files for a patent on his revolutionary oil-drilling bit.
Mid 1909	Sharp-Hughes Tool Company, a partnership, is organized in Houston.
Feb 1915	The Hughes Tool Company is incorporated in Texas..
1920	At age fourteen, Hughes takes his first flight in a Curtiss flying boat.
Sep 1920	Hughes is enrolled in Fessenden School, West Newton, Massachusetts, and graduates in the spring of 1921.

Sep 1921	Hughes enrolls in Thatcher School in Ojai, California.
Mar 29, 1922	Hughes' mother dies in Houston.
Sep 1922	Hughes returns to Thatcher, then withdraws at Christmas.
Sep 1923	Hughes enrolls in Rice Institute in Houston.
Jan 4, 1924	Hughes' father dies in Houston.
May 1924	Hughes acquires minority interest from his grandparents and uncle in the Hughes Tool Company giving him 100 percent control.
Dec 26, 1924	A Houston judge signs the order removing Hughes' "disabilities as a minor," thus eliminating the need for a court-appointed guardian.
May 30, 1925	Hughes executes a will at the age of nineteen, leaving the bulk of his estate to medical research. This is believed to be the only will he ever signed.
Jun 1, 1925	Hughes marries Ella Rice in Houston.
Fall 1925	Hughes leaves Houston to live in Los Angeles.
Nov 1925	Hughes hires Noah Dietrich as a financial advisor in Los Angeles.
Oct 1927	Hughes begins filming his World War I flying epic, *Hell's Angels* and spends $500,000 for more than forty vintage fighter and scouting aircraft, literally the world's largest private air force.
Jan 7, 1928	Hughes receives his pilot license and experiences his first plane crash at Mines Field, Los Angeles, during the filming of *Hell's Angels*.
Oct 21, 1928	Ella and Hughes separate.
May 1928	A silent film, *Two Arabian Knights* wins an Academy Award.
Dec 2, 1929	Hughes purchases a house at 211 Muirfield Road, Los Angeles.

Dec 9, 1929	Ella is granted a divorce in Houston.
May 24, 1930	*Hell's Angels* premieres in Hollywood; the aviation sequences remain unequaled.
	Hughes acquires 7000 Romaine Street, Hollywood.
Spring 1932	Hughes founds Hughes Aircraft Company in Glendale, California.
Sep 1932	Under the pseudonym "Charles Howard," Hughes gets a job as a baggage handler for American Airlines; Hughes advances to copilot within weeks.
Jan 14, 1934	Hughes wins a first-place air trophy in Miami in a modified Boeing aircraft.
1934	Hughes develops and tests the first retractable landing gear and flushed rivets to streamline airplane designs of the future.
Sep 13, 1935	Hughes proves, in a series of death-defying flights over the Sierra Nevada mountain range, that high-altitude flying greatly increases air speed, opening a new frontier for commercial aviation. He sets a new land speed record of 352.46 mph at Santa Ana, California, in the Silver Bullet, the world's fastest plane, built by Hughes Aircraft. (He had to make a forced landing in a beet field during its final run at 100 mph.)
Jan 14, 1936	Hughes sets a new transcontinental speed record from Los Angeles to Newark of nine hours and twenty-seven minutes. "All I did was sit there. The engine did the work," he explained.
1936	Hughes designs and perfects an oxygen feeder system that enhances pilot safety during high-altitude flights.
Jan 19,1937	Hughes makes the world's greatest long-distance speed flight, setting a new transcontinental record from Los Angeles to Newark, New Jersey, of seven hours, twenty-eight minutes.

Mar 3, 1937	Hughes receives the prestigious Harmon International trophy—as the world's outstanding aviator for 1936— in a ceremony at the White House. President Franklin D. Roosevelt presents the trophy, given by the Ligue Internationale des Aviateurs. Hughes is only the third American to receive the honor, following Charles Lindbergh and Wiley Post.
Jul 10-14, 1938	Hughes flies around the world in three days, nineteen hours, and seventeen minutes. With his four crewmen, in a Lockheed Model 14 twin-engine transport, Hughes establishes a new record and returns home a ticker-tape hero.
1939	Hughes perfects power-booster radio receivers and transmitters in contemporary aircraft.
May 1939	Hughes acquires stock in Transcontinental and Western Airlines, later renamed Trans World Airlines.
Fall 1939	Hughes begins working on an experimental military aircraft, the D-2.
1940s	Hughes builds Hughes Electronics into the single largest supplier of weapons systems to the United States Air Force and Navy.
Spring 1940	Hughes begins filming *The Outlaw*.
Jul 1941	Hughes Aircraft Company moves to a new plant at Culver City, California.
1941-1943	Hughes designs revolutionary ammunition feed chutes for fifty-caliber machine guns, doubling the rate of fire.
Nov 16, 1942	The Defense Plant Corporation approves an $18 million contract with Kaiser-Hughes Corporation to build three flying boats to aid the war effort.
May 17, 1943	A Sikorsky S-43 with Hughes at the controls crashes in Lake Mead, Nevada; two die.

Oct 11, 1943	The Air Force issues a letter of intent for Hughes Aircraft Company to build 101 photoreconnaissance planes.
Fall 1943	Nadine Henley becomes Hughes' private secretary.
Mar 27, 1944	The Kaiser-Hughes contract on the flying boats is cancelled. The Defense Plant Corporation issues a new agreement with Hughes to build one flying boat.
May 20, 1945	The Air Force cancels the contract to build the 101 photoreconnaissance planes. Hughes is to complete two of the experimental planes already under construction.
Jul 7, 1946	Hughes is critically injured but survives a fiery near-fatal Beverly Hills crash of the XF-11, which was designed for photoreconnaissance. He later redesigns the propeller configuration for the next prototype.
1946-1949	As principal shareholder of TWA Hughes designs the first cost-effective routes to Europe and the South Pacific.
Aug 6-10, 1947	Hughes testifies before the Senate War Investigating Committee probing his work as a defense contractor in WW II.
1947	Bill Gay and Wilbur Thain begin working with Hughes.
Apr 5, 1947	Hughes successfully tests the second XF-11 at Culver City.
Oct 1947	Frank William Gay goes to work at 7000 Romaine Street.
Nov 2, 1947	Hughes test flies the Hercules, HK-1 Flying Boat. The Long Beach, California, flight lasts less than sixty seconds, but it reinvents Hughes as an aviation hero and remains one of the most famous flights ever.

1941-1956	Hughes builds Hughes Aircraft from a four-man operation into an eighty-thousand-employee powerhouse that includes Hughes Electronics and Hughes Helicopter.
Nov 1947	Hughes testifies on November 8, 10, 11, and 14 before the Senate War Committee and afterwards states that he will never again appear in such a setting.
May 10, 1948	Hughes acquires control of RKO Studios.
1949	Hughes develops the "all-weather Interceptor," an electronic weapons control system with a combined radar set and computer capable of finding and destroying enemy planes day and night, in any sort of weather.
1950-1956	Hughes conceives and manufactures the "air-to-air missile," which seeks out its target and then locks in through a fail-proof system of radio impulses. Deadly and quick, this guided missile was considered to be the most important contribution to the defense of North America since radar.
1950-1956	Hughes invents, then mass-produces, the navigational control system for the F-102 interceptor—the backbone of American Air Defense Strategy in the fifties and sixties.
Apr 1951	Hughes fires Paul Jarrico, a screenwriter, after he was subpoenaed to appear before the House Committee on Un-American Activities.
Fall 1951	Gordon Bench begins working with Hughes.
Nov 20, 1952	Hughes testifies in Los Angeles Superior Court in the Jarrico case. This is his last court appearance.
Sep 23, 1952	The Chicago syndicate purchases control of RKO Studios.
Feb 10, 1953	Hughes reassumes control of RKO after the Chicago group forfeits a $1.2 million down payment.

July 1953	James J. Whetton begins working with Hughes.
Aug 11, 1953	Dr. Simon Ramo and Dr. Dean Wooldridge resign from Hughes Aircraft Company sparking a crisis between Hughes and the Pentagon.
Dec 17, 1953	The Howard Hughes Medical Institute is incorporated in Delaware.
Mar 31, 1954	Hughes acquires 100 percent control of RKO for $2.4 million.
1955	James Leo Wadsworth begins working with Hughes.
Feb 11, 1955	Hughes takes his last pilot's test in Miami, Florida.
Jul 19, 1955	Hughes sells RKO to General Tire Company for an estimated $25 million.
Feb 1956	Hughes orders the first jets for TWA—three Boeing 707s.
Jun 7, 1956	Hughes orders thirty Convair 880s from General Dynamics.
Dec 10, 1956	Hughes Tool Company makes a $205,000 loan to F. Donald Nixon.
Jan 12, 1957	Hughes marries Jean Peters in Tonopah, Nevada.
May 12, 1957	Hughes fires Noah Dietrich.
Dec 15, 1960	Lenders impose a voting trust, causing Hughes to lose control of TWA.
Dec 24, 1960	Hughes moves with Jean to Rancho Santa Fe.
1959-1964	Hughes revolutionizes the nations wartime helicopter capability through $440 million in government contracts. He builds the TH55A helicopter—the forerunner of maneuverable choppers for battle conditions.
1960s	Hughes pioneers and produces the unmanned satellite prototypes, virtually clearing the way for the onset of today's satellite era.

Spring 1961	Hughes hires Chester C. Davis as vice president and general counsel of the Hughes Tool Company.
Jun 30, 1961	TWA files an anti-trust complaint against Hughes in New York.
Nov 23, 1961	Hughes moves with Jean to 1001 Bel Air Road, Bel Air.
Feb 11, 1963	Hughes refuses to appear for a deposition in the TWA suit.
May 3, 1963	A Federal judge in New York awards TWA a default judgment over Hughes' refusal to give his deposition.
Jun 21, 1964	The U.S. Court of Appeals upholds the default judgment against Hughes.
May 26, 1965	The Army awards a contract to Hughes to build light observation helicopters in what would become the largest single business loss in Hughes' career.
May 3, 1966	Hughes sells his 6.5 million shares of stock in TWA for $546 million.
Jul 17, 1966	Hughes leaves Los Angeles by train for Boston to stay at the Ritz Carlton Hotel.
Nov 27, 1966	Hughes arrives in Las Vegas by train from Boston and takes over the top two floors of the Desert Inn.
Mar 31, 1967	Hughes acquires control of the Desert Inn Hotel and Casino, the first step in building his Nevada Empire.
Dec 27, 1968	Stockholders approve the sale of Airwest to Hughes.
Jan 15, 1970	Jean Peters announces she and Hughes will divorce.
Apr 3, 1970	Hughes acquires Airwest.

Apr 14, 1970	A Federal court enters a judgment of nearly $1.5 million against Hughes for damages to TWA in the antitrust case.
Jul 1970	Richard Danner delivers a $50,000 secret Hughes campaign contribution to "Bebe" Rebozo at San Clemente.
Aug 1970	Danner delivers another $50,000 check to Rebozo in Key Biscayne, Florida.
Nov 14, 1970	Hughes signs a proxy giving control of his Nevada empire to Chester Davis, Raymond Holliday, and Bill Gay.
Nov 25, 1970	Hughes flies from Las Vegas to Paradise Island, Bahamas, moving into the Britannia Beach Hotel.
Dec 3, 1970	Hughes Tool Company fires Robert Maheu as chief of Hughes' Nevada Operations.
Jan 1971	Hughes' organization employs a new Washington representative, Robert F. Bennett. Bill Gay assigns Francis Fillerup, a staff member, to handle negotiations to use Hughes as a front for the Glomar Explorer and the CIA Project Jennifer.
Jun 18, 1971	Hughes and Peters divorce is final in Hawthorne, Nevada.
Jan 7, 1972	Hughes conducts a telephone interview from the Bahamas with newsmen in Los Angeles to refute Clifford Irving's book.
Feb 10, 1972	Robert Maheu files a $17.5 million lawsuit in Los Angeles against Hughes for libel and slander.
Feb 15, 1972	Hughes leaves the Bahamas by boat to Miami, then by air to Managua, Nicaragua, moving into the Intercontinental Managua.
Mar 13, 1972	Hughes meets briefly with U.S. Ambassador Turner Shelton and Nicaraguan President Anastasio

	Somoza in Managua shortly before flying to Bayshore Inn, Vancouver, Canada.
Aug 29, 1972	Hughes returns to the Intercontinental in Managua.
Sep 25, 1972	Hughes signs papers authorizing the sale of the oil-tool division of the Hughes Tool Company.
Dec 7, 1972	Hughes holding company is renamed Summa Corporation.
Dec 24, 1972	Hughes leaves Managua for London, moving into the Inn on the Park.
Jan 10, 1973	The U.S. Supreme Court overturns the judgment and lower court rulings against Hughes in the TWA case.
Mar 17, 1973	Hughes meets with Governor O'Callaghan and Philip Hannifin in London.
Aug 9, 1973	Hughes falls in his room at the Inn on the Park, fracturing his left hip.
Dec 14, 1973	Hughes is inducted into the Aviation Hall of Fame in Dayton, Ohio. Officials hoped that he will show up to accept the honor, but he instead sends Ed Lund, the only other surviving member of the 1938 around-the-world flight.
Dec 20, 1973	Hughes flies from London to Freeport, Grand Bahama Island, moving into and purchasing the Xanadu Princess Hotel.
Dec 27, 1973	A Federal Grand Jury in Nevada indicts Hughes in the acquisition of Airwest.
Jan 30, 1974	The Airwest indictment is dismissed by a Federal judge.
Jun 5, 1974	Hughes' personal papers are stolen in a burglary at 7000 Romaine Street.
Jul 30, 1974	A Federal Grand Jury in Nevada re-indicts Hughes in the Airwest case.

Nov 13, 1974	A Federal judge again dismisses Hughes' indictment in the Airwest case; the Justice Department appeals. (The indictment is reinstated by the U.S. Court of Appeals on May 7, 1976, a month after Hughes' death.)
Mar 18, 1975	Hughes Glomar Explorer story is disclosed.
Sep 10, 1975	Hughes' aides and executives receive employment contracts that had been approved by Hughes.
Feb 1, 1976	Hughes is flown from Freeport to Acapulco, to a penthouse in the Acapulco Princess Hotel.
Apr 5, 1976	Hughes dies while being flown from Acapulco to Houston.

Some of these entries are taken from Chronology: The Life of Howard Hughes

In partial explanation for the listings regarding lawsuits in the chronology, it is told in several places in this book how Hughes dictated the tactics in lawsuits against him. It was easy for three of his longtime attorneys to accept this. They realized that they may know the law, but only Howard Robard Hughes fully knew his mental machinations and actions that may have caused the action. Hughes, of course, never made a wrong decision and HIS actions were legal and proper as far as he was concerned.

The tactics in the TWA lawsuit show one example of his attitude. He felt he was doing that which was most beneficial to his airline by delaying any purchase of jet transports. TWA was serviced by Super Constellation. They could carry 126 passengers at 300 miles per hour over 4,000 miles non-stop. This was almost 75 miles per hour faster than any then propeller-driven aircraft such as the military C-54. The Super Connie had a matchless safety record, was a beautiful aircraft, and pilots loved it. Why should Hughes have to change to jets?

He did not understand minority stockholder's rights and the power of a minority stockholder lawsuit. It had never happened to him, and he made sure it never happened again. Hughes never realized the fact that just because he was a large majority stockholder, that he did not own the airline. He couldn't see that he was doing anything wrong in refusing or delaying to buy jet transports to finally compete with the other airlines. By doing the purchase, it was assuring income from the stock lesser persons held. It was *his* airline, so why couldn't he take a plane out of service for his personal use? Why couldn't he order a passenger bumped to give a seat to a favored one? He just couldn't accept that his interference with the operations of TWA was wrong or even questionable. After all, it was *his* airline.

This was Hughes' stand when he was sued. He hired a prestigious law firm in New York to defend him. That firm designated Chester Davis, one of their principals, and a highly rated trial and appellate attorney. Shortly into the court action, the firm recommended settlement. Hughes hadn't done anything wrong, and besides, the money demand was unacceptable; therefore, Hughes refused.

He gave detailed instructions to Davis. Davis presented them to his firm. The principals of the firm disagreed with Hughes. Davis disagreed with the firm. Davis withdrew from the firm and established his own office. The suit was fought for years, with motions, appeals, trials and more appeals.

Hughes always believed he lost because he lost his airline. Davis always believed he won. He didn't allow Hughes to lose $200 million. Hughes was forced to sell his majority stock, but instead of ending up a big dollar loser, he was able to escape. He got almost $600 million for his stock and the last appellate court allowed him a tax status which taxed him at the lowest rate.

One last aside, Hughes was not a braggart. It appeared to us that he never admitted, even to himself, that any man was superior.

For instance, he had heroes in the field of aeronautics—people such as Lindberg, Wiley Post, Eddie Rickenbacker, and Claire Chenault. But none of these great men conceived, designed, manufactured, and then flew the results of those labors. Hughes recognized Noah Dietrich as equal, or perhaps superior, in intricate financial transactions—but, nonetheless, Noah was an employee. Even though Hughes never consciously thought this way, he didn't need to. He was Howard Hughes.

Howard Hughes (signature)

The Lord and His Vassals

Feudalism was a political and military system that dominated relationships and the 13th century way of life, and had long been considered dead by the bulk of the Western-thinking world by the beginning of the 20th Century. It was not, however, entirely extinct.

In these ancient times, there was a lord and master and his vassals. The vassals promised to serve their lord, to fight in battle for him, and to oversee and work the portion of land assigned to their care. In return, the lord promised to treat the vassals with honor and respect, and to supply them with some substance over and above that which the vassals could produce from that portion of the lord's land.

Howard Hughes came upon the scene early in the 20th Century, and from the 1940s to 1976, the world witnessed a giant of the industrial age, a brilliant inventor, a pioneer in all phases of modern aviation development and space exploration, a movie producer, and first and foremost, a great American patriot.

Hughes created a huge and diversified empire with a tireless work ethic and personal genius. But even with his own exceptional abilities, he realized early on that he would not be capable of handling his empire on his own. He needed his own type of feudalism (without the military aspect)—vassals who would be willing to be dedicated to his cause, men and women who would allow him to continue to control each facet of his realm, and yet be there for the many duties that went beyond just office help. The loyalty, up and down, really existed. The lord, Hughes, gave jobs, standing, and recognition and the Operations staff performed services beyond what office help were usually expected to do.

Only a select few were awarded the honor, over a period of years, of being known as "administrative aides" to Howard Hughes. It is almost unbelievable what the title of "aide to Howard Hughes" and the public recognition garnered from it did for these select few. And like the vassals of old, there was initially a salary that grew to reflect rewards for honored service to their leader and for loyalty and dedication.

Hughes treated his aides with courtesy and dignity—an actual display of genuine kindness toward his mid-level administrative and office help that was a rarity at the time. The aides, as well, demonstrated a deep sense of loyalty that many today might find difficult to believe. None of the vassals ever gave any information about Hughes to the media during his lifetime, and most of them have continued to respect his desire for privacy since his death.

James J. Whetton summarizes the desires of those who were closest to Howard Hughes in terms of this project: "Why now, at what seems to be this late time in history, are the five of us writing this story of the real Howard Hughes? We, who were closest to him, have for far too long honored his personal request for complete secrecy and personal privacy. He was one of the greatest patriots in the history of this, the greatest of all nations. His accomplishments have had a measurable effect on all of us and will continue to leave their mark and legacy in the field of medical research, the Howard Hughes Medical Institute. He meant for his entire fortune to be so used. Unfortunately, because of his lost will, the relatives he totally despised have shared in getting several hundred millions of his final estate. We finally decided that our pledge of silence needed to be broken, and the story told of the real Howard Hughes, as we know of his life from our personal, hands-on experience with this greatest of men."

Howard Hughes

A Great Man Remembered

What is it about the conclusion of life that brings old memories into sharp focus? The distinguished businessmen, the shrewd politicians, the colorful galas, and glamorous women?

1947 was such a time—a time of continued postwar building and a time where America became what it was meant to be—the apex of freedom, love, and prosperity. It was undoubtedly one of the greatest eras of our history, as well as the period in which the Howard Hughes' companies flourished: Hughes Tool Company, Hughes Aircraft, Hughes Productions, and other numerous holdings.

Changes were on the horizon for Hughes, and by 1947 everyone wanted a share in his success. He'd been the ultimate conglomerate business tycoon and his popularity, intrigue, and achievements ignited during the post-war era. Due to a variety of factors, including Hughes' chronic pain from his Beverly Hills plane crash in July 1947, he leaned more and more toward isolation.

Even before that, upon arriving on the tarmac after his 1938 around-the-world flight, a _News Reel_ reporter asked him, "Mr. Hughes, were you ever frightened during this history-making flight?" Hughes replied, "Not near as much as I am with all these people around me!"

In the skies, Hughes was alone with his thoughts, totally in charge and invincible. On the ground, he was hounded night and day. Everyone wanted something. A story. A dollar. A million. There was no end to the landslide of requests coming in.

From his early days, Hughes showed signs of distancing himself from unnecessary groups of people. This might have been a result of his very close companionship with his mother and no one else. When she died, followed shortly by his father, Howard Hughes was left to run Hughes Tool Company at the age of nineteen. Being so young and in control of a thriving business, he learned quickly who his friends were and whom he could and could not trust.

From the moment Hughes took control of the Hughes Tool Company, he also assumed complete and autonomous control of every event that he was to be involved with for the rest of his life, including his visions for the future of his country and everyone in it, his business operations, even down to his personal health and well being. For every minute of every hour of every day of every year, for the rest of his life, even to his death, Hughes was completely in control and dedicated to the outcome. He and he alone, unilaterally, for the most part, guided his destiny and even the destiny of many others.

The years since the Hughes' legend have flown past, and in the summer of 2009, three former Hughes' employees met with the purpose of compiling their memories—all Mormons (members of the Church of Jesus Christ of Latter-day Saints), and all part of a group whom Robert Maheu had termed the "Mormon Mafia." They are James Leo Wadsworth, Dr. Wilbur S. Thain, and James J. Whetton. The meeting took place in a sunny kitchen, caged birds on the counter chirping in the background. Thain, Wadsworth, and Whetton—their paths had intersected at various times throughout their employment for Howard Hughes, but now, it was time to bring their stories together.

This meeting was not just about Hughes' medical condition, or the four years Dr. Thain had spent with him at the end of his life. It was not about the Desert Inn that James Whetton had managed, effectively ousting various corrupt employees from Hughes' empire. Nor was it about Wadsworth and the litigation of the most important court cases in U.S. history in which he was involved on behalf of Hughes. This meeting had a much broader focus—that of *remembering the true Howard Hughes.*

Howard Robard Hughes, the *real* person, not embellished by exaggerations from outsiders and the media, not slandered by jealous and angry rivals, but the man who was a great patriot in his days of glory, those days when the public and the media noted his every move, his every business deal, and each woman with whom he appeared—*this* is the man whose story will finally be told.

It begins with the Operations Center . . .

)towardstypho

The Set-Up: Operations

The time came when it was necessary for Hughes to set up the ultimate communications center to handle the thousands upon thousands of incoming requests, both personal and business, of his ever-growing empire.

A change had been developing in Howard Hughes' personal business. He realized that the Hughes Tool Company was a separate and distinct entity from his movie role, from his lifelong love of designing and flying airplanes, and from his patriotic interest in the growing military upheaval of the late 1930s and early 1940s. He knew that he needed more space between his private, business, and public lives, and that the whole world would seek to read about him in print with little exposure to truth and facts.

The final realization of the need to separate these varying roles came to him as a result of a serious plane crash on May 17, 1943, in which two of his closest personal friends lost their lives. A Sikorsky S-43 amphibian, with Hughes at the controls, crashed after landing on Lake Mead, about thirty-five miles east of Las Vegas, Nevada. The ensuing probes into the event by the media were unwelcome and when he recovered from the psychological shock of this tragedy, he resolved to have a more private personal office to become a buffer between his public and personal life—thus, the birth of the Operations Center.

In the fall of 1943, Nadine Henley, a very accomplished secretary with unusual stenographic skills, became Hughes' personal and private secretary. She convinced him that he also needed a confidential accountant for his personal spending accounts. As a result, he engaged Lee Murin, a CPA. This was the beginning of Hughes Productions.

Hughes had owned a fairly large office/storage building at 7000 Romaine Street since June 30, 1930. He had a seldom-used apartment/office on the top floor. The second floor was divided into large office spaces. Divining his need, the efficient Nadine Henley began setting up a communications office with what was actually a private telephone system that had a separate line to the Hughes residence. She was very careful about who she hired to handle the phones. One of the first she hired was Wilbur Thain, son of a prominent Beverly Hills family. He was also a Mormon. (The "Mormon exclusivity" came several years later.) Thain had started as a temporary employee, working during the Christmas holiday in 1947, and continuing for several years. He worked on an off for Hughes after that.

James Whetton had started working for Hughes in 1953, and James Leo Wadsworth spent six months working for the Hughes/Peters personal staff in 1955 before returning to his Nevada law practice. But no one on the staff dared tell Hughes that Wadsworth had resigned. So as far as Hughes was concerned, Wadsworth was still his employee.

All three men had been counted on the Hughes' staff at one time or another, but were especially, and literally, at his side during the most active part of his business-related adventures into the world reserved for future billionaires.

The establishment of Hughes' Operations Center was the beginning of the true empire—an empire that could be compared to the political process of feudalism. By the mid-1940s, Nadine Henley's tireless efforts were no longer enough to handle the workload. Hughes trusted her implicitly; she was very intelligent and also understood his growing idiosyncrasies. As a result, Nadine was given autonomy over whom to hire for the Operations staff, and she looked for those who could be the most trusted. She knew that in order to effectively manage Hughes' conglomerate of

businesses and personal affairs, she needed a much larger staff—
one that operated around the clock.

Even when he began producing movies as actual director,
Hughes did not spend the usual director's time on the set, but
expected those whom he had chosen to do what he told them to
accomplish. This characteristic mode of operation became even
more established after the Beverly Hills airplane accident, which
to some extent made it difficult for him to function physically.

There is no doubt that Hughes' confidence in his own abilities,
combined with a dislike of working with strangers, led to the
establishment of the Operations Center. He found the constant
interference and disturbance to his normal routine became annoying
even with men whom he trusted and had worked with for years. He
went to great lengths to avoid these interruptions. However, he was
extremely loyal to his trusted executives, engineers, and personal
aides. He hated to assume responsibility for having to discharge
any such person. Since Hughes was quite passive-aggressive in his
communications skills, he relied on others to help him with these
issues.

In 1947, Nadine was asked by G. Wendall Thain (Wilbur Thain's
uncle, who worked at Hughes Aircraft) to find a job for Frank
William (Bill) Gay, a Mormon from Provo, Utah. Gay was married
to Wilbur Thain's sister. Bill Gay first started working for Hughes
in October in the personal office of Noah Dietrich, who was the
controller of Hughes' many holdings. Then Nadine brought him
over into the Operations Center.

Gay's career with Hughes was solidified at the end of 1947
when a real crisis came to fruition as Columbia, South America,
had been indicating that all forms of transportation within that
country were to be taken over by the central government. This
was a major concern for Hughes since the South American hub
for TWA was located in Columbia. The threat became a reality in

December 1947 when an attempt was made to take over all TWA holdings that included hangars, maintenance shops, supplies, and even the airplanes in the country. Hughes immediately contacted his attorneys, the U.S. State Department, and his Washington lobbyists. He was told on December 31, 1947 that if he could prove that he personally owned the stipulated items that they would all be returned to him.

That New Year's Eve, Hughes immediately began to assemble his documents. He started calling the office personnel for help, but found only Bill Gay at home. All of the others were out on their usual New Year's Eve debaucheries. Gay dropped everything, coming to the Romaine office, and the two of them worked through the night until 11 a.m. the next day. About that time, the rest of the office staff trickled in, a little worse for the wear. The work continued at a blistering pace until that evening on January 1st, when a packet was put on a plane bound for Washington, D.C.

Exhausted, everyone prepared to leave. Hughes was lying on the couch, also spent. But just before Gay stepped out, Hughes asked him to stay. He asked Gay why he had been at home the night before and not out celebrating like the others. Gay said, "Mr. Hughes, I'm a Mormon." Hughes asked him what he meant. Gay explained that Mormons believed holidays were family days, so he was spending the evening with his family.

Several days later, Hughes requested Gay to "come over and talk." When Gay arrived, Hughes asked him to explain more fully about the lifestyle of the members of the Mormon Church. Gay explained his beliefs about marriage, family, morality, abstinence from liquor and tobacco. Hughes remained quiet, again lying on a couch.

Days later, Gay was again summoned, and Hughes told Gay that he was to organize a communications office for his staff. The office would be staffed around the clock and would handle telephone calls and personal assignments. Not only that, but Hughes wanted Gay to hire men who had his same personal values. Most of those eventually hired were Mormons; two exceptions were Floyd Colglazier, an Episcopalian, and Roy Crawford, a Presbyterian.

During the early 1950s, Gay hired Hank DiRoma, a Catholic, who, as an attorney, had already established himself as a tenacious "bull dog" prosecutor. Gay and Wadsworth had previously known DiRoma on the tennis courts while attending Brigham Young University (BYU). The others following DiRoma were all Mormons.

When Hughes made his first request, Gay had only been working for him a couple of months. He had been hesitant in taking the job at first, as he had envisioned his future as that of a college professor in philosophy, not business. He had to work out a couple of problems. One, he still had a few quarter hours left at BYU to get his BA degree, which he solved, and second, he had an invalid mother who refused to move to California with him.

Gay's problem with his mother was solved when a former tenant, James Leo Wadsworth, agreed to come back to stay with her so he could finish his last quarter for his degree. Wadsworth stayed on longer for the winter quarter doing graduate work and instruction in a first year political science course. When he pulled out of graduate school, he called Gay and told him he could no longer take care of Mrs. Gay. This started one of the many periods of no communication between Wadsworth and Gay.

Hughes, the master negotiator, asked Gay for a six-month trial, and if, in fact, Gay didn't like his job, Hughes would pay for him to complete his education. Of course, history records what happened. Gay never returned to college, but spent the rest of his life working for Hughes and the Howard Hughes Medical Institute (HHMI).

After the request from Hughes, Gay started right away, carefully recruiting those with intelligence, administrative ability, morality, and above all, loyalty. Many in the original Hughes Operations Center continued to serve Hughes until the time of his death. Over the years, additional staff members were recruited as the workload continued to grow. The new hires were carefully screened, well educated, and expected to grow in their assigned positions. In fact, many continued their educational process and completed their degrees. Wilbur Thain, who had worked weekends for Hughes since December 1947, earned his MD, graduating from the UCLA School of Medicine; James Leo Wadsworth had finished law school, graduating with a Jurist Doctorate degree from Washington University in Washington, D.C., and became licensed in Nevada, and James Whetton was a graduate of the United States Naval Academy, Annapolis, Maryland.

Wilbur Thain was a young college kid in 1947 when his brother-in-law, Bill Gay, called him to help out with staffing issues at Hughes Productions during the Christmas holidays. Nadine Henley became Thain's temporary boss. "I was attending UCLA at the time and had been working in the student health center as a male orderly at nights," Thain remembered. "Supplemental income while the school was closed during the holidays was welcome."

By early spring of 1948, while Hughes was negotiating with Floyd Odlum to purchase his twenty-four percent interest in RKO Pictures (accomplished in May 1948), Bill Gay had organized a full staff of telephone and communication services for Howard Hughes. Thain became a part of the Hughes' staff in the Operations Center starting in July 1948 and worked there until June 1952, mostly nights and on weekends, during the four years he was going to medical school at UCLA.

In 1953, Whetton was counted as one of the highest-paid staff members when he started working for Hughes. He arrived on the staff with a list of credentials that justified his elevated pay scale. He'd received a BA and three engineering degrees from the U.S.

Naval Academy. During WWII and the Korean War, he'd served as Flag Lieutenant and personal aide to a high-ranking admiral in the Pacific Theater of Operations—all of which required top-secret clearance. From his start until 1958, Whetton seldom worked in the Romaine office with the rest of the staff except when specifically requested by Hughes. Almost all of his time was spent working directly with Hughes on projects for Bill Gay, and occasionally manning the Operations Center desk, again at Hughes' or Gay's request.

This highly specialized group of staff members became, for the most part, the only family that Hughes ever acknowledged. Whetton remembered one evening when he was manning the Operations desk at Romaine Street; he received a phone call from Rupert Hughes. "Rupert Hughes informed me he was Howard's uncle and wanted to talk to him. The following evening when the Boss called to pick up his messages, I gave him the names of the various callers. Then I finished by saying, 'By the way, your Uncle Rupert called.' This was followed by several minutes of silence. Mr. Hughes finally said, 'Jim, I want everyone to understand that as far as I am concerned, I do not have a living relative on the face of this earth.'" This was just a foreshadowing of future trials over control of Hughes' estate—the attempt to discredit the formation of the Howard Hughes Medical Institute, and the fight to control Hughes Aircraft by Hughes' relatives, both of which attempts failed.

The Operations Center was on the second floor of the building at 7000 Romaine Street in Hollywood. In 1930, Hughes had purchased the Romaine Street offices from Eastman Kodak and worked in his private office there until the fall of 1951. His personal finance officer, Lee Murrin, and Hughes' controller of many of his holdings, Noah Dietrich, also had offices in the building. Contrary to other published claims, Hughes himself used the plush apartment on the third floor where he kept several changes of clothes and personal papers.

After moving from his private Romaine office, he worked out of the Beverly Hills Hotel. Once in a while, he would spend the night at the Beverly Hilton, and when it was dedicated in August 1955, Hughes had the Hughes Tools Company lease the presidential suite on a long-term deal. He held business meetings there with Air Force procurement generals, other Armed Forces officers, Boeing staff and attorneys, etc. The small suite beneath the presidential suite was also leased. Whoever was charged with setting up the meeting would arrive several hours in advance, staying in the small suite, then going to the presidential suite during the meeting, and "cleaning up" afterwards. Wadsworth was the original organizer. These meetings were typically twelve to eighteen hour marathons.

The Operations Center was organized so that all phone calls and requested appointments went through an aide before the information reached Hughes. At Hughes' request, Nadine set up private telephone lines—a direct line between the office and Hughes' bungalow at the Beverly Hills Hotel complex.

Ellie Pugmire, one of Hughes' secretaries, remembers the Operations Center: "The Operations Center was referred to as "the nerve center" and was manned twenty-four hours a day, with two men on each shift. Every telephone call for Hughes was logged on yellow legal pads, showing the exact time received, and the complete messages taken down in shorthand were later typed on the Daily Call Sheets. Only when Mr. Hughes called in and asked for his messages were they given to him, however in very extreme emergencies, Operations would call him.

"Code names were given to very important persons, as well as the girls, or starlets, and actresses. There was no other way, other than by letter, to contact Mr. Hughes except by calling Hollywood 4-2552, the number at that time, and giving your message to one of the boys.

"Only those working in Operations were allowed in that office, except for Bill Gay and myself, and there were several occasions when I answered the phones when the boys were called away to do something outside of the building for Hughes. By this time Hughes knew my voice and wouldn't be too upset when I answered and explained why I was in there.

"There were times when the Call Sheets got out of hand, with more than a hundred calls listed that had not been taken care of, and we would try to call Hughes' attention to them when we were working with him at the Beverly Hills Hotel. On these occasions Bill Gay was with me, and once in a while we got the list down to a mere dozen or so.

"Calls at that time included such names as General Ira Eaker, Loughlin and Frank Waters, Robert Gross, Howard Hawks, General George, Charles "Tex" Thornton, Dr. George Thorne, Frank McDonnell, Glen Odekirk, Floyd Odlum, Del Webb, Walter Kane, Johnny Meier, Harry Cohn, Jerry Wald, Louella Parsons, Carl Byoir, Greg Bautzer, Cary Grant, Darryl Zanuck, and many others, plus calls from the girls."

Just as in a feudalistic society, if any one noun could sum up Howard Hughes, it would be loyalty. He was unfailingly loyal to his staff. As the Operations staff evolved, it eventually operated in primarily three diversified groups. The first group manned the Operations Center twenty-four hours a day, seven days a week. This group also screened all calls coming in for Hughes and received and executed his orders.

The second group was involved with delivering documents or transporting people in various assignments. For example, they would ensure that people, mostly young women under contract to Hughes Productions, were escorted to drama lessons, photo sessions, and dined or entertained as Hughes directed.

The third group handled legal matters—Bill Gay, James

Wadsworth, James Whetton, Ellie Pugmire, and Gordon Bench, among others—and spent most of their time working on various business or personal projects and legal matters that directly involved Hughes. These business sessions were very intense and often would last long hours, sometimes even several days.

Wadsworth only spent six months in Hollywood, officially leaving December 8, 1955. When Gay had hired Wadsworth, he was promised that after three months in Gay's office becoming oriented, he would be transferred to the legal staff at Hughes Aircraft in Culver City. But at the end of the three months, the transfer did not happen. Wadsworth spent several days trying to secure the promised transfer from Hughes through Gay. But on the morning of December 7th, Gay told Wadsworth that Hughes wouldn't release him from the Peters/Hughes meeting coordinator position that he held. Wadsworth attended his last meeting, one with Boeing's engineers and attorney, which ended at 2 a.m. on December 8th.

"I went back to the Operations Center after checking out of the luxurious apartment in Beverly Hills. After hanging up the office car keys, I told Gordon Bench to send my pay check to my Vegas address," Wadsworth recalled. "I never made my quitting more formal than that. Hughes found out when Jean Peters told him she couldn't get a hold of me on the phone. When Hughes called Gay he was told that I was on a special assignment in Vegas but was still on the Hughes personal staff."

For the next fifteen years, Hughes continued to call on Wadsworth to help him on projects, although Wadsworth was no longer on the payroll or compensated. "I did what Hughes asked me to do," Wadsworth said. "Anyone would have. During those years, I accumulated more than $50,000 in bills that I could have demanded payment on. But I never did. Working for Hughes put me on a pedestal in the eyes of others, and it opened doors that wouldn't have otherwise been open to me. Even though I didn't get paid during those years, I felt privileged that the public knew I was one of Howard Hughes' attorneys. He let me use his name, and in exchange, I worked for him at no charge."

Hughes would frequently call in for his messages, but if he didn't ask for them, it became a challenge to try to get in touch with him. For example, if Pat Hyland, the president of Hughes Aircraft, called to say he couldn't reach Hughes on his private line about an important deadline, the staff would try to track him down and give him the message—sometimes successfully and sometimes not. Thain recalls, "The art of running him down wasn't easy, but it became a learned behavior as many of us got to know his habits and where he'd most likely be at certain times of the day or night." Wadsworth remembered Randolph (Randy) Clark as the one who was most able to "run down Hughes or any other execs."

The Operations staff worked twelve-hour shifts. Thain worked the night shift—3 p.m. until 3 a.m. Occasionally he worked the day shift on holidays or weekends. On Christmas Eve he started work at 4 p.m. and worked twelve hours straight through Christmas Day. He and Ellie were put in charge of getting in the final orders for Hughes' Christmas flowers that he sent to close friends. "Everyone else had families. I didn't yet," Thain said. "I got married between my junior and senior years of college." Hughes sent red roses, yellow roses and "long stemmed gardenias, for which they had to cut down part of the bust. They were very beautiful. We had a standing order for his florist, Sid Mills, to keep roses and gardenias on hand at all times because we never knew when Hughes would want to send flowers to someone," Thain continued. "The Christmas list included not only Jean Peters, but other women and business people—Hedda Hopper and Louella Parsons were two I recall. There were fifteen to twenty people on the list, each getting four dozen long stemmed roses or gardenias;

needless to say, Sid always sweated this out because Hughes would never make a decision until late Christmas Eve or early in the morning."

"The first time I spoke to Howard Hughes on the phone," Wadsworth notes," he kept me on for hours. Later, Hughes called up Bill Gay to find out more about me. When Gay told Hughes that I was a former pilot and flew A-20 bombers (Hughes' favorite combat plane), the deal was sealed. Hughes wanted to meet me. I was told to be on a certain corner at a specific time. I waited for over an hour there. Hughes finally drove up in a Chevrolet and rolled down the window. 'Are you Leo?' he asked. I answered, 'Yes.' Hughes said, 'We know each other from the phone.' I replied, 'Yes,' again. Then Hughes drove away."

Wadsworth chuckles at the memory. "He just wanted to meet me. That's all. The next week I was asked to set up a dinner with Jean Peters. After that, my primary job was to arrange everything for Jean Peters and set up meetings at the Beverly Wilshire Hotel. I'd been taken out of the Operations Center for good."

During the early years of the telephone office, the daytime hours consisted of Bill Gay and one other person on the phones. Nights and weekends, only one person was in the office. This original staff consisted of Bill Gay, Charles Grindstaff, Wilbur Thain, and Bob Alder. Later Floyd Colglazier and Roy Crawford joined the staff. In 1951, others were hired but Thain specifically remembers two— Gordon Bench came during the fall of 1951, and Kay Glenn was hired to replace Thain when he left in the spring of 1952.

Thain recalls, "The office was originally furnished with a desk, file cabinets, and a couch on which the person working all night could sleep if Hughes wasn't working or asleep himself. There was a recording device, solid wire at that time, and a darkroom with a photographic copy machine where all copies had to be developed and processed like black and white film."

All of the memos going to Hughes were typed on a typewriter and then sealed in brown paper envelopes. The envelopes were fastened with sealing wax by an emblem embossed with the letter G in the wax so Hughes would know it came from Bill Gay's office. Howard Hughes could be very thrifty for a rich man. After he accumulated too many of the brown envelopes, he'd send them back to be reused. Thain recalls, "We'd have to scrape off the wax residue to reuse them. I also remember Hughes asking the phone company to return nickels or dimes if he got a wrong number when calling on a pay phone."

In addition to the many people taking care of Hughes personally, there were others working at 7000 Romaine Street, but most of these had no personal dealings with Hughes. They included film editors, bookkeepers, an accounting division with three to four people, plus four to six drivers, some reporting directly to Lee Murrin or Charlie Guest.

The staff's general assignment was to do whatever Hughes wanted, whether it was to run errands, call someone, or take dictation. For Whetton, sometimes it was just to keep Hughes company. "From my first interactions with Mr. Hughes, I was struck with the impression that he was very lonely," Whetton recollects. Most of the time when Hughes wanted to make personal or private phone calls he would dismiss whomever he had been working with in order to make the calls. For whatever his reasons, he never dismissed Whetton while making these calls. "I was there but just didn't listen in. I came to feel that because of my experience with top secret naval intelligence clearance, Hughes knew he could spend many hours involved in making those calls in my presence, not having to worry that I would ever betray his trust."

On the Road

Although the Romaine Street Operations Center remained functional until the time of his death, Hughes stopped using this portion of his staff as he had for the past nineteen years. His new mode of staff utilization involving his vassals changed completely with his move to Rancho Santa Fe, California, near San Diego.

As Dr. Thain noted, when Hughes settled into his new location, the staff members started the new era by traveling with him, with their living quarters nearby. This select few consisted of longtime and faithful vassals John Holmes, Lavar Myler, and Roy Crawford.

In July of 1966, Hughes left for Boston, traveling in a private rail car. It was at this time and for the rest of his life that Holmes, Myler, and Crawford added to their numbers Howard Eckersley, George Francom, and Chuck Waldron. During his stay in Boston, Hughes and his aides were housed in the Ritz Carlton hotel while Hughes underwent a series of physical exams at the Boston Clinic.

On November 27, 1966, Hughes, again traveling by private rail car, left Boston and upon his arrival in Las Vegas with his staff took over the two top floors of the Desert Inn's main nine-story tower for his extended stay where he remained until his departure on Thanksgiving eve in 1970. Howard Eckersley, a key aide, described to Dr. Thain their departure from the Desert Inn: "Shortly after midnight, we carried Hughes from his ninth story suite down the narrow enclosed stairwell to a waiting van on the ground level. From there, we drove to Nellis Air Force Base to his waiting jet and from there flew to Paradise Island in the Bahamas, moving with his staff into the Britannia Beach Hotel." Thus began Hughes journey into total isolation for the rest of his life.

It was during the Las Vegas stay that Hughes purchased the Desert Inn, the Sands, the Frontier, the Castaways, and the Landmark hotels, declaring Las Vegas his official residence. Hughes' influence completely changed the face of Nevada, and specifically the ownership and control of gambling in the state.

The staff at Romaine Street now had a completely new structure to serve Hughes. For the rest of his life, this select group would faithfully serve him both from the standpoint of his physical needs and well being, and with even more rigid standards of service in the conduct of his business practices. How could this happen when he had been so well and carefully served from Romaine Street? The answer? No more contact by telephone or memos to and from Romaine Street. Only those who lived with Hughes were serving him—face to face, twenty-four hours a day, seven days a week.

During the Desert Inn time, the close staff consisted of John, Lavar, Roy, and Howard Eckersley, George Francom, and Chuck Waldron. Sometime during this period, Roy got into disfavor and was replaced. Jim Rickard, who for years had served as a driver, joined the group in 1972. According to Thain, "The aides I knew from 1972 to 1976 were John, Lavar, George, Howard, Chuck, and Jim. We also had the barber, Mel Stewart, two cooks, Gordon Margulis, a former busboy from the Desert Inn, Cliff Wiseman, and two front office people, Allen Stroud and Eric Bundy."

Following his departure from the Desert Inn, those chosen to literally live with Hughes for the rest of his life were on permanent duty for two weeks, then off for two weeks. This was done to allow his vassals to have some semblance of family life, though it was still a great personal sacrifice for all of them. One redeeming feature was that from time to time, the men's families were allowed to join them on the road. In addition, Lavar Myler and John Holmes attended Summa board meetings as Hughes' personal appointees.

(Hughes Tool Company was renamed Summa Corporation in 1972 with Bill Gay at its head.)

By now Romaine Street only functioned to support travel and logistics. Meanwhile, Bill Gay had opened an office in Encino, California with a staff of four, but only Gay had direct contact with Hughes and Hughes' vassals.

Even near the end of his life, and despite his failing health, Hughes kept his remaining ventures organized by directing and preserving them as a part of his overall vision of the future. As for the development of his holdings in Nevada, he was involved almost daily in every detail of planning up to the time of his passing.

Hughes Tool Company & the Family

Hughes Tool Company (HTCO) was started as a partnership of Hughes' father, who was commonly referred to as "Big Howard," and Walter B. Sharp. Indications are that it started as a wildcat drilling company. The partners, especially Big Howard, saw the need for inexpensive drilling equipment as there was a serious lack that would allow fast drilling, especially through hard rock. Using the inventive genius that would be inherited by his son, Big Howard began to design and then manufacture various drilling machinery in a small blacksmith shop that soon became a manufacturing company of no small importance.

Big Howard knew from his own experience and failures that something more than what was then used was needed to drill through the rock strata that seemed to overlay the oil deposits in Texas. It would be pure speculation to say where his idea for a rock bit came from, but he began with drafting tools, pencils, and paper on his kitchen table. His tool bit, when finally on paper, had 166 cutting edges. It, of course, required harder metal than simple steel. The tool shop worked out the problems and the Hughes Tool drill bit came into existence.

Big Howard demonstrated another characteristic that was inherited to some degree by his son. In spite of the fact that the HTCO had received a very comprehensive patent on the rock bit, the secretive handling of marketing of the bit became famous throughout the industry. The bit was never for sale, but was only available through a rental or lease agreement. When an order for the bit was received, a bit was wrapped in burlap. At first, Big Howard and one of his trusted workers would take the bit to the drill site. The workers and drillers would be chased away from the drill. The bit would be attached to the drill rod and lowered into the hole before anyone was allowed to return to the site. A HTCO person would then remain at the drill site to make sure that the bit was never pulled up and available for examination by anyone except the HTCO employee.

When the famous rock bit was invented, HTCO was worth roughly $750,000. When Big Howard died, the published worth was $10,000,000. Howard Robard Hughes, "Little Howard," had not quite reached his nineteenth birthday, leaving him an orphan, his mother having died two years previous.

The state of Texas was more a civil law state than an English Common Law state. Texas had civil law leanings that allowed a minor who could prove himself knowledgeable and competent and able to inherit, to receive ownership of a business and the run it. Since he was an only child and because of his father's will, Hughes was left the majority of the stock in Hughes Tool Company. Even though by this time HTCO was a stock company, it was still somewhat a partnership. Big Howard had allowed certain members of his family to buy small amounts of stock. Not one individual or even a group of family members had a large enough share holding to gain control.

Little Howard engaged attorneys and filed suit to take advantage of the Texas law. The hearing was set in the courtroom of Judge Walter Montieth. Montieth was a long-time family friend and had come to know Howard at the local country club where they had played golf together a number of times. Writers and reporters, some fifty years after the hearing, have tried to make that friendship a more important part of the court's decision than it actually was. The reporters at the time the hearing took place knew that in the relatively narrow confines of business and politics of Houston in 1924, everyone knew everyone. Politicians were close friends to anyone who had money and influence.

The nearly nineteen-year-old Howard Robard Hughes amazed and actually astonished the judge, reporters, spectators, and family with his knowledge of the HTCO business left by his father—its methods, its finances, and its prospects for growth. The remarkable young man walked out of the courtroom in control of a company worth ten million dollars. In the mid 1970s it was worth $750 million, but was not without a substantial amount of debt.

A study of the court proceedings of that hearing in 1924 led those attorneys of Hughes' later years to believe that even at that tender age, Hughes instructed his attorneys as to how he wished the hearing to go and be presented to the court, and further, that he would present and conduct his own testimony.

It is, to this day, a mystery as to how Hughes became more than casually fluent in his ability to dictate legal documents flawlessly, as he later did on several occasions. One classic example of this was his dictation of the sales agreement between RKO and General Tire and Rubber Company, which is covered in detail in the chapter on RKO Studios.

It should not be surprising—his knowledge of the law—because for the better part of his life he hired and worked closely with some of the best legal minds in the country, one of whom was one of his vassals in Operations who worked with Hughes for a longer time period than any of the others—James Leo Wadsworth.

Shortly after the inheritance of his father's stock, Hughes bought out the remaining stock, most of which was owned by family members.

"Incompetents never control

the products of a genius."

Unknown

The Shaker Table

Life's experience forms character that distinguishes one from another. The combination of personal qualities and the moral, ethical nature of a person were invaluable to Howard Hughes. This multi-bit code was something Hughes used to access people and their use to him. He examined their character and prevailing spirit to see if they would be of benefit to him and his organization.

The shaker table used in mining strains the fine from the coarse grains with the hope of finding a rare gem or nugget. This technique was used by Hughes to separate the competent from the incompetent. He would scrutinize the evidence at hand and determine a person's usefulness in his personal and business bailiwicks.

Hughes' mind and his ability to absorb detail and remember those he considered important was a marvel to all of those who worked for or with him. This dismayed many of those he pigeonholed, depending on how the briefing of their background struck him. He wanted to know any special knowledge each may have, i.e., about automobiles, steno skills, language knowledge, etc. As information and backgrounds emerged he delineated in his mind the attributes and downfalls of a person. The process—of course most geniuses have one—went like this:

The shaking began with Nadine Henley and William Gay, or anyone else that would brief him on a new employee. They were often nonplused at what he would grab onto during a personal briefing. Some of what might be considered an employee's minor attributes could determine Hughes' concept of that person, and he would so use them as though it were a specialty.

James Wadsworth's first encounter with the mind of Hughes was in 1947 when he was asked to do some research on International Law and also to get some ideas from J. Reuben Clark III, professor of International Law and Political Science at Brigham Young University. There was amazement that Hughes would use a senior from BYU for research because he was gathering material per his own instructions from some of the most professional attorneys available. It was the beginning of many lessons that prepared Hughes to tell his professionals how to attack and solve complicated problems. His own solutions to problems and to life in general carried forward into every walk of his life—business as well as personal.

Although Wadsworth didn't work intimately with Hughes before 1955, he knew and became close to people who had worked with the man from 1928, such as Noah Dietrich and those through the 1930s movie years. Walter Kane, Perry Lieber, various Hollywood people, business and personal employees from the mid 1940s, along with Nadine Henley, and his accountant, Lee Murrin.

Of course there were over a dozen men and at least three women who were associated with 7000 Romaine Street. Hughes treated each one of them a bit differently. Some were admitted to his private life and some were strictly company employees. Among those who survived the shaker table were William Gay and James Whetton. Whetton had been involved as a General Manager of a General Motors dealership. When Hughes thought he might buy a Packard automobile, although wanting several persons to evaluate the make, the opinion he wanted most was Whetton's.

Some of Hughes' employees were just telephone, errand, and message assistants. Some he recognized for their professional knowledge, such as Wilbur Thain, MD, and attorneys Hank DiRoma and Marty Cook. He allowed certain people access to his private ideas because he recognized specialties such as Dr. Jack Pettitt's great scientific and mathematical mind. Wadsworth was more or less singled out for his special tasks, mainly because he had been an A-20 combat pilot, and James Whetton was an Annapolis graduate. One thing he felt they all had in common was loyalty. The assurance in his own mind that the loyalty toward him resided in his favored employees, even after they had left him, remained with Hughes until the time of his death.

This chapter deals primarily with the Romaine Street employees. The corporate officers and those actually hired by the Hughes Tool Company—such as Maheu—are another story.

The Romaine Street staff was, from the early days of Bill Gay and Wilbur Thain—mid 1947 forward—something special to Hughes. Since Gay and Henley did the actual hiring for the Operations Center, Hughes looked to them for backgrounds on all personnel. James Whetton, having been a personal aide to an admiral, was qualified to be executive officer material to Hughes. Using Whetton for some personal errands confirmed this, and Whetton was thereafter so used.

Though told in other portions of this book how certain persons were singled out and given special jobs, this can be illustrated here in the use Hughes made of James Leo Wadsworth. An unfortunate episode brought Wadsworth to Hughes' attention just days after he went to work at Romaine Street. The "straw boss" of the Operations Center, Charles Grindstaff, had taken an afternoon to go to a UCLA-USC football game. Grindstaff had a massive heart attack and died at the game. When the immediate word was received at the Operations Center, the entire staff on duty, including Bill Gay and Nadine Henley, left for the stadium. They saw to the body and went to the Grindstaff home to comfort the widow and children.

Left at the Romaine Street office was one driver/messenger and James Leo Wadsworth, who had been there less than two weeks.

Each new staff member was given a very thorough briefing as to policy, method, and especially how to answer and what to say if Hughes' personal phone rang. The phone was picked up on the second ring, followed by, "Hello, this is (first name)." Nothing more was said until Hughes stated the purpose of his call and the immediate details to accomplish that purpose. Very often, Hughes would just be calling for a phone number or a report on what he had last asked to be done.

Seldom would such a call be made unless Hughes was starting one of his protracted work sessions. Once the phone was answered and Hughes began to work, he wanted whoever originally started on the phones to stay on the phone until he was finished with what he wanted to accomplish. That could be hours. On the occasion of Grindstaff's passing, Hughes worked for about eighteen hours straight. This was not necessarily unusual, but eight to twelve hours was the more standard work period.

Hughes had become quite hard of hearing by 1955 and so had amplifiers on his phones. He could make out words from certain speech mannerisms. The best voice would be in mid-range, not too fast, and spoken with fairly flat vowels. It seemed that those who grew up or were educated in Utah had the speech mannerisms that most appealed to Hughes, which made the staffing of Romaine Street with Mormons a fortuitous happening.

On the day of Grindstaff's passing, about three hours after Hughes started working with Wadsworth, some of the staff began to return to the office. Hughes did not indicate that he wanted a change on the phones. After nearly eighteen hours, several half-eaten sandwiches and a lot of caffeine-enriched soda, that session came to an end.

Several days later, Hughes called Bill Gay and asked for a complete rundown on James Leo Wadsworth who was on the phones when he last worked. Gay responded, "I have known

Leo Wadsworth since 1939. Wadsworth went into the Air Force and became a pilot. After the war, he lived with my family for six months. He graduated from Brigham Young University, was from a small town in Nevada, had been elected to the Nevada State Legislature, went to George Washington University for a law degree, and received his Jurist Doctorate. He spent four years as a 'quasi-judicial officer' in the Civil Aeronautics Administration and returned to Nevada."

Since Hughes also liked seemingly insignificant aspects of a person's abilities, Gay added that Wadsworth was a ten handicap golfer and played a reasonable recreational tennis game. A few days later, further inquiry was made as to what planes Wadsworth had flown and his standing in the state of Nevada. Was combat flown? Gay gave another rundown. Leo's father was a power in Nevada and well known in National Democratic circles. Leo had flown combat missions in the Mediterranean and Italian theatres, both in A-20 and A-26 planes.

A few days later, as written in the chapter The Set-up: Operations Center, the office was told that Leo was to stand at a particular corner of an intersection and wait. About thirty minutes after the appointed time, a Chevrolet pulled up in front of Wadsworth and a window rolled down. Hughes asked, "Are you Leo?" When Wadsworth answered in the affirmative, Hughes said, "I wanted to have a look at you." He then drove off.

About a week later, Hughes called the office and asked for Leo. On getting him on the phone, Hughes said, "Leo, do you know I own an A-20B and it is parked out at Burbank?" No answer was expected and Leo was informed that twice a month, the plane was rolled out of the hangar and the engines revved up. Leo was told that he was to go to the field and supervise this maintenance. Of course, this was just a bit of a favor because the mechanics certainly were more capable than a pilot with only a few hundred hours. It was not unusual for Hughes to do little things for employees that would give pleasure and a break from sitting around the office.

Within a week, the office told Wadsworth that he was to set up a dinner at the Tale of the Cock restaurant for Hughes and Jean Peters. Every person who went to work at Romaine Street as part of the Operations staff—not drivers, security, or purely messengers—were briefed very thoroughly on how these dinners were to be handled.

There was to be no pork, cabbage plants, or dried beans in any form served. The person setting up the meal was to be at the restaurant at least two hours before the time that Hughes and his date would arrive. The kitchen and preparation of the food was to be watched—actually supervised. The several places Hughes ate all knew that his staff were to have access to the kitchen. The placing of the food on the serving trays was watched. The staff member was to stay until the meal was over and the party left.

The second reason that the staff member stayed until the Hughes party left was so they could carefully check the accounting, even to adding it up, and then to pay the bill. At some restaurants there was a standing charge account, others were to be paid in cash or by the staff. A very strict percentage for a tip was to be paid unless the Boss, by a sign or brief word, would indicate that it be more or less than that percentage. This seldom happened. The maître d' was especially tipped.

On this particular night, Wadsworth was motioned to the table. He was introduced to Jean Peters as "Leo Wadsworth." She was told that from that time forward, if she wanted anything or had any needs, she was to specifically call for and use Leo.

Jean Peters was ready to file her final pleadings for her divorce from Cramer, and an attorney prepared the papers. They were first taken to Hughes for his reading. If he saw something he didn't like or agree with, back they went to the attorney. After Hughes was satisfied, Peters was allowed to read them and sign and verify. The same person then took them to the courthouse and filed. They were then returned to the attorney for serving on Cramer and a court date set.

The day before the final hearing on the divorce, Wadsworth was called and told to take Cramer to the Country Club and play golf with him to make certain he didn't show up in court and disrupt the proceedings. Hughes had such a passionate interest in golf that he could not imagine any golfer would turn down a chance to play at the Los Angeles Country Club as a guest of Hughes. Poor Cramer couldn't.

The golf ploy was used more than once. The most startling use was with a Lieutenant General. In 1955, a Lieutenant General was as important as a four-star general is today. Hughes had an appointment with this particular Lieutenant General, who was in charge all of purchases or contracts for supplies for the Air Force. An appointment was set for the meeting. The general was met and picked up by staff and put in a complimentary suite at the Beverly Hilton Hotel. He was then told that Hughes could not see him that day. It didn't faze the general because this type of "put off" was expected from Hughes. The second day, however, was a different matter. No one did that to a Lieutenant General who was in the higher echelons of the Air Force. But the invitation to play what many called the Wilshire Golf Course was just too good for even a Lieutenant General to pass up. As an aside, even though Wadsworth was "on his game," he lost $20 to the General. Of course, this was reimbursed.

After Wadsworth quit without notice, Hughes demanded of Nadine Henley where Wadsworth was and what he was doing. He was told that Wadsworth was on special assignment to Las Vegas because of his political knowledge. True to the way others were viewed by Hughes, he just considered Wadsworth still on the payroll.

The following brief stories illustrate how many former Operations people were used by the Boss.

Shortly after setting up in a law office in Las Vegas, Wadsworth received a phone call.

Hughes: "Leo, Crockett called the office and said he had been notified that his lease/contract for the fixed base operation at McCarran was not going to be renewed by the county. We don't want Crockett to lose his operation."

Leo: "Yes, that has appeared in the newspapers."

Hughes: "Well, don't you know the commissioner? You are supposed to be politically knowledgeable in Nevada."

Leo: "I was in the State Assembly with one of them, and know the other two. One of them is a close friend."

Hughes: "Well, see them and get this stopped."

Leo: "The commission has already passed a preliminary resolution and it has been published in the papers. I don't see what can be done."

Hughes: "Leo, do you know how rich I am?"

Leo: "I have been told."

Hughes: "Well, you will stop this and I will back up any promise, within reason, you have to make."

There were no cash bribes, but a lot of political maneuvering and some business deals later, Crockett did not lose the operation.

For the next several years on personal calls from Hughes, titles were searched, flowers were delivered to some of Hughes' favorites when each opened on the "Strip," and several political errands were accomplished.

At a conference in December of 1970, Nadine Henley laughingly told Chester Davis and the Intertel people that Leo didn't need introductions. "He is still listed on the personnel staff at Romaine and had been so listed for fifteen years."

This continued "use" of Romaine Street staff was not confined to Hughes. The corporate office of HTCO also, on occasion, felt free to call on former Romaine personnel to do errands. When visiting Hollywood, they would ask for transportation. Holliday, Executive Vice President of HTCO, selected James Whetton and Leo Wadsworth for special jobs and favors. At that fateful meeting of December 1970, of course, Holliday was a necessary member. When he entered the suite and saw Whetton and Wadsworth in attendance, he said, "Well, I see the gold dust twins are together again." This was the nickname he used for the two.

The Romaine Operations staff had a special place in Hughes' heart. Whetton and Wadsworth were used to the day of his death. John Holmes and Lavar Myler were, at Hughes' instructions, made directors of Summa Corporation. Hank DiRoma was used to check out titles and assay reports of mining claims years after he had last worked in Hollywood. There was no doubt in Hughes' mind that these special employees had a lasting loyalty and he trusted them—modern feudalism to the end.

Howard Hughes

Introduction to Hollywood

Howard R. Hughes left Houston in the fall of 1925 to relocate in Los Angeles. It cannot be said that Hollywood and the movies were his primary reasons. At that time, Hollywood was not considered the world's movie-making center. During the early 1920s, most American movies were made in New York and Fort Lee, New Jersey. German filmmakers were also making very impressive movies at that time. The first movie made in the Los Angeles area was not until 1907, and it wasn't until 1911 that the first studio was built by the Nestor Company in a sparsely settled district of that city known as Hollywood.

People soon realized that the excellent year-round weather, the proximity of almost every kind of scenic location, and the then attractive tax structure made Hollywood ideal for movie making. By the middle 1920s and Hughes' arrival, most of the major studios had been established—Columbia, Metro-Goldwyn-Mayer, Paramount, RKO, United Artists, Universal Studios, and Warner Brothers were all in full swing.

Hughes found some Union Pacific Ranch acquaintances in the area. Hollywood's rich were drawn to the U.P. Ranch and the very welcoming atmosphere for anyone of fame. There was excellent sage hen and quail hunting in the heart of the ranch. Western stars such as Bronco Billy Anderson, William S. Hart (Bill), Jack Hoxie, and others visited this ranch and various dude ranches in Idaho and Wyoming. They relaxed, got publicity, and it didn't cost them anything but transportation.

World War I was still very fresh in the public mind. The Air War had its beginnings in the 1920s and thrilled the public patrons.

Although Hughes didn't receive his first pilot's license until January 7, 1928, he was already a very skilled pilot. He decided to get into the movie business and, of course, would make flying movies. He began filming *Hell's Angels* in October 1927.

In his learning process, he changed the script, scenes, and directions so many times he became somewhat of a legend early on. In 1927-28, Hughes' film *The Racket* was nominated but lost to *Wings* in the presentation of the first Academy Award for Best Picture. This caused Hughes to become even more determined to make great films.

He stepped up the hiring of WWI pilots and buying the right planes. It was during filming that he was forced to demonstrate his own flying skills for one of his more perilous scenes because his pilots said the flight was too dangerous and could not be flown. Needless to say, he proved them wrong when he executed the flight himself.

Besides the financial twists and personnel complexities of Hollywood, Hughes discovered the pleasant but dangerous aspect of romantic life in the new movie capital. Hollywood was filled with enchantresses whose favors were readily traded for advancement in the business. Hughes still believed that the man was the pursuer and the conqueror. He found out early in his movie career that the roles were often reversed in the movie business.

His first conquest was a silent film beauty, Billie Dove, who was several years his senior. This was probably the first time that he had ever experienced a romantic relationship with an experienced, accomplished bed partner. His relationship with her, lasting two or more years, led to his October 1928 separation from Ella Rice, whom he had married in Houston on June 1, 1925, just short of four months before he left Houston to live in Los Angeles. He and Ella were divorced, with Ella as plaintiff, on December 9, 1929.

Enter Noah Dietrich

Howard Hughes was barely into production on his first film, *Hell's Angels*, when he realized that filmmaking, specifically in Hollywood, was like no other business in the world. A promise, a handshake, and business morality did not rule the day as he had found in Texas and most of the West. It is not really known how Hughes found Noah Dietrich, but Walter Kane, who became a self-proclaimed Hughes intimate, on many occasions, suggested that perhaps Billie Dove might have put Noah and Howard together.

Noah was a public accountant and bookkeeper when he first went to work for Hughes. He had several accounts and was not really a financial figure in the movie business when Hughes discovered that all his own brilliance and genius had not prepared him for the infighting that permeated Hollywood. As with any new venture, Hughes did not remain an amateur very long. He also recognized early on that Dietrich was just the man he wanted and needed for the ticklish handling of money in this new world. He welcomed the insight that Noah brought to him, and Noah, very quickly, took over the financial chores accompanying Hughes' venture into the world of movie making.

Very soon, Hughes fell into the lifelong habit he exercised with people he trusted and who had an ability to do a job. By the time he moved from silent to talking films, he had established a routine of giving directives to Noah and knowing they would be done. Hughes then moved forward as though those things had been accomplished.

Except for his two years with Billie Dove, Hughes went five or more years without a personal friend in the movie business. He became more dependent on Walter Kane, a remarkable figure in the movie world. Kane was fast making a name for himself in the tricky business of finding talent—mostly young and lovely girls. Columnists fed their readers' gossip and tales of Kane acting as a pimp for Hughes, which was absolutely untrue. Kane, however, became a person whom Hughes used as a Hollywood social tutor. The society of wealthy Texas was no school to prepare a man for the rapidly growing movie society.

It wasn't long until Kane's peculiar personality quirks fostered feelings of jealousy with Noah. This is probably where the first tales of Noah not being quite honest with Hughes' great fortune developed. Hughes discounted the tales of Noah's involvement, but he never completely discarded them.

It was during Hughes' early years in Hollywood that he met less than a handful of what he considered to be close friends. Everyone Hughes really liked he never forgot such as Cary Grant, one of his first and closest friends, Dick Powell, June Allison, Kathryn Grayson, and one most notable, Katharine Hepburn, who first met Hughes in early 1936.

Howard Hughes (signature)

Katharine Hepburn

Hughes' eyes began to focus on Katharine Hepburn as she first appeared on the screen in 1935. As late as 1952 and 1953, while working at night with Hughes, James Whetton recalls that he would pick up and answer the private line to Bungalow 19 and inform Hughes who was calling. Most of the calls would be from those friends closest to him, many were from Hepburn to schedule their next golf game.

In a book, *Remembering Kate,* Hepburn described Hughes as a "practical dreamer prone to planned impulsiveness. He liked to act on the spur of the moment, but only after he had thought through the details of his action and the planned outcome." This was so true of everything Hughes did.

Hepburn recalls a change in Hughes and his movie making activities and, as she said, his newfound interest in "seeking fame." She had given him a lift to Beverly Hills after a golf outing. She learned that after he produced *Hell's Angels, The Front Page* and *Scarface,* he really had no great passion for picture making. "He was a brilliant man," said Kate, "but he did have a passion for movie stars . . . Howard was always up for adventure . . . Now he always liked to think things through and I was always more instinctive . . . But we always had a lot of common interests."

They began to talk with decreasing frequency. Hepburn's book states, "During one of Hughes' last calls, he asked me what time it was. 'Four o'clock,' I said drowsily, looking at my clock. 'Day or night?' he asked." Their friendship and fond memories never ceased.

Loyalty

The Operations Center personnel considered themselves the protectors of Hughes' privacy and personal security. Hughes also engaged a private security company doing business in the Los Angeles area. The head of this company soon gave up all other clients. Lee Murrin was now able to review the entire gamut of Hughes' finances. Because Kane was still with Hughes and now a personal friend, Kane became a familiar face at the Romaine office. It was not long until Hughes was hearing, and ignoring, hints of Noah Dietrich's not-quite proper use of Hughes' funds for his own enjoyment.

Shortly after Bill Gay went to work for Nadine, he, Murrin and Nadine actually went to Hughes in person to explain that Noah had purloined a large sum of money from Hughes' funds. Hughes said, "And how much are you saying he used for his own purposes?"

Murrin answered him, "We can pretty well make it one million dollars."

Hughes then replied, "And how much did he make for me during that year?"

Murrin answered, "About seven million."

Hughes then said, "It appears to me that a return of seven million for a smaller one million is a pretty good return on our money." He then turned his back on the talebearers.

Dietrich married in October of 1955. He had an open house for the entire Romaine Street staff. The house he and his new wife were now living in was a very elaborate home in the hills above Beverly Hills. By this time, he was aware that news about him was reaching Hughes. Noah took the most recent hire in the

Operations Center behind the large swimming pool and offered that person a sum equal to his salary if he, Noah, could receive reports of what was being said and going on in that office. This bribe attempt was reported to Gay and Nadine. Murrin evidently said something to Hughes, who received it rather brusquely. Murrin reported later to Hughes that Noah had negotiated for the house using the Hughes name and funds but putting the title to the house in his own name.

In the late spring of 1957, an article appeared in a Los Angeles newspaper accusing the Hughes organization of using bribes and influence to obtain drilling permits for oil in the Los Angeles Harbor. This was brought to Hughes' attention. One thing that just wasn't done was to use the Hughes name or connection in any way that would bring discredit on Hughes. Investigation revealed that Noah, in the company of several business associates and lawyers, had accomplished this for his own benefit. The Hughes name was never on the final documents. It is generally believed that this was the final blow to Dietrich's association with Howard Hughes. True to his lifelong personnel relationships, Hughes waited until Noah made the first move, which came on about May 12, 1957.

The above disclosures are some of which were developed for Hughes' defense in the slander case filed by Noah following his forced departure. It is now believed that with the demise of Ed Clyde and Chester Davis, Wadsworth is the only person alive who was instrumental in putting the defense together for Hughes.

Wadsworth opines that Marty Cook may also have firsthand knowledge of the slander case and the associated stories. Marty, as his associates knew him, had started his career with Hughes as a key member of the Operations staff. An accomplished attorney, Marty later managed and supervised the Los Angeles law firm for Chester Davis. His rise to prominence is typical of the pattern of success demonstrated by most of the original members of the

Hughes Operations staff, all of whom benefitted and learned a great deal while being closely allied with Howard Robard Hughes.

One typical, and somewhat humorous, experience in which Marty was involved occurred while the staff was in Miami in 1953 with Hughes. In carrying out any assignment for Hughes, staff members had to commit to flawless memory every minute detail of his instructions in order to carry out and complete the assignment to his satisfaction.

On one such important assignment, Marty was to lease an estate and meet with the property owners, again carefully following Hughes' instructed dialogue to the letter. Formally dressed in a white suit, he was to represent himself as a successful and recent college graduate (which he was) and to lease the house for one year.

He was successful in securing the lease, but when he attempted to back out of the driveway in Hughes' 1951 Chevrolet with a manual transmission, the car refused to shift into reverse. He called James Whetton, a car guy, who explained to him that a part of the transmission linkage had become disconnected.

Following Jim's instructions, he crawled under the car, white suit and all, reconnected the needed lever, and returned to the Columbus Hotel with a grease-stained white suit that had to be disposed of.

Howard Hughes

RKO

RKO, in the late 1930s, became a leader in doing things differently. In 1939, the management of RKO, in keeping with new and innovative programs they were trying to implement at the studio, hired Orson Wells to create and direct films. Wells had just startled the public with his exciting expose of outer-space beings that was broadcast over the radio. It was so real that the listening public actually believed an alien invasion was happening.

As a result of this overwhelming success, Wells immediately made changes to the way films were being produced, especially in the use of cameras and soundtracks. His direction of dialogue was also very unique. In *Citizen Kane,* his use of off-screen voices and other innovations broke with the staid Hollywood methods.

Hughes was intrigued by the new RKO. It seemed to be heading in a direction that his creative mind always seemed to run. On May 10, 1948, Hughes purchased RKO from Floyd Odlum, the president of the Atlas Corporation. Ellie Pugmire writes here about her duties as it concerned Hughes and his movies.

"One of the things vitally important to Hughes, which I handled, was his library of motion pictures, including every current film made by RKO. It was a common practice in those days for heads of other studios, as well as stars, to borrow motion pictures to be shown in their homes or studios for private parties. Certain old films were prohibited, and Hughes used every known process to preserve these films that were stored in the basement at Romaine Street. He never allowed anyone to see a picture he had not screened first, if it was a new one, and then the only persons permitted to see the new pictures were certain studio heads such as Harry Cohn, Sam Goldwyn, Cecil B. De Mille, Spyro Skouras, and Darryl Zanuck; and Hughes also wanted to know who would be screening with them.

"I had lists of films in Hughes' film library and those at RKO which showed the year the film was made, the stars, film classification such as comedy, drama, musical, western, etc., the producers, directors, and others associated with the film; and I knew which ones could be loaned and which ones could not.

"I kept a complete file on every motion picture which was loaned out, and this information included who made the request and for what reason, where the screening would take place, those to be present at the screening, who approved the request, and the data on the delivery and return of the film.

"Many times, when those heads of studios were extremely anxious to view a film, and I had turned down the request by their secretaries, they personally called me and explained the necessity to see the film. Occasionally I took their request to Mr. Hughes for him to make the final decision. When requests were granted, the film would be picked up at a certain time just prior to when they wanted the screening and returned to us, or the studio, promptly the next morning.

"Mr. Hughes had his own projectionist, Karl, who was on call at all hours, and sometimes Hughes would only loan a film if his own projectionist ran the film. Hughes used Sam Goldwyn's projection room located at his studio on Santa Monica Boulevard just a few blocks from the Romaine Street office. Hughes, on the other hand, borrowed from the other studios, and those requests were also handled by me."

Unfortunately, things deteriorated at RKO. Among the many reasons for this problem was that Hughes was in no hurry to have a production chief who could really run the show. Dory Schary was no longer affiliated with RKO, and Schary was the one man who could have made RKO a money maker. Instead, Hughes felt he could run the studio himself and make money and pictures at the same time.

The simple fact was, however, that Hughes did not have the necessary time or energy to guarantee the success of another empire such as RKO. Another reason for the abject failure was because of the Communist situation that occurred in the 1950s to which Hughes was committed to fight to the finish.

Hughes did turn out one picture in 1952 called *The Las Vegas Story*, starring Jane Russell and Victor Mature. The film did not win any Oscars. One reviewer was quoted as saying, "Miss Russell wore so many plunging necklines and strapless gowns that the actors had a difficult time focusing on their lines while on set shooting these scenes."

Since the picture did not do very well, it should have been forgotten and written off. However, it marked the emergence of Hughes, the fighter.

The writer of the screenplay was Paul Jarrico, who had been hired by RKO to do the screen writing. Jarrico was a member of the Screen Writers' Guild. It was in 1951 that the HCUA (House Committee on Un-American Activities) had subpoenaed Jarrico to appear before the committee in Washington, D.C. The subject of the committee was to determine the extent of Communist infiltration in the movie industry. As you may recall, the HCUA was just another committee until after World War II. It had been something of an embarrassment to the Franklin D. Roosevelt administration before and during the war because Russia was an ally.

After the war, the HCUA branched out as a champion, determined to stop the spread of Communism. What better place to start than the motion picture industry?

Howard Hughes was really passive about politics. As was observed by Noah Dietrich, it was not known if Hughes was a

Democrat or Republican. It apparently didn't make much difference to Hughes as he effectively played both sides of the political fence. It has been reported that Hughes never voted in his life, although there is no record to substantiate that.

When it came to making political moves, Hughes was always behind the scenes using skilled negotiators to press his point, but they always had to come back to Hughes for any financial strategies. Hughes usually only got involved in politics when one of his many business entities was directly affected in one way or another. He never hesitated to get deeply involved in any matter that potentially was a threat to his country, or anyone living in it. In particular, Hughes, to his everlasting credit, took on the issue of Communism right up front. He felt that this was a direct confrontation and genuine threat—Communism against the American free enterprise system.

Hughes immediately fired Jarrico in April 1951, even though the screenplay was not yet complete, because Jarrico refused to answer HCUA's direct questioning as to whether or not he was a Communist. Jarrico took the Fifth Amendment on the grounds that his answer might tend to incriminate him. This was enough for Hughes. He wanted no part of anyone with the slightest taint of "red." It could be said Hughes believed, "better dead than red." Now that Jarrico had been fired and a non-protect filed by Jarrico or the Union, the matter could well have died there.

Hughes, confronted a short time later with finishing the screenplay, hired other writers to finish the task. The writers were told that Jarrico's name would not appear on the credits of the film, although Jarrico had contributed substantially to the film. It was determined that he had written about one-third of the screenplay. The writers then protested. The Union agreement provided for arbitration in such cases, and the dispute was submitted to a panel consisting of three members of the Writer's Guild.

The decision, as determined by the panel, was to be binding on both sides. The writers, however, had not counted on Hughes' tenacity. Even after the arbitrators had reviewed the screenplay and film clips and, as might be expected, submitted that Jarrico wrote at least one-third of the screenplay, their decision was that Jarrico should be given credit according to the contract. Because of Hughes' resolve, when the picture was released, Jarrico's name was conspicuously absent. This happened in early 1952.

It would appear that Hughes was in direct violation of the Union contract that provided for credit to be given to those who participated in the making or writing of the film. This, then, resulted in an open, and what was to be a vicious, confrontation between RKO (representing the industry) and the Writer's Guild. The Union felt that it had been put on the spot. To them it was a labor dispute that had to be challenged, as they felt Hughes violated the contract to which Hughes' RKO was a signatory. Hughes knew it would, without doubt, boil down to an issue of Communism versus the American way.

From the outset, public opinion was decidedly with Hughes and against the Union and Jarrico. The Screen Writer's Guild was painfully aware that the entire matter would be viewed in a different light once the media began its reporting of the issue. They knew the public was against them from the start because the HCUA had raised the insidious issue nationwide of the threat of Communism, of which everyone was acutely aware.

Nevertheless, the Union felt it had to make a stand on the issue as they saw their contracts with writers being threatened. They considered the matter as strictly a labor dispute that should be resolved without the overtones of Communism. It was a calculated risk the Union took because it would be obvious to all who read about the issue that they were trying to defend one of their own, a man who had refused to testify before a Congressional committee, and, for his own protection from prosecution, had sought and invoked the Fifth Amendment for whatever reasons. The Guild felt it had no other option than to protest to RKO that the contract had been broken, and the possibility of a strike was in the offing. They were determined to take this stand for fear other studios would adopt the same tactic used by Hughes, and their position would be dangerously impaired.

Swift action by Hughes at this point took control of whatever initiatives the Guild may have had. It lost its momentum, if it really had any, at this time when Hughes filed his suit in the Los Angeles Superior Court in March 1952.

Legally, Hughes sought a declaratory judgment and asked to be relieved of any demands for damages that Jarrico might make. RKO took the position that Jarrico had violated the standard moral clause in his contract when refusing to answer the questions posed by the HCUA. It was RKO's point that the contract was rendered null and void when Jarrico declined, under oath, to answer those certain questions, thus cancelling his contractual obligations with RKO.

In an effort to end this portion of the Hughes/RKO episode, Paul Jarrico filed suit for $350,000 against Hughes and RKO, claiming he was illegally denied screen credits for *The Las Vegas Story*. In December 1952, Judge Orlando H. Rhodes, who dismissed the lawsuit contending that Hughes and RKO had done nothing improper, issued a ruling. During the interim period between March and December 1952, Hughes did appear in court to testify on his own behalf.

Ellie Pugmire recounts the following: "Mr. Hughes was an avid fighter of Communism and the first person I recall who was actively fighting it, and he started this fight at his RKO Studios. One of the members of the staff kept a "pink" file in an office set up at the studio, covering every employee who was known to be active in the Communist Party or who had attended such meetings. Hughes either fired them or blacklisted them from working in his studio or any other studio if he could. No one was hired to work on any picture at RKO until cleared by this special office. He was genuinely one of the most patriotic men I have ever known and for him to appear in public and testify was my proof of his dedication. I was very impressed with the man I would be working for the next six years. This was one of the last appearances in public by HRH."

Ellie also recalls the sale of RKO in 1954: "It was one of the longest and biggest projects I had worked on so far, and all of my time was spent at the Beverly Hills Hotel during this period in 1954. I typed the entire contract myself in the same room with Hughes, his attorneys, James Whetton, Mr. Tom O'Neil, and others, and I believe Ralph Stolkin was also present. I don't remember all of the names, but I remember Mr. Stolkin because he was smoking a big cigar at the time, and when Hughes came into the room he put it out.

"Mr. Hughes was clearly in control at all times, and I was amazed at his skill in not only telling the attorneys how it should be done, but his uncanny knowledge of the law.

"The contract was tremendously complicated and had to be revised many times. The thing that impressed me most was the fact that Mr. Hughes practically dictated the whole contract verbatim. He seemed to have a photographic mind and could remember exactly where an item or phrase could be found.

"However, after about three days of complicated negotiations and long hours, Mr. Hughes' beard was showing, and he had his dirty white collar turned inside. Obviously he had been working day and night and his appearance didn't bother him at all. He was looking through the typed pages and couldn't find an item he thought was in the contract. He looked directly at me and said, 'You left out such-and-such when you typed this.' I knew that it had been discussed at one point but never was dictated. I started to explain to him that it hadn't been dictated and none of the other men came to my rescue, but he interrupted me and said, 'Well, we won't stand here arguing about it.' I think that even he was a little tired at this point. Later, when he was out of the room, several of the men came up to me and said that they knew I hadn't left it out. But it was soon taken care of and forgotten. That's the only time Mr. Hughes ever said anything like that to me.

"The lengthy contract was all finished, neatly typed with no erasures, with the copies placed in their blue backings, and were ready to be signed.

"It was then about 9:00 p.m. and Mr. Hughes announced that we were going to go to Las Vegas where the documents had to be signed. He wanted me to go also as we would have to get out a press release as soon as they were signed.

"As we walked out the door, he looked at me, and said to the other men, 'She's a damn good stenographer.' I was well rewarded."

Ellie continues: "The others went to the Santa Monica Clover Field Airport, where Mr. Hughes kept his Convair, and they flew with him at the controls to Las Vegas. I wanted to pick up an overnight bag at home and freshen up, so I had the office make a reservation on the next flight available and had a driver pick me up at home to take me to the Los Angeles Airport. I met the others at the Flamingo Hotel around midnight.

"I didn't have time to be tired, and by the time everything was organized and a typewriter found for me to type on, it was getting close to morning again.

"Mr. Hughes dictated the press release over my shoulder, and I typed directly from his dictation. The press release was two pages long when it was finished. He picked it up and read it, and I couldn't believe it when he handed me back the second page to type over. There was a flaw in the bond paper and it wasn't acceptable to him. Yes, he was a perfectionist.

"About 6:30 a.m., when the work was finished, he turned to me and said that I had done a good job and that he appreciated my help and said that I could go and get some rest now."

When the RKO sales was complete, Ellie recounts the following: "After the RKO transaction was over no one seemed to know what happened to the check for several million dollars. This went on for days, everyone was extremely nervous, and the office was in an uproar. Mr. Hughes claimed he gave it to someone, but it had completely vanished. He called James Whetton to see if he had seen the check. Jim reminded him that he had not accompanied him to Las Vegas and had not seen the check.

"A couple of weeks later Mr. Hughes gave his old sport coat that had patches on the sleeves to Don Alder to take to the cleaners. Don was standing there as the cleaning attendant went through the pockets. He pulled out a crumpled piece of paper and the missing check was found."

Howard Hughes (signature)

The Starlets

Much has been made, through the years, of Howard Hughes and women. With regard to the starlets Hughes placed under contract for possible use in his movies, Gordon Bench recalls: "Mr. Hughes had a number of starlets under contract in the 1950s. To keep them active and away from the Hollywood "vultures" it was necessary to schedule drama lessons and other activities to avoid boredom on the part of these young girls from all over the United States. It was up to us, in Operations, to schedule the arrival time at the drama coach's home or studio, make certain the lesson only extended a certain time, and that the young starlet would go out the back door as another came in the front door.

"The drivers were very adept at this and at no time during my stay with the Hughes organization was there a serious slip-up. But it was close many, many times. Hughes knew of this delicate balance and would call from time to time to check up to make sure schedules were being adhered to. This was a very serious part of the job assignment but it had its humor too. The humor may not come across to readers, but to us it was almost hilarious. Especially when the drivers would come back and tell us that they saw driver A pull up thirty seconds ahead of schedule and driver B was not quite ready to depart. Of course, the drivers knew all of the different starlets because the driving assignments were changed often. This was so the starlets couldn't quiz the driver too closely because they didn't know quite enough about the operation. They were all so thrilled about being in Hollywood and taking drama lessons that they didn't always understand the scope of the entire program."

"These incidents are unknown to most of the public and particularly to these starlets, but were of interest to us in that we could picture Mr. Hughes behind a master chessboard plotting the moves of these starlets. And then the impression came to us that he was running his empire in much the same way with a definite overview of what was going on in the different companies.

"Mr. Hughes, in our opinion, was still interested in the possibility of getting into full-scale movie productions again, and that is why he sponsored and signed these girls to contracts with RKO Studios. In the long run they had a lot to gain and, by comparison, little to lose. One interesting fact to remember is that Hughes had no personal contact with any of them. One 'garbage collector' said in his writing that Hughes had an intimate relationship with one Yvonne Shubert. We know this to be totally false.

"This process did afford us some more pleasurable moments when it was necessary to take these starlets to a social event such as the ballet. This would involve one of us and our wives and the starlet for dinner and an evening out. This was indeed a treat for our wives who were kept busy at home with our children. Often we would use the Cadillac limousine with a driver, and it was very impressive to the young starlet to get such treatment."

An important part of Hughes' program was to expose these starlets to the finer things in Hollywood. As Gordon relates, "During one of these evenings, I had my first trip to Perrino's on Wilshire Boulevard, one of the truly outstanding restaurants in Los Angeles. It was there I first tasted caviar, which I think is great for the Russians, but I understand you have to cultivate a taste for it.

"Through the course of the years we got on a first name with most of the maître d's in Hollywood, Beverly Hills, Los Angeles, and Santa Monica. Obviously when we came into the restaurant we always got the red carpet treatment because there was always money in it for the maître d's, the waiters, and the restaurant. But the service was excellent and the food superb, hard to really tell which restaurant was finer than another one. Several favorites, one of ours was the old Tallyho on Beverly Boulevard with absolutely the finest cheesecake ever. The wife of the owner made it herself and was so proud of her accomplishments, but she was not willing to share her recipe with anyone. Also, the Beverly Hills Hotel where the cuisine was marvelous. Of course, none of us ever drank any liquor items, which must have hurt the hard hearts of the maître d's because that is the money maker in the restaurant business.

"After I left Hughes employ, my wife and I went to the Tallyho a time or two but were always quick to tell them we were not with Hughes any longer, and we were paying. However, the maître d' continued to treat us as if we were still with Hughes, but with a more modest check for us to pay.

"While Hughes was spending, or should we say investing, a considerable amount of money in the future of the young ladies under contract, it is even more interesting to disclose his personal interest in their safety and security. It has never been known by anyone, except for his vassals, the details of how they were protected by having them under highly professional surveillance. This was in addition to providing them with everything they needed for their comfort and well-being. Hughes was never, regardless of their progress or lack thereof, unkind to them, nor did he just get rid of them. If they left the program, it was only because they felt their progress was not fast enough to satisfy them."

According to Ellie Pugmire, "The girls were all under surveillance at one time or another and some of them had their phones tapped when it was suspected that they were 'playing around.' Mike Conrad was doing most of this work during the time I worked for Hughes. His real name was Jeff Chouinard, but he was known as Mike Conrad after he started his contract. He had his own company and he hired as many operators as necessary. Mike had a panel truck equipped with all kinds of electronic equipment. They could keep surveillance from this truck, as well as listen to what was going on in the house they were watching.

"At one time, while I was living in Westwood, they were keeping surveillance on Joyce Taylor, just a couple of blocks from where my home was, and I saw the parked truck when she went to the office and when she returned. Mike laughingly told me once that one of the residents used to come out and bring him coffee after he'd been there awhile."

James Whetton was assigned by Hughes to read all surveillance reports daily and to notify Hughes of anything in the reports that in his judgment it should be brought to his attention.

Ellie also remembers: "Bill Gay had to hire many more employees to take care of the girls. They were always assigned to work in pairs when they escorted the girls to dinner, to their drama or singing lessons, shopping, or to the theater. They followed a rigid schedule, which was set up in the office. Hughes hired the best drama and singing coaches in the industry to train the girls—and also to keep them busy.

"They lived in nice secluded apartments or homes where surveillance was made easy. Hughes spent very little time, if any, with them, and he wanted reports so he would know what was going on. He was also watching the escorts.

"Any messages the girls had for Hughes were relayed by these young men. Almost every detail of their activities was reported to the office and it was a monumental job to keep them all under control. Bit parts were gotten for some, and Joyce Taylor got to star in a movie, but the others never made it.

"They were under contract to Hughes Productions, so when Hughes sold RKO they still stayed on. Hughes also had connections with the other studios. While the girls were being trained they received $200 a week and their contracts usually were for two years. They seemed to have a certain amount of security and they, too, were well taken care of."

> *"My affections were first for my country,*
> *then, generally for all mankind."*
>
> *Thomas Jefferson*

Patriotism

One hundred and sixty years ago, Daniel Webster said, "Let our object be our country, our whole country and nothing but our country. And by the blessing of God, may that Country itself become a vast and splendid instrument, not of oppression and terror, but of Wisdom, of Peace and Liberty, upon which the world may gorge without administration forever!"

Patriotism runs in the blood, be it blue or otherwise. An essential part of the entire adult life of Howard Hughes was his love of America. His approach to his industrial activity, his inventions, and his improvements on those of others, his expenditure of the enormous funds to develop industry with America in mind, his antagonism to Communism, and his political support of those who he viewed as true patriots—these things have never been fully explored in all the thousands of words that have been written about him. Hughes believed that Communism fed on aggression, hatred, and the imprisonment of men's minds and souls, and he fought with passion to keep it from taking root in America.

Hughes was not an isolationist as was Burton K. Wheeler. (Burton K. Wheeler served in the United States Senate from 1923 to 1927. He came to the attention of America by helping to expose the scandals of the Harding administration. He was an extreme isolationist until World War II and had a large public following.)

Hughes was not an Internationalist, One-Worlder as was Henry A. Wallace. (Henry A. Wallace was Franklin D. Roosevelt's second Vice President. He was an outspoken one-world exponent. He was not re-nominated for Vice President in 1944 because of his social idealism and internationalism. Truman asked for his resignation from the Cabinet partly for his outspoken support of Russia. Franklin D. Roosevelt sent him on a wartime mission both to Russia and China. Wallace was regarded as a Communist.)

There is no better way to describe Howard Hughes in short terms than "American Firster." He received the Congressional Medal of Honor in 1941 for the Glomar Explorer work.

Although much can be said and written about Howard Hughes' patriotism for his country, there are also many examples of his equal patriotism and deep concerns for his countrymen and women. One outstanding example of this was displayed prominently during the period of atomic testing that took place in Nevada during the 1960s and into the 1970s.

Hughes was deeply concerned about the inevitable tragic outcome that would result from exposure to radiation generated by the atomic tests. He was very disturbed regarding the health and safety of people and animals living downwind from the tests. The prevailing winds in the area were primarily from the west and south. As it turned out, Hughes was a hundred percent correct.

Studies have since proven that, without doubt, a large and yet undetermined number of people, particularly from southern Utah, along with thousands of sheep and cattle, have died, in many cases from cancer, as a result of this exposure. Hughes went so far as to instruct his own people—employees and vassals—in Nevada, to avoid any areas of potential exposure and also to note and report any damage that might occur as a result of quake-causing tests. One such event was reported to him when earth movement, as a result of a test, broke a high-pressure water line at the Desert Inn, resulting in substantial flooding of the project.

In January of 1971, Hughes hired, as a new Washington, D.C. representative, Robert F. Bennett, later to become a U.S. Senator from Utah. At that time, Bennett was a proprietor for the Central

Intelligence Agency (CIA) and he negotiated with Hughes to use Hughes as a front for Project Jennifer, which was the mission name assigned to the Hughes-owned Glomar Explorer.

Briefly stated, this ship was designed and especially equipped to explore the possibility of mining deep-sea areas of the Pacific Rim for valuable minerals. This was merely a front for the CIA's search for a sunken Russian atomic submarine. The sub was found and documents retrieved which, to this day, have never been publicly exposed.

Much has been written and said about Hughes' research and personal involvement with the mighty flying boat, the Hercules, but very little is known about the fact that while the Hercules was tied to a Long Beach pier, it was for years a floating research laboratory. Modern-day aircraft radar was developed, along with many other amenities for modern-day aircraft flying comforts. After all of the fallout from the government's funding of the project, only a few insiders are aware that Hughes had invested $25 million of his own money on the Hercules.

Although Hughes maintained for years that he was a citizen and resident of Nevada, like most native Texans, he never quite got Texas and those early teachings out of his personality. He claimed to the time of his death the friendship of several Texans. However, his first and lifelong loyalty was to the United States of America. He was a red, white, and blue American patriot.

This did not keep him from being greatly admired throughout the world. For instance, even though he gained great publicity for "kicking the Communists out of Hollywood," when the State Department was dealing with Communist China to allow President Nixon a state visit to China, one of the U.S. demands was to allow a satellite positioned that would cover all of the President's appearances in China. This was to keep China from publishing its own version of everything.

After months of meetings and communications, China agreed to the satellite only if Hughes placed it and gave his word that after the visit, the satellite would either be destroyed or that the control, including transmissions, would be transferred to China. China would accept the word and work of Hughes before it would that of the United States.

It can well be argued that no other wealthy American industrialist has been as concerned as Hughes in keeping money, industry, and especially defense-related inventions and weaponry in the United States and out of the hands of potential enemies. Even during the Korean and Vietnam wars, Hughes did not agree that his heat-seeking missiles and air-to-air sighting systems his companies had developed should be given to other nations, even allies. He, of course, had little direct control over this because so many of his defense systems and weapons had been transferred to the United States Defense Department.

Throughout the prime period of his life—primarily the 1950s—Hughes' vassals were privileged to see first-hand his deep involvement with the dynamic growth of the Hughes Aircraft Company, and his never-ending search and recruitment of the country's top scientists for employment with Hughes Aircraft. They were proven and known for their abilities to invent, develop, and manufacture the top-secret needs of the military and the masses of "ordinary" people involved in air travel. His focus was mostly concentrated on the design of the aircraft of the future, conveniences, and safety items such as aircraft cabin pressurization systems, military and commercial radar, missiles, guidance systems, and satellites, all of which required investments of billions of dollars for research, development, and final production of the end product.

Volumes have already been written about Hughes' famous exploits, but have been reviewed here to establish his evolution as a true and dedicated patriot. All of these achievements were publicized worldwide and established and solidified America's world image as a leader in all fields of aviation and later established America's undeniable leadership in space exploration, all of which established Hughes Aircraft as a partner in the space program. Howard Hughes was inducted into the Aviation Hall of Fame on December 14, 1973, just two years and four months prior to his passing.

An early disclosure of Hughes' lifetime of patriotism was clearly displayed in the contents of a copy of his first will, which was prepared in the early 1920s and was later modified. He never wavered from his constant love and loyal, idealistic support for his country. Many incidents during his life are reminders of this distinguishing quality. One could say it first became apparent as he attempted to prepare a will, to his historic fight against Communism, to his numerous contributions to aviation, and to his final legacy, the Howard Hughes Medical Institute.

Some of Howard Hughes' awards include:

- The Harmon trophy for Outstanding Aviator of 1936 and 1938
- The Congressional Gold Medal awarded in 1941 in recognition of his achievements in advancing the science of aviation and thus bringing great credit to his country and throughout the world. According to the *New York Times*, he never bothered to come to Washington to pick it up. Later President Harry Truman mailed it to him.
- The Collier trophy, given in 1938 to Howard and his crew for their successful around the world flight
- The Octave Chanute Award in 1940 for outstanding contribution made by a pilot or test personnel to the advancement of arts, science and technology, and aeronautics

- Induction into the Aviation Hall of Fame (Dayton, Ohio) in 1973
- Induction into the International Aerospace Hall of Fame posthumously in 1987
- Induction into the Nevada Business Hall of Fame posthumously in 2003

The Airplane Chronicles

Much has been written about Hughes' various accomplishments in aviation so some of his more famous issues and flight problems are not detailed here. Those less known incidents recorded in logbooks from the mechanics that worked on planes and times when Hughes would actually speak one-on-one are very interesting.

There is a world of difference in the ability to modify an existing plane and the genius to engineer and manufacture a completely new one. Because one can do the first doesn't mean he can do the other. Howard Hughes was a genius at both.

As with most boys growing up in the 1910s, especially in Texas and California, flying and airplanes became almost an obsession. By the time Hughes was ten years old, the U.S. Army was experimenting with aircraft. Planes not much more than winged kites with motors and propellers carved of wood were being tested by the Army. Balloons were used as early as the Civil War to spy on the movement and locations of enemy troops. Although none of the hide-bound, Napoleon-worshipping military brains in Washington D.C. accepted anything but cavalry to furnish intelligence, Pershing did make nominal use of two planes in his pursuit of Pancho Villa. Any boy living close to an Army base became fascinated by the flights of the planes the Army was testing. Hughes was no exception.

When his parents enrolled him in school in Ojai, California, Hughes was just a few miles from Santa Maria where one of the first schools of aeronautics was established. Big Howard took Little Howard to Boston when Hughes was nine years old to witness the annual rowing race between Harvard and Yale.

Big Howard, a Harvard grad, was so pleased with Harvard's victory over their arch rival Yale that he made a promise to Little Howard that he could have anything he wanted. Little H had seen a hydroplane in the harbor. He pointed to it and said he wanted a ride in that plane. Big H wasn't happy with the choice, but he kept his word. Hughes had a fondness for seaplanes, hydro and amphibian, from that day forward.

By late 1919, the warplanes from WWI were beginning to appear everywhere in the U.S. in the hands of the test pilots and veteran flyers of the Great War. Any place there was a field, grass strip, straight road, even occasionally a bladed-out airstrip, and a chance that a crowd would gather, one could bet that barnstormers would set down hoping to pick up a few dollars.

The United States was only able to put 196 U.S. manufactured planes in Europe during the war; however, over 1,200 planes were built. The famous "Jenny," which had been developed as a light bomber, was sold to the public. At first slightly underpowered, it was later equipped with the dependable Liberty Engine. This plane, with reinforced wing surfaces, was used for wing walking and, with its large front cockpit, to give rides. Although no records still exist, there appears to be no doubt that Hughes was an excited and eager passenger. The Deviland, DH 4, and toward the middle of the 1920s, the Jenny, were used by the Army to fly the beginning of the Airmail service.

In the middle of the 1920s, Hughes was an accomplished pilot although it was several years before he ever applied for and received an "Airman's Certificate," or pilot's license. From his first ride in the seaplane in Boston, Hughes was fascinated with "what makes them fly." This led to a deep interest in plane design and engineering. The WWI fighters he bought for *Hell's Angels* intrigued him. Why could a Spad X111 out-dive any of the others without shedding fabric or wings? Why could a Fokker 7, slower by ten miles per hour in level flight, out-climb a SE 5? Why was a Fokker tri-plane so much more maneuverable than any other fighter? Did the rather early design of the cowling on the Sopwith Camel and French Spad allow greater speed with the horsepower in each?

Hughes had purchased roughly eighty WWI fighter planes to make *Hell's Angels*. He had many pilots available from that war—British, Canadian, American, and German. These pilots knew the planes very well, and they knew the planes were getting old and untrustworthy. New vassals at the Operations Center were impressed with the story told that during the filming, one of the pilots had refused to do a stunt Hughes had dreamed up for a dog fighting sequence. Hughes grounded the pilot, got into the plane, and performed the flying stunt himself.

What was left out of the telling, meant to impress the new man, was that there was more than one such incident. On more than one occasion when the stunt pilot refused to pilot one of the old relics, Hughes would take the plane himself and demonstrate the airworthiness of the plane and the feasibility of the stunt. After several attempts to film a squadron take-off when all but one of the planes would get off the ground, Hughes, believing as he did so many times in his life, that people or circumstances were deliberately thwarting his desires, took the defaulting pilot from the plane. He got in it and the multi-plane takeoff was to be filmed again. Hughes got the fifteen- or more year-old plane about a hundred feet in the air and it lost control. The resulting crash, the first of many Hughes survived, put him in the hospital, seriously injured.

Attempting to capitalize on the great success of *Hell's Angels*, Hughes followed with two more WWI movies—*Cock of the Air*, and *Sky Devils*. By the filming time for these two films, which were poorly received, the planes used in his first great success were really worn out, rickety, and dangerous. Substitute look-alikes and trick photography were the order of the day. There were, by this time, quite a few home-built, three-quarter size copies of the WWI planes— some were undoubtedly used. For years, a three-quarter Spad was flown from the Burbank airfield. The plane problems forced Hughes to become even more interested in their design and engineering.

His fascination with seaplanes reared its head again in late 1933 or early 1934 when Hughes became interested in a hydroplane he saw in the Los Angeles Harbor. He bought it and had it transferred to a repair shop in Burbank. He had already reamed up modifications he wanted to make to the plane. One of the many fortuitous incidents in Hughes' life occurred at this time. The shop assigned Glen Odekirk to work with him. Odekirk was a real flying "nut" and an accomplished pilot. Glen was one of comparatively few men in Hughes' life with whom he formed an almost instant liking. Odekirk got along very well with the man.

Although it was never really dormant in Hughes, his mental, egotistical, rather selfish, and secretive nature became overpowering. Seemingly out of the clear blue sky, he decided to fly that plane east. He never, at that time, divulged any plan or purpose for the trip.

Odekirk found that he was looking for a mechanic to go with him and asked to be that man. Hughes told him that as a married man, perhaps he shouldn't go because it could last a couple months. Odekirk still wanted to go. As the two men separated, Hughes hollered over his shoulder to the effect that Odekirk should pack since they would leave the next morning. This was the notice that so often prepared persons who Hughes allowed to accompany him.

The trip east lasted several months longer than two. Hughes and Odekirk were next located in Florida where they took part in the All American Air Meet of 1934. Hughes entered an amateur pilot event and won his first award.

Hughes' underlying self-esteem and his ever-present patriotism were aroused when a professional French pilot, Raymond Delmonte, set a new land speed record of 314.219 miles per hour. It took a war and the knowledge of how the Germans had secretly developed the Luftwaffe for nations to realize the need and great benefit of secrecy in development of machines and weapons that may aid in fighting a war. It didn't take even discrete inquiries to discover that Delmonte's plane had been developed by the French government at the unheard of cost of $1 million dollars. The government involvement by the French annoyed Hughes' and he resolved to recapture the speed record that had been held by James Wadell, an American. Hughes sent Odekirk back to California to find the facilities to manufacture a plane of Hughes' own design with his own money.

Upon returning to California, Odekirk found a place for Hughes at the Glendale airport. He began to lay in the tools and equipment to accomplish the outlandish hopes of a true dreamer. Hughes followed Odekirk and, on arriving and approving the location, looked for those to help with the dream. From the California Institute of Technology, Hughes selected Richard Palmer. He then hired ten or more skilled workers and a meteorologist, W. C. Rockefeller.

Hughes then began a style of work that stayed with him the rest of his life. He began the round-the-clock workday that became familiar to his staff. He would exist on sandwiches and milk with seemingly no sleep. As the Boss and doing it himself, he seemed to expect his whole crew to do the same. Again, as he did the rest of his working life, if he just couldn't go any longer, he would disappear for a few hours in the daytime for sleep and return refreshed. It is to be noted that this was daytime, and not at night, as would most men.

Hughes was discovering that mental concepts and knowledge "out of the air" wasn't enough to design and build his dream plane.

When problems developed that seemed to be beyond him, Odekirk, or Palmer, Hughes would disappear for a day or two without notice. When he returned he would be filled with knowledge and ideas to solve the problem. Word of what Hughes was doing leaked out and was even written in periodicals. This probably made him more attractive to Army aeronautical engineers, private individuals such as university professors, and knowledgeable pilots such as Lindberg, Wiley Post, and others who were already aeronautical heroes.

There is no doubt that Hughes did not go to Wright Patterson field in Ohio. He had already made enemies at that field responsible for most of the research and development of the Army Air Force. Hughes had no sympathy for the military mentality that was keeping the U.S. development of air power tied to the conceived use of planes prevalent in WWI. He made no secret of his public criticism of that mentality. His public statements made a lifelong enemy of Major General Myers, the commanding general of that field.

Starting with his study of WWI planes while making *Hell's Angels,* the monocot wing and streamlined cowling of the Lockheed Vega, he made a careful study of all the so-called racing planes. Hughes' many interviews and consultations with aeronautical engineers, airflow, and other experts, fixed in his mind what to do about streamlining and the problems of air resistance.

One of the first solutions he discovered was the thick chord of the wing. For the lift necessary for low-powered engines, and to give the plane maneuverability, the chords in both the top and bottom wings of the WWI fighters were thick and in the front of the wing. Undoubtedly, Hughes had the brains of his staff to aid him, but he made the first steps in what was to become known as the "laminar flow" wing as it appeared on the Consolidated B-24, and more widely known on the P-51 Mustang. For his H-1 racing plane, Hughes moved the chord back almost to the middle of the wing, thinned the chord, then shortened the wing far beyond what his experts advised, then calmly told them that the power of the engine he would use would provide the necessary lift.

Hughes attacked the tail assembly. The struts and wire bracing would have to go. Certainly for a plane that was built for speed and not aeronautics, the usual large tail elevators and vertical assembly (fin and rudder) were not needed. On his plane, they therefore were reduced and streamlined.

Hughes and his experts studied the problem of the air "bubble" around the exposed nuts, bolts, and joints. It is not really known if a certain individual drew attention to the problem, but Hughes and his assembled experts devised a counter-sink for the nuts and bolts and a streamlining of the joints and flight controls.

The idea of retractable landing gear had been bandied about in aviation circles for several years, but had never been developed. Landing gear had been streamlined as far back as the Great War. Rudimentary spats had been put on landing gear. The axles and the braces had been worked over and the Fokker DVII was equipped with a flying surface axle. If a retractable gear had ever been engineered, it had never been put on a plane. The French-engineered plane of Delmonte had landing gear sheathed in metal that made the gear smooth and streamlined. Hughes conceived a gear working on a pivot and bringing it up into the fuselage.

In August 1935, the crew decided that the newly dubbed H1 was ready for testing. Now began the fights over who would test the plane. As with many later instances, the crews who worked with Hughes to develop this plane and the later ones tried to keep Hughes from testing such an innovative machine. Hughes had one argument that always prevailed: "It is my plane and I intend to test it." And so he did.

The test flight lasted for about fifteen minutes and was smoothly landed. The only problem encountered on the flight was the momentary heart wrenching when it appeared that either the wing or the field was too short. The plane lifted smoothly just before the runway ran out. Though there were no flight problems, the test flight revealed to Hughes that some slight changes were necessary. He and his mechanics immediately made them. The nearly too-short field caused Hughes to have the plane towed to Santa Anna where Martin Field offered plenty of runway length with no problems in climbing out.

On Friday morning, September 13, 1935, Hughes, in the H1, made four perfect passes over the course the timing officials had laid out and was unofficially credited with a speed near 350—well over the existing record of 314 mph. True to the perfectionist that he was all of his life, he thought he could do better so he made a fifth and sixth run. On the last pass, his engine quit, and Hughes lowered the gear and set down in a grass strip. He calmly got out of the plane and, when the worried observers raced to him, he was sitting in the grass making notes.

The two aviation associations that were officially timing Hughes agreed on an official time of 352.388 miles per hour. Much to the prestige of American aviation and to the discomfort of Major General Meyers at Wright Patterson, the plane had been engineered and constructed at the unbelievably low cost of roughly $120,000.

Due to the simple fact that he did not reveal his thoughts or plans to many people, if any, his interest in long-distance flying with passengers was not known to even his work crews. He had a passion for speed. He closely watched the assault on the coast-to-coast records and attempts to lower them. He had been refused entrance to the Bendix races on the ridiculous challenge that it would be unfair to the other entrants to allow him and his H1 racer to complete. It was of no consequence—there were other challenges to conquer.

During the 1934 Bendix Air Races, Roscoe Turner broke the

existing coast-to-coast record by breaking the then existing record with a flight of a bit over ten hours. Hughes found his next mission in the world of air speed.

He knew the limitations of his H1. As it was configured, the racer didn't have the carrying capacity for the fuel to make a high speed run of 2,400 miles. He studied his problem for some time and realized that the airmail planes then being flown could be his solution. He decided to extensively modify the Northrop Gamma, a mail plane.

He had a Gamma installed in his Glendale hangar and began his modifications. By the time he was satisfied, he had turned it into a drastically turned-out new model. He was able to borrow the latest Wright Cyclone engine and one of the variable pitch propellers that Hamilton had developed and sold to the Army Air Force. He solved a major problem in installing long distant tanks.

True to the work habits that had developed in the building of the H1, he ignored everything but the present problems. He slept when he could go no longer. He drove his crew to the limits of their endurance. He would have worked right through Christmas Eve of 1935 if Glen Odekirk had not questioned him as to the day. Hughes was pleased that someone had remembered his birthday, but Glen reminded him of Christmas and suggested the men should spend some time with their families. Hughes insisted that his crew be ready to get back to work the day after Christmas. Until near mid-January 1936, the workdays were long and hard.

Hughes now had a plane that would carry a load of 10,000 pounds, a record for planes of that type. His plane problems and physical hardships on that flight have been written numerous times and need not be repeated here. It should be sufficient to say that on January 13, 1936 at 12:15 p.m., he took his highly modified Northrop Gamma off the Los Angeles Union Air Terminal and touched down at the Newark Airport at 12:42:10 a.m. Eastern Standard Time. His flight time (elapsed time) of 9 hours, 27 minutes and 10 seconds took a bit more than a half hour off of Turner's time.

Although many of Hughes' peculiar work habits were never fully explained to his vassals as each started working at Romaine Street, it seemed as if many times the next problem and solution came to him "out of the blue." It was not really that way at all. He had many things he wanted to do in his life and something he either read or heard about often caused him to decide to do one of those many things immediately instead of later. It was so with various speed records. "That should be kept in the U.S; it will not last long and the U.S. should keep it. I'm going there anyway, so I may as well take care of it," was his excuse, explanation, or reason for starting something new. If for no other reason, he couldn't resist a challenge, whether it was one that had been thrown in his face or generated internally.

He was never a publicity-seeking ego. As with most of his endeavors, his cross-country speed flight was conducted without any notification to the press. After his landing and the time were made official, the news leaked out. Hughes was already one of the best stories the media had. The record time made the Northrop Gamma almost as famous as the H1. When the news leaked it took no time for the press to find him. In answer to the question, "Why?" he made one of the many laconic comments which the press picked up and for which he became famous: "I wanted to go to New York, so I decided to see how fast I could get there."

Hughes was reluctant to say anything about his modifications to the Northrop. What he did was his own. To end the prying, he gave the credit for the endurance and speed of the plane to the Air Force Wright engine and the variable pitch propeller. He had taken one of the better single-engine mail planes and made it a record-setting aircraft for single-engine carrying capacity, for endurance, and for cross-country speed. How he accomplished these remarkable records belonged to him, not to the general public and certainly not to his competitors, whom he considered his enemies.

Hughes never liked New York in the winter. In fact, he never appreciated cold weather, ice, and snow. As soon as he could get away from the publicity, he climbed into the Northrop and headed to Miami, one of his lifelong favorite retreats. While he was there he discovered that America's cross-country speed pilot, James Wadell, had set a new record from Miami to New York. Here was another personal challenge, and another time that he sought to accomplish a personal goal without hours of planning. In the middle of the next day, he got back in the modified Gamma and set down in New York about forty minutes faster than Wadell's time.

Now the press had an international field day. The officials who had to certify his record time from Miami to New York of 4 hours, 21 minutes, and some seconds for the roughly 1,200 miles couldn't keep such an accomplishment a secret. Without Hughes wanting it, in fact, to his annoyance, the press was off again. "No speed record is safe from the hottest pilot in the world!" Hughes was really irritated. His remarkable mind was now set to developing methods of besting the press and publicity. Disguises were invented. He began using aliases when registering in hotels. He was even able to evade Federal regulations and file flight plans in fictitious names. Later, even the vassals at Romaine Street used various names to escape public notice. One of the most used was "Uncle Howie." Usually, however, questions, inquiries, and snooping were simply ignored.

On his way back to California, Hughes put the Northrop down in Chicago. He met a friend for various business discussions. The friend was full of talk about Hughes' speed accomplishments. Hughes tried to make light of his records, saying that with the advance in plane design and power plants, passengers would soon be able to eat lunch in Chicago and supper in Los Angeles. His remark was laughingly challenged and a bet was offered to prove it. It would become known that it was dangerous to dare, bet, or imply that Hughes was lying or mistaken, especially if money was involved. The friend offered a fifty-dollar bet that Hughes couldn't prove the lunch and dinner statement.

Commercial airliners of the time were taking over twelve hours to make the trip. Hughes put up his $50, climbed into the Gamma shortly after the two had finished lunch, and at 7:15 p.m. Pacific time, he landed in Los Angeles and went straight to the lunch counter and ordered. He had won his bet.

Hughes was never happy with one of his newsworthy accomplishments when he believed that he was to be bettered in a short time. He had conceived modifications to the H1 that would allow him to better his own LA to New York time. Odekirk was ordered to take the H1 to the Hughes Aircraft plant, as the Glendale hangar was now being called.

The wing was modified, not so much the design but seven feet was added to the span, and the anticipated load called for strengthening the fuselage connection. A new engine was installed—the recently developed one thousand horsepower Wasp.

The problem of the lack of oxygen in his previous distance speed flights had never left Hughes' mind. Indeed, that problem stayed with him the rest of his life, leading to pressurized cabins and individual oxygen systems for every person in the plane, but that is another story. For the flight he contemplated next, he would have his own high-pressure system.

Hughes ascended to the cockpit of the considerably modified H1, now being classified as H2, and flew it from the west coast to New York at the average speed of 332 miles per hour. His elapsed time of 7 hours, 28 minutes and 25 seconds for the measured distance of roughly 2,400 miles broke his own record.

Howard Hughes

Hughes Aircraft Company

It was on a day in the spring of 1932 that Howard Hughes made a decision that would eventually change his business environment and leave behind a legacy unmatched by any other individual born in his century

As noted in the chapter, The Aircraft Chronicles, Hughes' many record-setting flights took place from January 1934 through July 1938. The work on all of the planes involved was accomplished at his newly established Hughes Aircraft Company (HAC), which he had founded in the spring of 1932. From this humble beginning in an aircraft hangar with only a workbench, HAC began its journey into the unfathomable future. It was in these facilities that Hughes, with Glen Odekirk and his small group of skilled workers, began what would evolve and later become Howard Hughes' lifetime legacy.

During its first few years, HAC was not known for its profitability, but it was known for designing and building aircraft that broke every known flight record and showed to everyone Hughes' generosity at work in the world, and in the future of aircraft.

It wasn't until after WWII and into the 1950s that profitability was to be attained. During the war years, HAC was basically a small, run-of-the-mill defense contractor primarily in the business of reconditioning aircraft with a small contract to manufacture ammunition belts, a far cry from what eventually was to become one of the most inventive and successful producers for not only military defense, but a wide range of consumer products worldwide.

Progress was somewhat impeded for HAC in November 1947 when Hughes had to take on the late Senator Owen Brewster and his political cronies, which, before it was over, involved Brewster's infamous attempt to protect Pan America's exclusive right to be the only intercontinental carrier. At this point, TWA was to become a competitor of Pan Am as a new international carrier.

Up to that point, Hughes had enjoyed and earned a fair reputation by being awarded several military contracts. However, after these Senate hearings in which Hughes was decidedly the victor, if one can really be considered a winner when the press is involved, Hughes lost favor with some of the military people who awarded most of the lucrative military contracts. Since HAC was a subsidiary of the Tool Company, Hughes was advised by Noah Dietrich to sell Hughes Aircraft. At the time, Dietrich had a strong position in Hughes Tool and was somewhat jealous of the fact that he had little or no control over the aircraft company. Hughes had other plans about which nobody, including Dietrich, had any knowledge. Had Hughes followed the advice to sell, Hughes' multibillion-dollar legacy, the Howard Hughes Medical Institute, would never have become a reality.

Instead, beginning in the early 1950s, HAC was launched and a growth pattern continued unleashed up until its sale to General Motors in 1987 which enriched the Howard Hughes Medical Institute coffers by about $7.6 billion plus General Motors H stock. This sale, at the request of Bill Gay, was initiated with General Motors Chairman Rodger Smith by James Whetton, who was a member of the G.M. president's advisory board.

So from the end of the Senate hearings through the formation of HHMI, there was a very critical series of ups and downs for HAC. It all began as Hughes recruited a new management team. General Harold George was a very logical choice to head up the restructuring of HAC, since during WWII he had literally built the now-famed ATC (Air Transport Command) into a recognized giant. He was an aggressive leader with the valuable military background that was desperately needed by what was to become a giant in the world of defense contracting.

Aided in a fast start, George had working for him two electronic geniuses—Dr. Simon Ramo and Dr. Dean Wooldridge. They were a product of Cal Tech, which had established a reputation for producing the very best in the realm of scientific research.

Ramo and Wooldridge immediately occupied their time developing the first stages of an electronics weapons control system, as well as radar systems for commercial and military aircraft. These weapons were to be used by fast flying aircraft as interceptors that had a deadly combination of radar and a computer that could seek out the enemy in any kind of weather and deliver a fatal blow. As important as these contracts were, they were peanuts when compared to the multimillion-dollar contracts that were evolving under the guidance of former General Harold George. Another former military general was Ira C. Eaker, who had been the deputy commander of the U.S. Air Force and had many of the necessary credentials vital to HAC's success. A third man, Charles "Tex" Thornton, was hired to be the general manager of HAC.

Faced with the need for expansion, it was also recognized that the home base of HAC would have to be relocated. In late 1953, Hughes began his search in Miami, Florida. The details of that venture are discussed in the chapter, The Ordinary Side of a Genius.

The Miami plan was scrapped and consideration surfaced to examine Las Vegas as a possible site. Hughes had been buying property and had already acquired several acres on the west side, known as Hughes' Site. Hughes quickly responded and vetoed this idea because of the exposure HAC employees would have had to the Las Vegas environment. He emphatically stated that because of the secret and highly sensitive defense work with which they were involved, the lure to compromise the type of work involved would be too tempting in that environment.

The major restructuring and transformation of Hughes Aircraft from its humble beginnings to its phenomenal growth and eventual sale to General Motors is chronicled in the chapter, Howard Hughes Medical Institute.

It became apparent to all that HAC was on the threshold of becoming a giant and would, no doubt, surpass in profits the fabulous returns displayed by the Tool Company. Hughes began to take a more personal interest. It must be noted that as Hughes did so, he also created a great deal of frustration and numerous delays, and in some ways, slowed the rate of progress his new management team desired to create. Unbeknownst to them, his plans of creating his legacy, HHMI, was prominently involved in structuring the future of HAC. In retrospect, he should not have been faulted.

Many people were sometimes critical of Hughes' unorthodox management style, but it also must be recognized that he always wanted the final word in the decision-making process. His long-range plans were unknown to most and beyond conventional thinking. The events of the critical period from 1950 to December 1953 follow.

In 1950, HAC needed to expand. Ramo and Wooldridge had made a proposal that went through the normal channels and wound up at Operations on Romaine Street in Hollywood. And that's just about where it ended too. Hughes did not respond. It was then that the staff began getting calls from both Ramo and Wooldridge asking for an audience with Hughes. Hughes put them off in his deliberate style, which did nothing to enhance his role in the eyes of these two men who had worked so hard to put HAC where it was since they had come on the scene.

Hughes balked about the expansion but after finally communicating with both Ramo and Wooldridge, he agreed. It came about that there was more to the proposal than just expansion.

In conversation with the two, Hughes felt that they wanted "a piece of the action." Hughes would have none of this. He knew what he had in HAC—a potential defense giant. It could well be worth billions. As usual, Hughes didn't want to part with ownership. Everything else that he was involved with was in his name, so why should he divest himself of the greatest potential money maker he would ever have? His logic told him not to give away any part of the ownership, although, frankly, if anyone ever deserved recognition for ownership it was Ramo and Wooldridge.

Of course, hindsight is always 20/20, but had Hughes given some control to these men, HAC could have been even more successful than it was. Although had he acquiesced, the highly successful firm of TRW—Thompson, Ramo and Wooldridge—would not have been created and the world might have been denied some of its great contributions in the electronics field.

Hughes began to interject himself into some of the day-to-day decisions, and things got somewhat problematic at the aircraft plant as Hughes tried to control his newly hired den of tigers. However, prior to this interjection by Hughes, an agreement was reached whereby Hughes expanded into Tucson, primarily for the production of the Falcon missile. This was in 1951, and it appeared that HAC's expansion was to boom.

General George was finding it increasingly more difficult to get upper-level decisions from Hughes. This was brought about by Hughes becoming fascinated with Las Vegas, where he flew in and stayed for extended periods of time. It was, for his new tigers, difficult to understand how Hughes operated unless you were one of his vassals, and then things would become somewhat clearer. The question arises—why didn't General George or his successors just go ahead and initiate those things that would enhance the operations at HAC? The answer was simple to his vassals—because Hughes, without question, insisted on being in charge. Whetton states, "We are reasonably sure he had a verbal understanding with General George that George would not do anything involving great capital expenditures without Hughes' express approval." One of the things that rankled George, Eaker, Ramo, and Wooldridge was the fact that Hughes would not readily respond to their communication efforts. The vassals were somewhat sympathetic with them and would make a solid effort to have Hughes return the calls.

At this crucial time when Russia was feeling its muscle, many at HAC were disturbed by Hughes' apparent lack of concern for the future of his great company. Prior to joining with Hughes, they had been accustomed to operating with relative freedom in initiating research and development. An air of tension developed as they felt their research was threatened by their newfound leader. There was concern that delivery schedules would be interrupted, costly delays would take place, and the overall efficiency of HAC would become questionable.

There was deep consternation on the part of George, Eaker, Thornton, Ramo, and Wooldridge that their authority was being questioned through some of the tactics introduced by Noah Dietrich, who during this critical period allegedly created friction with some petty actions on his part. It was said by some that Dietrich was jealous of the success of HAC after being a "baby brother" to the enormously wealthy Tool Company of which HAC was a budding division.

Things finally came to a head and Hughes agreed to meet with Eaker, George, Thornton, Ramo, and Wooldridge where it was alleged that they insisted that Dietrich be curbed in his petty dealings with key people at the aircraft plant. Ramo and Wooldridge also expressed their concern related to Hughes' apparent lack of action. Three of them, Thornton, Ramo, and Wooldridge, along with George and Eaker, were certainly in a position to know what would happen as a result of their taking direct action to Hughes and facing him. Five on one, as it were, did nothing to change Hughes' undisclosed plan of action, which, in three short months would come to be known by all. However, the employees' well-expressed intent and meanings were very sincere.

A major crisis was bound to happen, and it did. In the summer of 1953, despite herculean efforts on the part of interested parties, Ramo and Wooldridge submitted their resignations. The full extent of this loss could never be totally evaluated but it had a temporarily paralyzing effect on the aircraft plant. When they announced the formation of their own company, Ramo and Wooldridge, which was financed by the Thompson Products Company of Cleveland, a chain reaction was in the making at the plant. Starting at the top and reverberating through the entire chain of command, HAC was stunned. Hughes knew that he could replace Eaker, George, and Thornton, but to replace Ramo and Wooldridge was a most difficult task. They had done so much and had built such a winning team that it was sad to see what was happening.

It now was inevitable that the next thing that would happen would be the possibility of the departure of the cadre that Ramo and Wooldridge had built over the years. Their real loyalty was to Ramo and Wooldridge rather than HAC, and this certainly was understandable when all of the facts were taken into consideration. As we all soon knew, Ramo and Wooldridge were eventually to become TRW and were instrumental in the building of the first intercontinental ballistic missiles for defense and have been known since as giants of the space and technology industry.

Hughes now found himself in another typically self-induced crisis—that of having to straighten out HAC to the satisfaction of the Air Force, who was by now, thoroughly involved. The intensity of this involvement was fostered by the Secretary of the Air Force,

Harold Talbot. Talbot's attitude toward HAC now assumed a tough line. In effect, he gave HAC an ultimatum. "Shape up, or ship out." Hughes turned on his charm and received ninety days to get things on a even keel. Two more resignations took place—that of General George and Charles Thornton. Later, another executive, Roy Ash, resigned and formed his own company—Litton Industries.

In September, just a month after Ramo and Wooldridge left, Hughes received word that a host of the senior scientists were about to pack their bags, fed up with the way things were progressing, or regressing, at the plant. They expressed concern about the future of the plant and the possibility of slowdowns that could affect progress in our defense system.

This threat, considered a serious one, brought under-secretary of the Air Force, Roger Lewis, to the plant in Culver City. His first act was to appeal to the employees to delay their decision to leave en masse. This could damage the country's defense effort, Lewis told them. From this timely visit and message, most of the scientists stayed and Hughes Aircraft went on to lick its wounds and heal beyond measure.

As Hughes himself put it, a mass walkout of the remaining top scientists would have certainly blackballed his public image, as well as that of the associated aviation industry. Finally, on December 17, 1953, the 90th day of the extension granted by the Air Force, Hughes dispatched his in-house attorney, Tom Slack, to Delaware where two history-changing documents were delivered.

The documents set up two new corporations. One of the documents declared Hughes Aircraft Company a separate corporation, no longer tied to the apron strings of Hughes Tool Company. The second corporation eventually became the Howard Hughes Medical Institute. Hughes' longtime dream was designed solely to conduct medical research as a not-for-profit entity. Hughes told his vassals, at different times, that he fully intended for his will to provide that most all of his assets, without question, were to go to this institution for medical research. Paraphrasing congressional publications, the Tool Company signed over to the Howard Hughes Medical Institute all of the patents, trademarks, and goodwill of the Tool Company's division for aircraft, and all of the stock of the new HAC. This gift came to $36,463.

The Tool Company then sold to HHMI the assets of the aircraft division, inventories, and accounts receivable due from government contracts, amounting to the sum of $74,618,038.

HHMI was without funds and to obtain the assets, the institute assumed $56,574,738 in liabilities of the Tool Company's aircraft division. In turn, HHMI signed a promissory note for $18,043,000, which represented the difference between the assets it bought, and the liabilities it incurred. This promissory note was to run for three years with an annual interest rate of four percent.

The Tool Company then leased to HHMI some real estate holdings and fixed assets of the aircraft division; this mostly involved the land and buildings at the aircraft's facilities in Culver City, California.

The lease obligated HHMI to pay Hughes Tool Company $26,000,000 over a ten-year, six-month period. HHMI subleased the Culver City land and buildings to the new corporation of Hughes Aircraft Company (HAC). The sublease provided that the HAC would pay $33,600,000 to HHMI in this same ten-year, six-month period.

From this point forward and until HAC was sold in 1987 to General Motors Corp., the trustees, Davis and Gay, and the selected officers of HHMI assumed the main responsibility for Hughes Aircraft Company. This continuance is covered in detail in the chapter on the Howard Hughes Medical Institute and Whetton, Wadsworth, and Thain's firsthand knowledge of its history.

Jets, TWA & Complex Relationships

Gordon Bench remembers: "I was with Hughes in Miami, Florida for the startup of what turned out to be a project destined for failure, but eventually ended up as a very profitable venture for Hughes.

"There were times when Hughes would want one of us to be with him and give him assistance in whatever project he might be working on. It fell my lot to be with him, alone in the house in Miami Beach. He had me get Bob Rummel, who was TWA's chief engineer and a close confidante of Mr. Hughes, on the phone. Hughes talked for what seemed like hours with Rummel. Though I could only hear the conversation from one end, it involved the placing of orders for jets for TWA's system. It was amazing to listen to Hughes talk to Rummel in that Hughes was so knowledgeable about a new thing called 'jets.'

"Hughes quoted facts and figures to Rummel that were beyond my comprehension. Now, I'm sure Hughes got these figures from Rummel or from some other very good source, but I was impressed. One of the main concerns was how he was going to handle the financing of the planes.

"In 1955, Hughes had been warned, by Ralph Damon, the President of TWA, that TWA needed to have the planes, and that the financing had to be arranged for. Hughes, though Damon, and no doubt others had warned him, went into a holding pattern before making a decision. It was obviously to TWA's advantage to be first with jets, but this possibility became bleaker and bleaker as Hughes procrastinated. So in February 1956, after the death of Ralph Damon, and the worsening of TWA's position in the industry, Hughes finally ordered the planes, and I was a part of history—an unrecorded part, but nonetheless a part of aviation history.

"Though Hughes had ordered some Boeing 707's, the full complement of planes was unfulfilled, and so, in a sense, it was back to the drawing boards. Hughes, it seemed, had come up with a plan to build airplanes, and there were many conversations between Rummel and Hughes about this possibility. This plan never came to fruition, and Hughes ordered his planes from Boeing to satisfy the needs of TWA.

"But now Hughes needed additional planes—the short-range variety—and once again Convair was back in the picture. Convair, having been burned by Hughes, knew to a large degree what to expect, but they apparently had no choice but to sell to Hughes and run the risk of his paying for the planes. Hughes and Jack Zeverly entered into clandestine negotiations, and finally a deal was made. Hughes was really in the driver's seat because Convair had no other sales for its jets. They were literally forced to sell to Hughes and at whatever price they could get. They were very concerned about how Hughes would finance the planes.

"The situation could have been alleviated had Hughes arranged conventional financing through banks and insurance companies, but the peril of this was that these institutions imposed tight controls and Hughes might not have full control of the airline company, TWA. Since Hughes was in command, he extracted an agreement that precluded him paying for the planes until they were delivered. He did make a down payment of $25 to $30 million for the first planes but the total contract was well in excess of $100 million, and that, coupled with orders from Boeing, put Hughes in hock for upwards of $400 million. How to pay? Hughes had committed and the only source was his 'golden egg,' the Hughes Tool Company.

"Hughes definitely wanted the normal loaning institutions to be involved, but eventually the HTCO was going to have to come up with this huge amount of money. HTCO was profitable, but they were over extended even then, and their cash flow was inadequate to pay for the some sixty jet airplanes that Hughes had ordered. But Hughes had to order them or TWA would have been in even worse shape.

"It was at this point that Noah Dietrich entered the scene. He was Hughes' money man and had always been able to bail Hughes out of tight situations, but this was a real test for Dietrich. Dietrich did not always see eye to eye with HTCO's upper echelon, and whether this was because of his close association with Hughes or not, no one knows. Suffice it to say that HTCO was the only way to raise the money unless Hughes would relent and seek institutional financing.

"Enter now Raymond Cook, an attorney with the law firm in Houston of Andrews, Kurth and Campbell. Cook was a fine attorney, skilled in negotiations, more than adequate with finances, and so he and Dietrich teamed up to see what they could do to get Hughes to borrow money from the eastern sources. It seems that Hughes had not been too friendly with the eastern bankers. This came about because they, being a new breed of bankers, wanted to meet Hughes personally. Heretofore the old bankers were willing to accept Hughes on the phone. TWA was in a money-losing situation with no way out but to have cash transfused quickly.

"The new president of TWA was Carter Burgess, the former Assistant Secretary of Defense and a well-regarded and capable executive who was of a strong mind. One of the quotes from this era came from Defense Secretary Charles E. Wilson with whom Hughes had many conversations and who had apparently recommended Burgess to Hughes. When Wilson was asked how Burgess would get along with his new boss, Howard Hughes, Wilson turned it around and said, 'You mean how will Howard Hughes get along with Carter Burgess?'"

TROUBLE WITH NOAH

Gordon Bench continues, "In late 1956, Dietrich, who had been originally hired by Hughes in November 1925, had an ongoing argument with Hughes about Hughes giving him stock interest in one of Hughes companies. Hughes would have none of it since the concept of self-ownership was sacred to Hughes. He jousted with Dietrich, keeping Dietrich happy by paying him a salary of $500,000 per year with lots of fringe benefits such as a staff, expenses, cars, etc. But Dietrich complained that he was being taxed by the IRS too heavily and wanted relief via a stock option. Such an option would, of course, carry a lower capital gains rate.

"Something was to come of this confrontation and all of us on the staff were well aware of it. The question was when. We had to be diplomats because business had to go on, and Dietrich was an integral part of this business." Dietrich was agitated too because the TWA financing had not been arranged for and it was a deadly serious problem.

Bench: "I remember Sunday, May 12, 1957, because it was when the confrontation between Hughes and Dietrich came to a head. The purpose of their visit on this Sunday, which turned out to be a telephone visit, was for Dietrich to go to Houston and arrange the financing for TWA's planes. Dietrich agreed but his agreement was conditional. The condition was that Hughes would grant him a stock option. Dietrich's thinking was geared, I believed, so that he might have Hughes over a barrel, because if Dietrich didn't go to Houston and arrange the financing, Hughes would be even deeper in the soup."

Their conversation, though not recorded, probably went along the lines of Hughes accusing Dietrich of blackmail and Dietrich said if the agreement wasn't signed then "everything between us is through." Hughes probably said, "Effective when?" And Dietrich said, "Immediately." Then, no doubt, there was a short silence, and then the sound of two different phone receivers clicking off. And Dietrich was unemployed.

Bill Gay and James Whetton, who had been called by Hughes immediately after the firing, were told to get all the locks changed on the buildings that Dietrich and his staff used. Bench adds, "I was on duty that night and called in the locksmith, Grover, who changed all the locks on the entire building of the Romaine Street office. This moment of truth showed to me that Bill Gay should have asserted himself and taken command of the businesses for Hughes, replacing Dietrich. He had the staff and the wherewithal to handle this, and Bill was a very bright man. However, because of his intense, vassal-like loyalty to Hughes, he lacked initiative at this decisive moment, and he would never have another opportunity. All of us suffered from Bill's lack of initiative. But then that was academic since a short time in the future, Summa Corporation became a reality."

One of the most difficult assignments now faced the staff—letting those people who were associated with Noah Dietrich know that they were being terminated. Working in tandem, Raymond Holliday and Raymond Cook, the attorney from Andrews, Kurth, etc., and the staff had to arrange for severance pay and figure in vacation pay for those who were entitled to receive it. Hughes wanted this accomplished quickly and with efficiency.

Dietrich was a capable person who knew the ins and outs of the Hughes empire from the start until this memorable day in 1958. It was Noah Dietrich who had asked Gordon Bench to go to the aircraft company to help them out. This was at a time when he was spending a lot of his time there trying to get Hughes Aircraft squared away.

It was at this point in time that Hughes was married to Jean Peters. Hughes had seen pictures of Jean Peters as a beauty queen, which she truly was—a real beauty. Hughes made overtures to her to get her under contract to do motion pictures. The wedding, a very well kept secret, took place in Tonopah, Nevada, January 12, 1957.

There had been speculation that Hughes was on the verge of a nervous breakdown at this time of his life. Since this was the rumor around Hollywood, there had to be a reason behind it. Now it followed that as there was a break between Hughes and Dietrich, perhaps Dietrich might be entertaining thoughts of having Hughes committed as being incompetent. This was pure speculation and there was nothing to substantiate it. It is only mentioned here to show what rumors were being bandied about in the industry.

Regarding this speculation, the one thing that would stonewall it completely was that of Hughes marrying someone, making it impossible for Dietrich to try to take control of the Hughes empire.

Bench recalls, "I knew Jean Peters, and in my way of analysis, she was a fine young person with many outstanding qualities. She was considerate of others, especially her sister. Shirley was going to be married and Jean had made a lot of preparations, some of which included having the use of Hughes' Cadillacs which Noah Dietrich had control over to some degree.

"Jean called the office prior to the wedding and I happened to be on duty. She fully explained the situation with regard to the Caddies and wanted it made perfectly clear that if anything happened and the Cad's were not available, Hughes would be the first to hear of it. I assured her that she would have whatever she wanted, and we would have rented Cad's had the need arisen. However, everything went off without a hitch, at least with regard to the cars Jean wanted for the wedding. I cannot recall a time when working with Jean Peters Hughes that I had a difficult time. She was a fine person and one who could have initiated the well-used expression, 'Have a good day!'

"But for those who advanced the idea that this was a marriage of convenience, I cannot agree. I sincerely think that Hughes loved

Jean and she loved him. I do know that it was difficult for her because she was used to being socially involved—the opera, plays and the like. This, of course, was not Hughes' cup of tea. He was at a point in his life that he didn't want to socialize any more than he absolutely had to."

Shortly after his marriage, Hughes planned a trip to Canada, ostensibly to fly some English-made planes he was considering putting into the TWA system. The night he was ready to leave, quite a few of the staff were with him at the airport making sure everything was in readiness for the trip. The TWA Constellation had been outfitted with a bed for Hughes to sleep on. All of the things he needed were stowed on board. The only thing that was not totally definite was who would accompany him on the trip. No one really looked forward to these trips because no one knew how long the trips would take.

Bench says, "I was fortunate this time that I stayed home, and was grateful for that blessing. Hughes had told us that he would be gone for no longer than a week or two at the most. Well, we grinned at each other because we knew his pattern. The stay in Montreal lasted into the weeks, not days."

Bankers

Gordon Bench: "One day Mr. Hughes called and asked that a meeting be set up at the Beverly Hills Hotel involving some very prominent worldwide bankers. A Swiss banker by the name of Walter Germann was there, and the others were solid members of the international banking fraternity, the old guard, if you will. It really took some doing to get all of these people together from the four corners of the world. The purpose was for Mr. Hughes to pick their brains about what the economy was going to do over the next several months or perhaps a year. It was a luncheon meeting, and those of us from his staff were invited to join with them. Now this was quite an honor to be in such company. I had the distinct pleasure of sitting and eating at the same table as Howard Hughes. Of course, we were there in an official status of making sure that everything went smoothly for these VIP's. And it did too.

"One incident that took place was impressed in my mind indelibly. Mr. Hughes excused himself from the table and asked me to join him, which of course, I did. He took me aside and explained that he wanted to be sure that one of the bankers got a particular dessert that Mr. Hughes knew the banker would be fond of. Now this may seem a small thing to those not knowledgeable about Hughes, but this banker was really impressed and Hughes made points with him, as well as the other bankers.

"During the meeting, exchanges of ideas took place among the bankers with the end result being that Howard Hughes was in a commanding position to know what the prime rate would do, all other things considered, and had the best possible information directly from the source. This meeting probably cost about

$3,000, covering airfare, accommodations, and incidentals, and in exchange Mr. Hughes got information that a real price tag couldn't be attached to.

"During this meeting Mr. Hughes just didn't sit idly by and listen and observe—he did that too—but he participated by putting in his ideas and thoughts, and the bankers loved it. And those of us on the staff were really caught up on the whole project. It had taken a couple of weeks to really put this thing together but it was definitely worthwhile, and we did enjoy ourselves. Unfortunately, I didn't have any cash to invest; seems like my lot was to have the foresight but not the cash, or vice versa.

"Due to the confidential nature of this meeting there was a security system set up that was unique at the time. Today such a meeting would be sort of ordinary, but Hughes was the master of mystique, and I think the bankers, as conservative as they were, really got into the whole thing and had a good time. And in addition to contributing to Hughes' knowledge, they learned and were deeply impressed by Hughes' foresight and his practical approach to problem solving."

Baseball

Gordon Bench: "There are many instances of my personal involvement working directly with Hughes on many major and never-disclosed projects that, much later in time, because of Hughes planning, became very important realities. One particular project involved the future of Major League Baseball.

"When Hughes wanted publicity, he certainly knew how to go about it in a first cabin manner. But he was selective in how he used his power to get things done. It was sometimes our job to work with the advertising agency and public relations firm to get a project worked out, often some public announcement about a forthcoming movie or a TWA project. Bill Utley was one of the contacts and Elliston Vinson another—both high-powered people with lots of connections and the ability to get Hughes the 'print' he wanted or needed at the precise time he wanted it to happen.

"The following is an actual situation of which the public was never totally aware. It occurred when the Brooklyn Dodgers and the New York Giants were entertaining ideas about leaving New York and coming to the west coast. Hughes, a sports-minded individual, learned about it and began getting involved to the point of possibly arranging for the financing to purchase the New York Giants who wanted to move to San Francisco. I was involved in this project, making calls, inquiring of bankers about financing, determining the pros and cons for acceptance on the west coast for such a move. Now these kinds of things cannot be kept totally quiet no matter how hard you try. This situation, at least as I observed it, created the desire for the first move of a major league baseball team to the west coast from the east coast.

"Hughes had a close tie to Del Webb, an old golfing buddy and baseball man of some ability, who later purchased the New York Yankees. I had the pleasure of meeting Webb when he was in Phoenix and I was a liaison between Hughes and Webb on a real estate deal involving both of them. But I think Hughes stirred up enough interest to assure the arrival of Major League Baseball on the west coast. In fact, Bill Utley and I had reservations on a plane to go to San Francisco to talk with the mayor of San Francisco about this project.

"The deal for bringing the Giants to San Francisco did not materialize at this point, but the groundwork was laid for Horace Stoneham to move his Giants to San Francisco and Walter O'Malley to bring the Dodgers, 'dem Bums,' from Brooklyn to Los Angeles.

"Whatever those thing were that motivated Mr. Hughes to get involved in the transfer of Major Leagues to the west coast, they were good ones, and I'm only sorry that the deal wasn't consummated in San Francisco. You can see what Major League Baseball has done on the west coast since that time."

Howard Hughes (signature)

Supposed Eccentricities

Gordon Bench: "Much has been said, particularly in the later years of Hughes' life, as to how eccentric he was. Let me say to you that at no time did I ever see Mr. Hughes in a pair of 'sneakers,' nor did he have toenails that were six inches long. He was neat and well groomed. When he decided to put on a suit and go out, he struck an imposing figure. He insisted on being well kempt and knew that each of us would do the same. This was never a problem with any of us in presenting that kind of an image.

"While talking about Tom Slack, an interesting bit of trivia occurs to me. One late night, or early morning, Hughes had asked Slack to meet him at Marion Davies' Ocean House in Santa Monica to transact some legal business. Hughes had asked me to be in attendance too. This home was right on the oceanfront and a well-known landmark that Hughes had leased for a time. When we arrived at the home and I reached for the doorbell, Slack stopped me and said, 'Don't ring the bell, I'll show you how to get Hughes attention quick.' It seems that Hughes and Slack had encountered problems of Hughes having Slack wait and wait for interminable periods of time and then telling Slack he hadn't heard the doorbell.

"You see, Hughes had a slight hearing problem. Sometimes it was a convenience for him not to hear. At any rate, Slack took a silver dollar out of his pocket and said, 'Now, Gordon, watch how quickly Hughes answers the door.' Well, it so happened that Hughes must have been anticipating Slack because the instant Slack rapped the dollar on the door, Hughes opened it and, with a few well-chosen words, chastised Slack for being so noisy. But

Slack just brushed off the remarks, and we entered and transacted the business and left Hughes at the ocean house.

"From that point on I carried a silver dollar in my pocket should such a situation arise that I needed to get Hughes' attention, the silver dollar would be handy. And it was, too, on more than one occasion. Incidentally, that silver dollar, minted in the year 1923, is in my safe deposit box. That dollar is significant in two ways, one as a memento from my days with Howard Hughes, and that year is also the year in which my 'baby doll' wife was born.

Bench continues: "In various parts of the country, from Palm Springs to Miami, when Hughes traveled, he would lease or rent homes for an extended period of time. Palm Springs was one of the places he liked to go from time to time because it was easily accessible with a short flight from Clover Field in Santa Monica. He eventually set up a mini-staff arrangement there and included on that staff was a cook named Bill Comeau. Comeau was quite a character and an adequate chef (we referred to him as a fry cook).

"One time Hughes wanted something special made, and as usual, for it to be done with a minimum of persons involved in the handling of the food itself. Comeau reassured Hughes that it would be 'untouched by human hands,' which brought a chuckle from Hughes. Of course, Comeau meant that it would be him alone that would do the preparation. While speaking of preparing food, Hughes really used to enjoy crepe suzettes. Now I had never tasted this delicacy before and found them to be very delectable. Well, Hughes checked me out on the preparation of these delicacies and then gave detailed instructions as to how to observe and instruct whoever prepared them at the Beverly Hills Hotel and supervise the preparation of this and other special delicacies.

"Of course, we would personally go to the chef and tell him what Mr. Hughes wanted, and the chef was always very obliging. You see, Hughes had a real sweet tooth and would on occasion order a chocolate mocha cake and could often consume the whole cake in one sitting. But for the most part, when he so desired, he would plan a well balanced diet consisting of steak, vegetables, and some breads and either milk or water to drink. There were only one or two times that I ever saw Mr. Hughes order any liquor. One evening when he was out with some people he ordered a daiquiri that, as he requested, was not heavily laced with liquor. He didn't approve of liquor usage for himself and especially his staff. However, Hughes was not prudish about this, but he did have a real aversion to over-indulgence by anyone in the use of liquor. He detested smoking and found it very offensive, and we certainly were happy about this.

"There have been endless volumes of phony comments about Hughes and his odd ways, eccentricities or idiosyncrasies or whatever, but we looked at it this way. He was rich enough to afford being as eccentric as he wished. But in all honesty, he wasn't nearly that different while we were working with him, and what happened after 1959 is, as far as we were concerned, just speculation and information taken out of context, second, and third hand information—anything to report for the sake of sensationalism and selling newspapers or magazines or books.

"Everyone has no doubt heard stories about him and his 'germ warfare' phobia. At no time while I was employed, did he ever ask me to do anything that required the use of Kleenex in transmitting things to him. I was never asked to capture a fly as one trash book has said; 'I caught flies for Howard Hughes.' We were, from time to time, asked to do menial tasks but that didn't bother any of us because that was part of our job.

"For instance, Hughes, when traveling or even when staying at the Beverly Hills Hotel, wanted his beds made a certain way to accommodate his long frame. I recall vividly one time being with him at the Beverly Hills Hotel and the question of making a bed came up. I told him I knew how to make a bed Army style with the hospital corners and he said that was fine but there was another part. Then he showed me how he wanted to have a pillow or two placed at the foot of the bed and the sheets and the blankets placed in such a manner as to provide warmth at the bottom of the bed as well as the top. Now I had another qualification to put on my resume.

"Hughes had been flying with a feminine guest and they had food on the plane. Following the flight Hughes called and asked that I come up and pick up the dishes and tidy up. Now that was the extent of menial tasks given me during my nine years of duty with Hughes.

"Working the night shift in Operations was never without a challenging event. It was not at all uncommon, since Hughes mostly worked at night, for him to call Operations and to say that he needed someone to pick him up and to meet him at 240th and plowed ground. One such event occurred one night when he called in and asked Garth Frazier to meet him in West Hollywood with a cab as he was without transportation. Garth left immediately and met Hughes with the cab at the appointed rendezvous. Hughes and his guest entered the cab with Garth and started out for Beverly Hills.

"Well, Hughes had a very sensitive nose and the car leaked fumes. Hughes told Garth to stop the cab and they'd get another. This was about 3 a.m. and cabs were not easy to come by. This particular cab circled the block and since it was dark and early in the morning, neither Garth nor Hughes noticed it was the same cab. Well, one whiff and Hughes knew it was the same cab so he waxed eloquent, according to Garth, but they had no choice then and so they suffered until they arrived at their destination."

Gordon recalls one time when Hughes ran out of gas and called: "I was on duty, and as usual, it was early in the morning. He had borrowed one of our Cad's, one of the few times he ever drove a Cad, and ran out of gas at La Cienega Boulevard at Sunset. He had backed the big, long Caddie against the curb with the wheels cramped against the curb. He saw the overall situation and bailed out and asked to get some gas, get the car started, and meet him in half an hour. Well, the car was totally out of gas—there were no fumes even—and it was parked so the gas tank was downhill. Trying to get gas into the carburetor, prime it and start it was one long time of frustration. There was no one else in the office, it being after midnight, so I knew Hughes could not call to find out where I was, and he'd just have to sweat it out until I got there.

"As all successful situations go I got lucky, got the car started, and headed for the spot where Hughes was to be. To add to the morning's frustrations he wasn't there. He had probably gotten a cab and headed back to the Beverly Hills Hotel. I cruised around looking for him, and then headed back to the office to see if he would call in. No call, so I went about the duties left to wind up before going home. When we had a changeover in shifts we always brought the person up to date on what was going on so we were always conversant with where Hughes was and what he was doing. This time it worked out fine and Hughes didn't call at all but getting the Caddies started will long be remembered."

Hughes & Golf

Hughes' interest in golf came quite naturally, as it did for all young Texans from well-off and prominent families. Golf was an expectation—almost a requirement. Being athletically gifted, unusually tall and slender, he quickly developed a long, easy swing that was necessary in the days of the then popular wooden-shafted clubs. We do not know much about his golf history but we do know that by the time he was nineteen and was about to assume personal ownership of the stock of the Hughes Tool Company, he was on his way to earning a two to three handicap as a member of the Houston Country Club.

As a regular player and student of the Club Pro he had, on occasion, played a round or two with the Federal Judge who, after his father's passing, was to preside over the hearing that resulted in Hughes being declared an adult and taking over the stock of HTCO.

When he reached Los Angeles in his late twenties he was an accomplished golfer. Also, by this time he had made a name for himself in Hollywood and had been accepted as a member of the prestigious Los Angeles Country Club off Wilshire Boulevard.

The Club, as it was known, was well manicured and a great test of golf play. It attracted the well-known pros of the game as well as some of the top tournament players. Though Hughes was not known as a habitual gambler, he, of course, would take any and all bets offered. Most typically he hated to lose and even more especially he hated to come out second best. He would take his strokes, which of course was the difference between his and his opponents' handicap, when he played with the pros, sometimes for rather large stakes.

The challenges, like so many others in his life, became an obsession. So he began taking lessons from the best teaching pros available. He worked his handicap down to a very respectable two. He consistently stayed at that level but was secretly embarrassed that he still could not play to the pros at scratch or less. He finally hit upon the Club pro and his teaching pro as to when he was going to play any one even up. Both informed him that he was probably never going to play in the same league as the pros. He reluctantly accepted this, put his shoes and clubs in his locker. Though this was not the end of his playing elsewhere, they remained in his locker for years. He still kept his locker well into the fifties. He never gave up his membership in the Club. He used it as a social entity, mostly as a getaway and a relaxing place to meet men, play cards, and talk. His membership was effectively used in ways that were a mark of his control over people.

Few golfers who were visiting could resist the chance to play the Club. It was luxurious, very exclusive, and as a guest of Howard Hughes! He had an arrangement with the Pro Shop that he could call any time and get his guests a tee time without a great delay. He would never play with his guests but always sent one of his personal staff, usually Wadsworth, who played an acceptable game with them. He used it very often to keep track of military men particularly, to keep them occupied or to delay a scheduled meeting. Perry Lieber, Hughes' personal press spokesperson and a famous Hollywood publicity agent, used the Hughes membership, at Hughes instructions, to delay the media—the movie people Hughes wanted to see but wanted to pick his own time for the meetings.

Several entertaining episodes involving Hughes and casino-type gambling occurred after a round of golf at the Long Beach Country Club. In the early forties, Hughes was involved in the research and the construction of the Hercules in Long Beach, California. It was therefore convenient to drop by and play a round at the local country club.

After finishing the game, on what is known to golfers as the 19th hole, a game of craps was in full swing in the locker room of the clubhouse. Hughes' was naturally drawn to participate, given his instinct for looking for any source where there was a chance for a profitable venture. No one there recognized Hughes as he got into the game on a small scale of betting. He was badgered to up the ante by one of the participants who had no idea who he was. Hughes tolerated this for a period of time and then when the pot got to a pretty good size, his antagonist challenged him to up the ante or get out. The story goes that Hughes then wrote out a check for $1,000,000, dropped it into the pot, and quietly said, "Fade any or all of it!" Well, his foe was then observed as he slunk into the fading sun of the Pacific Ocean and was never seen around the clubhouse again.

The club pro at the L.A. Country Club told Wadsworth that Hughes did the same more than once betting on golf. If the Boss ever made a mistake and got in over his head he could always raise his game up a notch or two.

One rather long-lasting episode involving Hughes and golf was after his introduction to Katharine Hepburn as told by her in her biography, *Remembering Kate.*

In early 1936 while she was filming *Sylvia Scarlet*, Kate and George Cukor used to have their staffs prepare picnic lunches for them and selected members of the cast and crew. One day during their break, a small plane circled overhead, zeroed in on them, and then landed a short walk away. Kate suddenly noticed Cary Grant looking sheepish. "That's my friend Howard Hughes," he said. As Kate said, she was so angry about the false and staged introduction that she ate her lunch without looking at either of them.

As it turned out this was the beginning of a long and valuable friendship that involved a lot of golf together over the ensuing years. As late as 1955, working with Hughes at night, James Whetton had just gotten off the phone with Miss Hepburn, having arranged a golf game at the Bel Air Country Club for the next day, when Hughes remarked that he considered Katharine to be the brightest female he had ever met. According to him, she could successfully run any corporation in the country.

Shortly after the airplane introduction, Kate was playing golf at the Bel Air Country Club, and Hughes was late for his golf date with her. Hughes performed a similar stunt, this time landing on the seventh fairway. Out of the plane he hopped with his golf clubs and finished the round with Kate and her instructor. At this point it should be noted that she, like Hughes, was an excellent golfer. As Kate said, "He was an excellent golfer, but you see, Howard was a man of action, not words, and I think this was simply the best way he could think of expressing his feelings."

In this instance, his plane was sitting in the middle of the golf course which had provided enough room to land but not enough to take off. As expected, Hughes had thought of everything. He simply had his mechanics come and dismantle the plane and cart it off. As Kate further recalled, he had not considered how he was to get home. He had just assumed that Kate would take him. As she said, "What gall. He was exciting and great fun."

One escalated golf game took place with Katharine and her father in Fenwick where her family often played and where a friend named Liddy, who always seemed to have a movie camera in his hands, often joined them. As they were playing, Hughes shied away not only from Liddy's presence, but also to ensure his privacy with the camera clicking away. "Howard," Hepburn interpreted, "Liddy has been taking pictures of all of us for years before you got here, and he'll be taking them for years after you're gone. He's part of this family, now drive."

It could be said, looking back at the long lasting friendship and mutual respect between Hughes and Kate, that they had more golf games together than with all others combined.

Golf in Las Vegas

By the time of Hughes' 1966 re-entry into Las Vegas, he had long since given up actively playing the game because of physical distress. He never did abandon his interest in the sport, however. This interest continued up to within two years of his passing as he launched his campaign that was about to change the face of Nevada.

Many stories have been told about his Nevada operations and particularly his acquisition of the Desert Inn and Country Club— stories typically full of enough garbage to fill a Los Angeles or even a New York City landfill. Coincidentally, his buying the Desert Inn did involve golf.

Hughes and his staff had taken over the two top floors of the main nine-story building. As it happened, those two floors made up the hotel's finest "high roller suites." A major PGA tournament was scheduled, known as the "Tournament of Champions," which was then, and still is, considered to be one of the Professional Golf Association's best.

Typically when such a major event was scheduled, the hotel would invite some of their high rollers as guests and reserve their finest suites including free room, food, and beverage so that these people could then drop a few hundred thousand at the casino tables as well as enjoy some of the finest golf to be played and witnessed.

Hughes was comfortably settled in while planning to invest his $546,549,171 from the sale of TWA, so in order to avoid intervention, he bought the Desert Inn. The story is then told that Hughes, in retribution, ordered that the Tournament of Champions must find a new home and the Desert Inn was closed to them for that and all future tournaments. This is a total lie and fabrication. The tournament was literally owned by Moe Dalitz, the retiring "Godfather" figure in Las Vegas who moved the tournament to the Las Vegas Country Club, and for the following years, up to La Costa, a premier course in southern California of which Moe Dalitz just happened to be a major stockholder.

As late as 1974, Hughes was still brooding over Las Vegas losing this tournament. At that time, James Whetton was general manager of the Desert Inn. Jim received orders from Hughes to do everything possible to bring a new PGA Tournament back to Las Vegas. Through Hughes Sports Network that had recently been acquired, he sent Tom Harmon to Las Vegas to consult with James Whetton and Leo Wadsworth in an effort to devise a plan that would return the PGA to Las Vegas, preferably at the end of the season.

The three developed a plan approved by Hughes for the return. The plan was new to the PGA and the LPGA. It was to be an end of the season tournament where a select group of the top players of the PGA and the LPGA would be invited to compete for a high stakes. By the time the former was accepted and approved by the PGA, Hughes was no longer available to sign off on his favorite of favorites—golf. The tournament did come to fruition but moved to Florida.

In 1973, the Desert Inn, Sands, Frontier, Castaways, and the Landmark general managers presented a plan to Hughes for the start of an annual golf tournament to be named in his honor, the Howard Hughes Invitational. Each property was allowed to invite up to 150 guests and, in typical Hughes' first class only style, each contestant would be given a prize, which in the year Whetton was chairman consisted of a Hughes Invitational embossed red and white golf bag, a full set of Ping golf clubs, a pair of slacks, a gold shirt, and a pair of orange and tan leather golf shoes. The tournament was played on the Desert Inn and Las Vegas Country Club courses. By design that year, all prizes were awarded in a leather bag with cash to be sure every guest left having a great golf experience. But as you might guess, most of their winnings were left in the casino cage.

Wives or friends of the invited guests were hosted in a separate tournament of their own at the same two courses, and they also received a lavish gift as the prize. One year, the Sands invited Sammy Davis Jr. He notified them in advance that he would be willing to participate but only if his golf cart could be equipped with a TV set. Another guest, who considered himself to be of prima donna status, received his golf bag with his stage name on it. He refused to accept the bag unless his real name was engraved. Immediately the correction was made. As a reward for his arrogance he was never invited to return.

One of Hughes final involvements with golf was a hotel complex with 15,000 rooms to be known as The Howard Hughes, and he wanted a golf course to be constructed for the Sands Wing. He instructed Whetton to contact Arnold Palmer and Jack Nicklaus as potential golf course architects. As it turned out neither of them was available at the needed time, so Billy Casper was brought in to consult on the property.

His chance to bring in Palmer and Nicklaus was interesting, because over the years golf magazines had presented stories that Hughes was jealous of both and was seeking to somehow destroy both of their careers. Again, these stories were totally fabricated garbage to sell magazines. Hughes had never expressed anything but total admiration for any and all involved with the professional golf association, for what was probably the only achievement in his proactive life in which he had not excelled and conquered. From his golf course view on the ninth floor of his Desert Inn suite, he could only wish that he could be on the ground during his more youthful days, able to conquer the course as he eventually conquered the rest of Nevada, and conquer and change he did in his own carefully planned and executed manner. But it must be said that with the faith and help of his dedicated and loyal vassals, he was able to complete his destined conquest and change forever the face of Nevada.

Howard Hughes

Property Acquisitions

Details from rare family correspondence indicate that Hughes' interest in Nevada started when he was sixteen years old.

In the summer of 1921, Hughes' mother became very ill, and for the first time, his father suddenly took an interest into how his son was being raised. He was concerned that his wife was raising him as a loner, and possibly even a sissy. So just before Hughes Sr. died, he bought a ranch in Elko County, Nevada. He then put one of his trusted cowboys in charge, and the young Hughes spent the summer of 1922 working as a ranch hand.

In close proximity was the very large Union Pacific Ranch, located in the northeast section of Nevada. The UP Ranch was not a dude ranch but was known for attracting and catering to important visitors who used it effectively for publicity. During the 1920's, most of the western movie cowboy stars such as Bill Hart, Ken Maynard, and Tom Mix were known to be frequent guests. No record exists that Hughes met any of them at that time, but it could have been his first contact with Hollywood.

Sometime later, Hughes Sr. acquired a parcel of land which Hughes Jr. later traded for a ten-thousand acre plot of BLM (Bureau of Land Management) land bordering Red Rock Canyon on the west side of Las Vegas, later known as Hughes' Site. This was Hughes' first entry into his long history of acquiring land in the Las Vegas area.

Hughes' introduction to the future of the new Las Vegas actually had its start early on. From the middle of the 1930's he had used Nevada as a place to relax and let off tension. None close to him knew for a certainty that he kept women in Las Vegas, but many people in Vegas preferred to believe so.

Hughes' visits to Nevada were mostly made by airplane. In the early 1940's he used a dirt landing strip between the old Last Frontier and the Union Pacific Railroad as a place to set down, rather than the paved field that later became Nellis Air Force Base. That dirt strip was the original fixed base location for George Crockett. Hughes and Crockett became fast friends, and over the years he frequently used Crockett's fixed base operation.

Hughes had always had a special feeling for fellow aviators, one of whom was Charles Lindbergh. (He consulted with Lindberg on fuel conservation and long-distance flying before his flight around the world. Later, he showed Lindberg some of the plane he was working with Boeing on, which turned out to be the Boeing 707.) The accident on Lake Mead in the amphibian he was flying, instead of souring him on the State, seemed to make him feel closer.

When Hughes made the land swap with the BLM, he was contemplating moving the location of one of his plant facilities to Clark County. The international espionage so widely prevalent at the time of the Cold War caused him to rethink the location. He told some members of his staff that the lifestyle available in Vegas was not suitable for persons who held not only corporate secrets, but also secrets essential to the United States' defensive establishment.

As his staff, we do not have firsthand knowledge as to when Hughes started to buy up his early acquisitions of numerous individual plots of land in and around the Las Vegas landscape, but during our time from the late 1940s on, we were not only aware but were actively involved in the property acquisitions, their changes, and the future construction and development of these properties. By this time, if you were to step out of your car on the highway north of Las Vegas and west of Nellis AFB, you could walk on Hughes-owned property all the way to McCarran Field airport.

As with so many of the non-security/military/aircraft plans

that developed in the mind of Howard Hughes, the plans he began in the 1940s to develop the Las Vegas area were not shared with many others, if shared at all, until the 1960s.

Hughes had a special feeling for Las Vegas, indeed for Nevada. He had a vision when he made the fabulous land swap to become owner of those 10,000 acres in the Las Vegas valley. His original plans—more schemes than actual plans—were to locate Hughes Aircraft on those acres. The professionals and scientists that ran the Aircraft Company were violently opposed to locating there. He then toyed with what was to become Hughes Electronics. By the early 1950s, both of these companies were involved in super secret work for the United States Defense Department.

Hughes was a frequent visitor to Vegas. He was a serious student of people and their environment. He soon became convinced that a gambling/liquor environment was no place for security programs; just as he believed that homosexual persons and those with Communist leanings were susceptible to blackmail, he could see that alcohol and gambling debts laid a person open to the same blackmail problems. He gave up any plans he had to move one of his sensitive companies to Nevada.

He would seldom explain decisions and would only give a reason if he thought one was absolutely necessary. He told those in charge of Electronics and Hughes Aircraft and those at Hughes Tool Company in Houston. He told Romaine Street officers and explained his decision to Bill Gay. Leo Wadsworth always thought his close ties to Nevada and the fact that he was doing confidential work for Hughes caused Hughes to explain in some detail why he backed out of his development plans for the Vegas valley. This explanation came years after the decision was made. At the time, no mention was made for other development.

There was much more to the Hughes' "New Las Vegas" than four inter-connected hotel/casinos. He had for years dreamed of a large international air terminal that he would own and be subject only to the least interference from the Federal government. He would manage and run it according to his own concepts with his own handpicked base operators. This was a variation on his feudalism.

In the late 1960s, Hughes bought the North Las Vegas Airport. He installed an old time pilot, Wes Durston, as the fixed base operator. Durston was in operation there when Hughes bought it. The Clark County squadron of the Civil Air Patrol used it as a base. Hughes certainly knew Durston as all the old-time, long time commercial pilots knew each other. He probably knew the squadron commander who was a retired Air Corp flight surgeon. This doctor's Air Corp ID showed that he was the sixth doctor to be certified in the Air Corp as a flight surgeon. Hughes also knew the Operations Officer of that CAP squadron, James Leo Wadsworth.

In keeping with his vision of a development that would be a full service area where there would be no reason for one to ever stray, Hughes envisioned a full service spa on the vacant ground immediately south of the Desert Inn tennis courts. In keeping with his bent for having those he knew and trusted in control of the businesses where he, and no one else, was in complete command, he instructed that Wilbur Thain, one of the doctors that had connections to Romaine Street and who had personally attended him for years, be in charge.

Hughes also owned a residential/apartment hotel on Twain Avenue just east of the entrance to the Desert Inn Golf Course. In the late 1960s and from December 1970 to the time it was sold by Hughes' relatives, Loren Bunker, a Mormon and former undersheriff of Clark County, was the manager. This property, to be known as the Manor House, was meant to be remodeled and kept for visiting managers of other businesses and some permanent Las Vegas employees. Situated on the Manor House property was a small private residence known as the "Green House."

The purchase of the Manor House, as so named by Hughes, took place in the early 1950s. As with other things he named for himself, the Green House was never mentioned when speaking to Hughes. Hughes never told any of his close associates, except perhaps Walter Kane, what he had it for. It appears he meant to house Jean Peters there when he wanted to visit Vegas. Before he left Los Angeles for Boston he had it sealed up. Literally sealed. The doors and windows were locked and taped. It was fenced and posted.

In 1972 orders came from someone to unseal the house and to really strip the interior of anything that could connect it to Hughes. Only Bill Gay, Kay Glenn, and the security boss from Hollywood were allowed inside. James Whetton was allowed inside the fence but not inside the house. Wadsworth was instructed to sit in a car about fifty yards from the front door so he could make a report of the unsealing if he were called. The sanitized house was then sold.

It is important that all through these grandiose plans, only certain people were ever given the insight into Hughes' mind and the working of it. When he decided that he could not move one of his security-necessary businesses to Nevada, he started to evolve other schemes to benefit the area that was one of his favorite destinations. It is evident that Hughes Tool Company in Houston knew something of his plans. It is apparent that that knowledge made it easier to get the Tool Company to advance the funds for all of the purchases that Maheu thought he had dreamed up. These acquisitions were made with Hughes' detailed instructions as to when and how. Maheu was to follow Hughes' instructions to the last word.

As previously told, Hughes used the dirt strip between Highway 95 and the Union Pacific Railroad and spent many days in one of his El Rancho, Vegas bungalows, and ate and gambled (low stakes) in the El Rancho Casino. Wadsworth remembers, "I always enjoyed a story from Joe Foley, who later became a partner in the law firm of Morse, Foley and Wadsworth, where he told of his homecoming in the fall of 1945. Sgt. Foley, as with most of us, was having a tough time adjusting to civilian life again. He went to El Rancho one night for supper and to play a little. He was 'hitting' on a pretty girl when he was warned by a dealer who told him that girl was with Howard Hughes. Sure enough, Hughes was playing at the same table that Joe was. Hughes was pointed out, and this was the only time Foley ever saw the man in person."

Howard Hughes

Nevada

Even Hughes did not predict the final outcome of his contributions to Nevada's future, and the fact that, ultimately, his presence and his personal investments in 1967 would forever change that future and, even to this day, the face of Nevada and the methodology of its dynamic growth. When talking of growth, keep in mind not only the growth of the Las Vegas strip, but even more importantly, the development of the property known as Hughes' Site on the west side, and development planned prior to his death, now known as Summerlin, named in honor of his grandmother, Jean Amelia Summerlin.

Hughes, prior to 1974, had already initiated plans for the development of Hughes' Site. Throughout many years, Hughes had as a close personal friend, Del Webb, who was already heavily invested in Nevada. They planned a mutual investment, for starters, to build a typical Del Webb adult retirement community center that had already been successful marketed in Arizona. Initially, the schedule had called for the construction of as many as 250,000 homes, complete with commercial centers to virtually create a new city.

The completion of this plan was interrupted by Hughes' death when in 1978 the intestate heirs, the family Hughes intensely disliked, came out of the woodwork and, through the courts, assumed control of the daily operations and the carrying out of Hughes' instructions, devoid of Hughes' most trusted confidants, Bill Gay, James Leo Wadsworth and James Whetton. Those relatives were not the least bit interested in hotel operations, but only in money and the development of the sale of the undeveloped land. The future of his legacy, The Howard Hughes, passed from the picture of what might have been, the hotel of all hotels, not just in Nevada but also in the world.

Hughes' changing of the face of Nevada began when he bought the Desert Inn to avoid his threatened eviction at the end of his planned ten-day stay. At the time, Moe Dalitz and his partner, Ruby Kolad, owned the Desert Inn. It is interesting to note that during this same time, the former U.S. Attorney General Robert Kennedy had commissioned a study to establish a blueprint for extracting the "mob" from Las Vegas, and thereby eliminate, or at least reduce, crime in Vegas. This theory was of special interest in that the mob actually controlled crime because they would only allow crime to be committed by themselves.

It is believed that Hughes was aware of this study, and since he was comfortably settled in, the best way to solve the problem was to buy the Desert Inn. As we all know, the proceeds from the sale of his TWA stock totaled $546,549,171 less tax in his Hughes Tool bank account. He was also fully aware that the IRS had taxed that money as "passive" income which was a higher rate than "active" or working income.* He also was aware that gross receipts for casinos were considered as active income. This tax on the TWA proceeds was changed from the IRS plan by the courts. Hughes was allowed to spread the sum over all of his ownership and over a period of years. This discovery, without a doubt, spurred him on as he bought up all of the remaining mob properties except the Stardust. To most investors, corporate or otherwise, such negotiations were considered to be a trying exercise while to Howard Hughes negotiations of any kind were a form of recreation. In the end, Hughes and Dalitz agreed upon a price of $13.5 million.

In Hughes' acquisition of the remaining mob properties, the

---

* "The court involved in the TWA lawsuit and the appelate courts allowed the tax on the TWA proceeds as lower than regular tax. This was one of the things Chester Davis delighted in telling me on more than one occasion."

—James Leo Wadsworth

next purchase was the show place of the strip, the Sands. Again Dalitz was consulted and Hughes made the purchase for a mere $14.6 million, but this included 183 acres of prime property, all of which since Hughes' death has been developed into a very first class complex made up of five high-rise buildings, a bank, and high class restaurants with the finished product now known as the Howard Hughes Center.

Following the Sands, Hughes acquired the Castaways and the Frontier. Both of these properties came with enormous parcels of empty land that were later developed into expensive high-rise condominiums. Hughes owned the Silver Slipper in his own name. This caused some considerable problems with getting rid of Maheu. It must be remembered that every time Maheu needed cash for one of his schemes, he went to the Slipper cage and drew it out. This is detailed more fully in the chapter, Betrayal.

With the purchase of the Desert Inn, Maheu really held from Hughes many of the detailed provisions of the purchase. The only thing that was actually purchased was the main building of the hotel, which included the casino. It was not known by Hughes that all of the remaining property was on a lease favoring the owners, D.I. Associates. Through some of the Whetton/Wadsworth friends in casino management, Moe Dalitz, the real mob boss, became quite friendly with the two over the years. Moe laughed on more than one occasion at how he led Maheu around as though he had a ring in his nose at the end of a leash.

The rest of the actual buy was the purchase of an existing lease that would come up for renewal in 1976. In addition to occupying the Desert Inn, it soon became apparent that ensuring the improvements required by the lease could create a very expensive long-term maintenance problem with a lease that would have to be renewed and renegotiated by November 30, 1979.

From the ninth floor of the Desert Inn, Hughes instructed

Robert Maheu by handwritten memoranda and phone calls which had to go through the aides who attended him. Edwin Fadiman Jr. classified these aides—Lavar Myler, Howard Eckersley, George Francom, Roy Crawford, and John Holmes—as "silent, incorruptible, non-smoking, teetotaling Mormons." Maheu, in his frustration and inability to gain any influence or even social contact with the five, called them the "Mormon Mafia."

Maheu never did understand how Howard Hughes had chosen and developed his own work pattern since the late 1940s. He never understood the Hughes mind and the workings of his "modern feudalistic" system. The system Hughes established at the Desert Inn was patterned after and an extension of the Operations Center at 7000 Romaine Street that had existed for almost twenty years.

From the purchases that began in March of 1967 until December 1970, the properties were operated under Maheu's contract with top-level management changes at each of the properties. With Maheu's departure, Hughes' master plan began to be implemented but did not become a reality until December of 1972. At this time the Oil Tool Division of Hughes Tool Company was sold for the sum of $150 million to a publicly held company in California and was to be called the Baker-Hughes Tool Company. The Hughes Tool Company continued as the owner of all of Hughes' remaining holdings, which included all of his Nevada and other assets worldwide, including Hughes Airwest.

Nevada had been on Hughes' mind for an extensive time as a place to establish his personal residence, especially regarding his personal security. He had learned from years in Hollywood how important this was and it continued to be even more important. He thought Las Vegas would provide a place where he could bring his personal staff of vassals whose skills had been honed for guarding and ensuring his privacy and security.

A story is told by Benny Binion of the Old Horseshoe Club that demonstrates how even Hughes' acquaintances protected his privacy. Benny, who knew Hughes from his early days in Texas in the 40's and 50's, related this personal experience with James Wadsworth in February of 1972, the day after its occurrence. "As you know, kicking Maheu out and leaving Las Vegas the way Hughes did was nationwide news. Several days ago, I was visited by an anchorwoman for CBS News. She said, 'We understand that you have known Howard Hughes for many years. We are told that you probably know as much about him as anybody.' I replied that I probably knew him as well as anyone still alive. She then asked if I would then consent to an interview about Hughes on tape to be in a television program. I consented, told her I would be happy to tell what I knew, and the interview was set up to be done in my office the next day. So the following morning, she showed up with an entire crew of two cameras and cameramen, lights and operators and people to handle the sound. She then said, 'Now, Mr. Binion, you have consented to this interview. You have agreed that you know as much about Howard Hughes as anyone. Now please tell us what you know of this mysterious man.' I looked at the camera and said, 'Not a G—damn thing.'"

From 1972 until his death, the Summa Board and his Las Vegas managers had a direct line to Hughes. In the same December period of 1972, the remainder of Hughes Tool Company was renamed Summa* Corporation which, though solely owned by Hughes, would begin to function as most of his other corporations except that the day-to-day operations continued to be tightly controlled by upper level management selected by Summa, with

---

* "When the Hughes Tool Company was sold, the contract allowed the buyers to use the Hughes name for ten years and there couldn't be a Hughes Corporation. I was personally involved in this. Bill Gay chose "Summa" because it meant to be the 'greatest' or 'highest', not because of Billy!"

—James Leo Wadsworth

Hughes' personal approval. Some flexibility was exercised by its officers and board of directors who were put in place with Hughes' approval. Chester Davis was selected as Chairman, Bill Gay as President and CEO, and John Holmes and Lavar Myler, along with Nadine Henley, made up the Board of Directors. Since Holmes and Myler were living with Hughes as part of the vassal's rotation schedules, they were able to communicate to him details of the board's activities as well as relaying Hughes' orders to the Board. The entire process now allowed the management of the individual properties to have open access with Hughes through the Board and to expedite the need for day-to-day management decisions especially where funding was involved.

With regard to Summa Corporation, Ellie Pugmire remembers, "The first time I heard about Summa Corp. was in London. Bill Gay, Nadine Henley, and Chester Davis were the ones responsible for setting up the corporation, which was headquartered in Las Vegas. The major holdings of the company were Hughes Airwest, the Nevada Operations—the Sands, Desert Inn, Landmark, Frontier, and Castaways Hotels, the Paradise Country Club, Silver Slipper, and Harold's Club, KLAS-TV, Hughes Television Network, the Xanadu Princess hotel in the Bahamas, and other properties and companies.

"As directors of this corporation they were managing all of Hughes' empire. Their dreams came true.

"On a trip to Las Vegas in 1974, I was taken on a tour of their offices that are located on the underground level of a building located on the outskirts of Las Vegas. The center of the wide hallway that separates the offices had a long narrow pool filled with water, walkways going over the pool, and various potted plants for décor. I had the feeling I wouldn't care to be working there underground with no outside windows. The security guards saw that the place was well protected."

Of particular interest was the Desert Inn, because unknown to

Hughes and not disclosed by Maheu at the time of the purchase, the entire property was in a major state of disrepair. The Desert Inn Associates issued a formal notice of leasehold problems on November 6, 1974 addressed to Howard R. Hughes. James Whetton received this letter, and along with Leo Wadsworth, had already inspected the property and notified Summa of most of the major problems that needed to be handled immediately. One particular and urgent problem was a section of 350 rooms that Wadsworth informed Whetton was about to be condemned by the County Health Department. Ahead of condemnation, Whetton caused the section to be fenced off and demolition began. Since this action created a violation of the lease, it would require that the destroyed building be replaced in kind.

When informed, Hughes immediately decided that before starting any major renovation and building program, a new, long-term lease had to be in place. In 1974, James Whetton and James Leo Wadsworth, accompanied by Chester Davis, made a trip to New York and negotiated a new 21-year lease with a 27-year renewal option of the Desert Inn property with Desert Inn Associates.

But here again, as a result of the prior briefings, Howard Hughes was way out ahead with his planning. He had already bought a major architectural firm in Van Nyes, California. The firm, Archi Systems, was already staffed with some of the very best in their fields. They had the in-house capability of not only the remodeling of existing structures, but also the design of new structures even to the point of recommending everything from carpets to complete furnishings along with bid preparations and on-site construction supervision. In fact, they had already designed a replacement building whose unique design lit up the night sky and reminded one of a large white pyramid. Airline crews as guests remarked that upon approach to McCarran, it was considered a catalyzed landmark. It was now critically important to get funding from Hughes for the renovation and new construction involving a total rebuilding of existing structures, but the construction of the pyramid, a new high rise, and a first class health spa was to be supervised by Dr. Wilbur Thain.

Again, Hughes quickly and quietly had acquired all of the property connecting the four hotels, which were each to become wings of the finished product to be known as The Howard Hughes, with a final room count of 15,000. Each wing was to be designed to accommodate a specific type of customer. The Desert Inn, with its Championship golf course, an ultra modern health spa and eight tennis courts was to be oriented to the sports crowd with primarily top female entertainers. The Sands Wing, with the construction of a new golf course immediately to the east, was to be oriented to the high rollers and convention customers with a convention center. The Castaway was to be known as the "Gardens" and would be family-oriented with an appropriate theme park. The Frontier would maintain a frontier motif and appeal to the "western" residents and guests, again with convention accommodations. Between the Gardens and the Frontier, one of the finest high-end shopping malls was built to accommodate four nationally famous anchor stores. Today this mall is the envy of every other mall in the nation. It is known as Fashion Place Mall.

In all, the four wings of The Howard Hughes were to occupy the length of three football fields from north to south on Las Vegas Boulevard and were to be connected by a tram for free passenger conveyance between the four wings and Fashion Place Mall. Since Hughes' passing, his grand concept and plans have been adopted and used by the different corporate owners of the now existing strip hotels, all built on the Hughes-owned property.

Howard Hughes had always had trouble with ownership of any major industry being controlled by "the mob" or "the family."

He most certainly recognized that gambling, as it was organized in Nevada right after WWII, could not have existed except by the men who ran Covington, Kentucky, Memphis, Tennessee and the illegal houses in most of the major cities from the east coast to the Mississippi River.

He knew, firsthand, of the various gambling enterprises in the western cities, but his experiences in Nevada and what he saw in his four years in the Desert Inn led him to believe that legitimate hotels with gaming casinos had become the way to go. No longer would the major income be a result of the mob and their concentration on gaming money. The real income would be realized from hotels and restaurants by the people who knew how to run them. Before he ever really lived in Las Vegas, he was familiar with the Flamingo, El Rancho Vegas, the Last Frontier, etc. He knew the right person who just might see the same thing—Conrad Hilton.

Bill Gay knew Hilton personally and Hughes began his personal pressure on Mr. Hilton to have a look at Las Vegas. The pressure and Hughes' individual influence worked. Baron Hilton, whom Conrad had brought up in the hotel business, was sent to Nevada. Thus corporate influence in the gambling hotel mecca of Nevada had begun. The still-existing Las Vegas Hilton tells the rest of the story. Wadsworth and Whetton had contact with the Hiltons to come to Vegas.

All of this planning was completed with Hughes' direct involvement to the smallest detail prior to his death, and most certainly with his personal approval and funding. Howard Hughes completely, and on his own, changed the face of Nevada forever from the standpoint of daily operations in Las Vegas in 1970 until his death in 1976. Hughes also owned all the property between the Frontier and Sahara Avenue. This included the site of the closed and later demolished El Rancho Vegas. In speaking of changing Vegas for the better, it was his influence along with corporate ownership being allowed to operate gambling that brought the Hiltons to

Vegas. If the mob had not been kicked out and corporate control of gambling allowed, Hilton would never have located there. Also, remember that Del Webb was Hughes' builder and Hughes brought him to Vegas.

The duplicity of Maheu in some of the purchases in Vegas needs to be told. For instance, for some time the Landmark had been in bankruptcy. The court had it for sale for $12 million. To initiate the possible purchase by Hughes, Maheu sent a memo to the Penthouse stating that, in effect, too many small businesses would not be paid as a part of the proceeds at that price and would be left out in the cold. He finally recommended a purchase price of $17 million. From that escrow, Greenspun and his Washington D.C. lawyer gleaned a finder's fee of $200,000. The property had been advertised on the open market for months. Why did it have to be found? Morgan, the lawyer, didn't do a thing but some of Greenspun's fees to him were paid. The very persistent and open remarks were that Maheu also got a fee. Some say the event was court approved. The Paradise Valley Golf Course, which was owned by Greenspun, and the Sands were also purchased under similar circumstances.

The Stardust was the final mob-owned property Hughes attempted to buy. The purchase price of some $30 million again included additional property and the Desert Star Laundry, which was jointly owned by the Stardust and the Desert Inn. As a part of the new pyramid building, Whetton had built a new laundry that, with the future expansion, would be capable of furnishing all 15,000 rooms of the Howard Hughes with all of its laundry needs. In 1975 Whetton had negotiated the sale of Desert Inn's fifty percent ownership of the Desert Star for $169,000. The same night of that sale the Desert Star Laundry had a fire and collected an insurance settlement of $1.25 million from the Teamsters Insurance Fund.

The Securities and Exchange Commission refused to allow

Hughes the Stardust purchase saying they could not allow Hughes to have ownership of over thirty percent of the Las Vegas room count.

In 1979, the Nevada gaming commission moved in and closed the Stardust down for unrecorded violations. The commission then contacted James Whetton, who still had a class A gaming license, to return to Las Vegas and take over as General Manager of the facility for the state. His answer was simply put. Once you have worked for a boss like Hughes, you will never find another like him.

More than three decades have come and gone since the public address system of the Desert Inn was turned on by James Whetton to tearfully request that a minute of silence be observed in remembrance of the passing of everyone's long-time friend and benefactor, Howard Robard Hughes. The entire hotel and casino went completely silent probably for the first and only time in history. The shocking news was such that several minutes actually passed before normal activity resumed and despite his passing, his quest to completely change the face of Nevada would continue.

The Nevada Operations

Changing the face of Nevada was a game that long since Hughes had honed his skills to accomplish. His entre to Hollywood, followed by twenty-five years of building what was eventually to be a multibillion-dollar empire, was, to Hughes, a walk in the park.

Fortunately, he recognized early on, as a result of his previous years of fun and games while frequently visiting Las Vegas, that the gaming industry from the standpoint of ownership and management was a whole new world. The difference is easily understood since the main commodity or product in all of Las Vegas is the control of huge amounts of money, twenty-four hours a day.

Under mob control, honesty was a forgotten word and only practiced by losers. Prior to Hughes entering the gaming arena, the mob controlled the huge sums of money that came their way. Skimming was a form of producing great personal wealth. There was no end to the skimming that took place in the casinos in the form of cheating from hustling of tokens, to payoffs to designated agents, and regulating slot machine payoffs.

These problems were handled to favor the house (the mob) with the use of the famous eye-in-the-sky surveillance. When a dealer was caught cheating against the house, one casino owner, who will go unnamed, had on his desk a small replica of a baseball bat. A dealer caught cheating would be escorted to his office for a stern lecture. If a second incident occurred, both of the cheater's hands were placed on the desk where all fingers of both hands were broken by the bat, causing permanent disability and no more dealing cards.

Moe Dalitz, it is told, was somewhat more tolerant. As he lectured the dealer in his office, he would put his arm around the dealer's neck while he lectured, then squeeze the neck with the stern advice that should another incident occur, the dealer's head would be separated from his torso.

The rest of the skimming took place in the casino cage or counting room at the end of each shift. The count would go with three piles of the shift winnings. The first pile was the winnings, the next pile was one for the house, and the third pile was "two for me or us." With Hughes and his new rules, the count was conducted with at least three cage managers, ensuring that the house got one hundred percent of the win.

A secondary source of individual income, which could be substantial, involved kickbacks to purchasing agents, likely general managers. And it revealed that a previous general manager was receiving a five percent kick back from an advertising agency. It doesn't sound like much, except that the advertising budget was $5,000,000 per year.

A typical example of "honesty does not pay" involves an experience related by James Whetton soon after he became general manager of the Desert Inn. He found that there were three major meat suppliers in Las Vegas, yet the Desert Inn was buying all meat products from only one company. He immediately ordered the food and beverage manager, who was simply following the previous general manager's orders, to get a bid from all three suppliers on a daily basis. Very soon thereafter Whetton was visited by the previous meat supplier who informed him that if he would buy his meat from him, an envelope would delivered to him each month containing ten thousand dollars cash. The visitor was immediately escorted from the Desert Inn and removed from the bid list.

Thus the first order of Hughes' business was to seek out key people in the chain of command who were of a different breed of people who he knew he could totally trust from past experiences. This assignment was logically entrusted to Bill Gay and Nadine Henley soon after the firing of Robert Maheu and his group of associates. The first to be brought back in were James Leo Wadsworth, James Whetton, and a newcomer, Steve Savoldelli, who had previously been a president of Pepsi Cola of Mexico. Steve, assisted by Bill Gay, had the prime responsibility as controller of all of Hughes' Nevada hotels and casinos, except for the Desert Inn whose management reported directly to Bill Gay and Hughes with the close involvement of Wadsworth during the entire rebuilding of the Desert Inn facilities.

Following the firing of Maheu in December 1970, Hughes conveyed to Bill Gay, in great detail, his desire to start an immediate house cleaning of all employees who could be identified as "mafia family" in all of his casinos. Gay asked Wadsworth for recommendations and with advice from long-time prominent Las Vegans George Franklin, Ralph Lamb, and others, initiated the house cleaning process. From this beginning, Wadsworth hired Modica as general manager of the Desert Inn. Meanwhile, as part of his assignment and with the approval of Hughes and Gay, he also hired James Cullen, who was known as one of the best undercover agents there was in the Las Vegas area. Wadsworth had known Cullen for several years before being called to Vegas. By 1973, the house cleaning was well under way.

Others involved in the transition were Frank Wilcox, a first cousin to Wadsworth, and Dick Woods, who was the youngest son of a great uncle—both could be highly trusted by all concerned. During the tenure of Modica, Speer, and Whetton at the Desert Inn, Woods was the chief cashier in the casino cage, and Wilcox was assistant cashier. In 1973 and for several previous years, Modica had been General and Casino Manager of the Showboat Hotel on Boulder Highway. In spite of the fact that it was not on the strip, that hotel/casino was very successful.

In 1974, Cullen reported to Wadsworth and said that there was going to be a union election at the Desert Inn and that it was very apt to be successful. Wadsworth took that information to Gay and they shortly had a meeting with Modica. In that meeting, Gay suggested to Modica that Cullen and others could help in beating the union. Modica flatly refused to consider the help. Gay told him that his job was on the line if the union won. Remember that Hughes was adamant about thinking that the gaming industry should not be unionized.

Modica lost the election by a vote of 86 to 80. Gay called Wadsworth in and said, "You hired him, you fire him," which he did. It was not more than a week until Modica was back at the Showboat. Speer and Whetton were hired to fill the vacancy left by Modica. Frank Wilcox then discovered a large amount of money missing from the cage and reported it to Wadsworth, who put Cullen on the problem. Ten thousand dollars was easily found, but Cullen said that fifty thousand was actually missing. The word got out and the money was returned in a paper bag.

Cullen continued his valuable services to all of the Hughes properties until the departure of all of Hughes' faithful in 1978. He was particularly effective in assisting Wadsworth and Whetton at the Desert Inn when the union was soundly defeated in the final attempt to unionize the casino personnel.

The spring of 1971 was the beginning of Whetton's direct involvement in Nevada. It began with several discussions with Bill Gay regarding the current and future of golfing operations in Las Vegas. Of particular concern were problems at the newly purchased Paradise Valley Country Club, operating at an annual loss of about $250,000 per year, that obviated a top to bottom restructuring. The most important changes there involved appointing Dave Johnson as head pro and general manager, and, although the course was open to public play, a private dues-paying membership roster was formed. The golf cart operation, which was on a lucrative lease contract, was cancelled. New golf carts were purchased and a very profitable center established for Paradise Valley. All of this was accomplished with personal approval from Hughes. Because of Hughes' long-term experience and interest in golf, the transition to profitability was easier to implement.

With the success of this project, Bill Gay recommended that a country club division should be set up to oversee all future golf operations for Summa Corporation, including the Desert Inn, however changes in management of the hotel properties delayed and preempted implementing this.

About September 1971, Gay requested of Hughes that Whetton become involved with the hotel management process. Since Perry Lieber, a long-time loyal employee of Hughes, had been assigned as general manager of the Landmark Hotel, this was the obvious place to start. And so began Whetton's intense indoctrination into the hotel/casino management process as assistant to the general manager of the Landmark. This learning process was a pleasant experience because Whetton had known and worked with Perry when Perry was involved years before as a publicist for Hughes and Twentieth Century Fox. Whetton was able to direct and initiate his own involvement with the various departments while learning the hotel and gaming business.

While at the Landmark, Whetton spent about a month in housekeeping with the best in Las Vegas, Mrs. Bellasco, who later became head of the Desert Inn housekeeping department. Next was six weeks with hotel management and reservations under Jack Shannon, who was taken away by the Imperial Palace and then brought to the Desert Inn by Whetton. Training in food and beverage took place under Bill Jaeger at the Desert Inn. Jaeger was the best in all of Las Vegas. Later, after Whetton's departure in 1978, Jaeger went on to handle the food operations for all of Steven Wynn's operations in Las Vegas and Atlantic City. All of these people were extremely loyal to Summa and its president, Bill Gay.

A management change at the Landmark resulted from Summa's hiring a Holiday Inn Manager of the Year. Whetton left the Landmark shortly thereafter.

In 1974 following Modica's casino election loss, there was talk about a need for management changes at the Desert Inn. Whetton recommended to Bill Gay the consideration of Don Speer as general manager. Speer was a long time casino host and assistant casino manager under Harry Goodheart at the Sands. Whetton discussed the matter with Speer, who had a long career in casino operations.

Bill Gay then appointed Speer general manager with the understanding that he would assume the primary duty of overseeing casino affairs and Whetton would become assistant general manager with the primary assignment of assuming administrative duties involving the hotel, restaurant and golf course operations.

In October 1974, a section of rooms was closed down that were unfit for occupancy. During this process, the building had to be destroyed. Whetton called in Deseret Industries who was happy to accept the donation, and effect the removal, of toilets, tubs and basins. This independent act, along with Whetton's close working relationship with supervisors, personnel, and department heads caused Speer to resent Whetton's administrative controls and to request Whetton's release. Until that release, Whetton was placed on a leave of absence. This act doomed Speer.

Late on a Saturday night, Whetton received a call from Bill Gay requesting that he meet with him and Steve Savoldelli in Los Angeles the next day. At that time Savoldelli had been placed in charge of business administration of the Las Vegas properties.

After lengthy discussions, Whetton agreed to return to the

Desert Inn as general manager. The reasons Gay gave for his selection of Whetton was twofold. First, casino activities were difficult to control at best, and the presence of a potentially unionized casino would add to management problems and activate the spread of the Union movements to other casinos. And second, the Desert Inn, or portions of it, was in a state of disrepair and Gay, consulting closely with Hughes, had already developed plans for upgrading all of the Hughes' properties in Las Vegas. He further felt that Whetton's background in engineering would be helpful in the rebuilding process.

The following Monday, Whetton replaced Speer as general manager. At this time, the Desert Inn began a strong working relationship with Archi Systems, a subsidiary of Summa Corporation, headed by very capable Dave Clark, whose Archi Systems had an excellent staff of architects.

Plans were already underway for major renovation of some of the existing buildings and for destruction and replacement of the condemned section of rooms that were known as the Country Club, as well as for a new six-story building which would replace the dilapidated area occupied by engineering, housekeeping, and purchasing.

Most of 1973 was spent working in meetings with Gay and Archi Systems on design concepts for each structure while demolition and construction was going on. The most constructive planning included an order from Hughes requiring that a mock room be built for each new or renovated section of rooms before construction started. Each of these rooms was completely constructed as a finished product and then inspected and criticized by the key hotel apartment heads. During this inspection process, many things needed to be changed, such as light switches, lamps, etc. In one section of suites there were wall mirrors and a sliding mirror door between the tub and bathroom and the living room—a great idea but Mrs. Bellasco, the housekeeper, objected to the mirror over the bathtub stating there was no way her girls could clean it. Needless to say, her input, as well as suggestions from others prevailed.

The project started by closing down one entire section of rooms at a time, just a step ahead of being closed by the Health Department. Two weeks after closing down the section known as "The Cribs," the County Health Department came in to find the section not only closed, but also fenced off.

Then began a fast track process of destruction of single floor rooms known as the Country Club section, rebuilding and refurbishing of a section of rooms adjacent to the golf course into two-story suites with several outdoor Jacuzzis, and a three-story structure on the north side of the property converted to luxury suites with up to three bedrooms. The famous nine-story building from which Hughes launched his Nevada acquisition was expanded into luxury suites on the 8th and 9th floors, while the casino moved to the first floor, and the old casino was completely rebuilt.

Bill Gay required that the new casino design be signed off on by a special committee made up of the general managers and casino managers of the Sands, the Frontier, and the Desert Inn.

Harry Goodheart, casino manager of the Sands, was an effective contributor to the design and layout of the new casino and was later recognized by Hughes who awarded Harry with a lifetime employment contract.

A major part of the project was the construction of the new pyramid-shaped six-story structure with three wings. Hughes had personally approved of this building's design. The rooms were all mini-suites with a large suite and a swimming pool at the end of each wing, and on all six floors. The staff expressed concern about the reliability of the construction of the upper floor pools and the difficulty of maintaining them, finally convincing Bill Gay and Hughes to confine pool construction to the ground floors.

The basement portion of the building was designed to have the various departments such as engineering, housekeeping, and a laundry capable of handling linen service for all of the Las Vegas properties.

During the entire construction and refurbishing project, Bill Gay was deeply interested and involved; in fact, he and Whetton would tour the entire project at least three to four times each month, always between six and ten p.m., while none of the contractors and crews were on site.

It was on the occasion of one of these tours that Whetton requested that Gay consider topping off the new six-story building with three super deluxe "high roller" suites. With the help of John Aldefer, Desert Inn Controller, they put together a proforma of construction costs and income forecast that later proved this addition to be a valuable asset for the property. Gay was very involved with the design and décor of these luxury suites. He was later accused, by Hughes' relatives in their lawsuit filed in Los Angeles, of being involved for his personal use of these suites. This accusation was totally false since he had no intention of occupying or ever using one of these suites. In fact, whenever he did stay at the Desert Inn, he used one of the small suites in the old three-story building.

Bill Gay, while continually keeping Hughes involved, continued in a very active role with Archi Systems in selecting everything from the color schemes to furniture, to carpeting, etc.

During this process, it was very urgent that the Union situation with the casino be solved. The root of the problem was that the casino employees felt isolated. Casino management necessarily had to involve very strict rules and discipline; but dealers were just ordinary human beings who had little or no dialogue with management.

A casino committee was started made up of the general manager, the casino manager, one shift manager, and a pit boss. The dealers were represented by three of the oldest in terms of service and one dealer from each game section. This group met in the general manager's office at 11 a.m. on a monthly schedule. The group immediately opened up discussions on issues from dress code, to rules, to personal problems. The bulk of Desert Inn employees were Union, but it didn't matter to management whether they were Union or not. The major difference was that Whetton preferred to operate in a family atmosphere rather than by Union rules. As far as he was concerned, his door was always open to any employee except when it involved a Union matter, in which case they might get an appointment in a year or at the next contract time. This worked well for management and the employees and the Union was defeated soundly.

When negotiations came up for the Teamsters and culinary contracts at Paradise Valley, Hughes took a hard-nosed stand that a small country club like Paradise Valley could not survive paying the Union prices of the Strip. It was a nasty battle of about three months but the Club employees voted to decertify both unions. Here again, good employer/employee relationships paid off.

Union strikes were a way of life in Las Vegas, particularly since the demise of mafia holdings. But strikes were never a serious problem at the Desert Inn because of the loyalty of the Desert Inn employees. This was vividly displayed when the Union brought in a bunch of goons to harass management as they entered and left the property. In fact, when Whetton went through the picket lines, he always made a point of stopping and having a friendly chat with his people. The goons weren't even allowed to come close to his car. One goon finally did start to rock the car but a cattle prod to his belly knocked him backwards as the employee pickets cheered.

The Ordinary Side of a Genius

On or about June 1953, Whetton read an article in *Time Magazine* about the people who worked as the staff for Howard Hughes. Mentioned in that article were two key people, Bill Gay and Nadine Henley. "I was headed for San Diego for two weeks of Naval Reserve duty, and I managed to locate Bill Gay and spent a couple of days in interviews with him and Ms. Henley. As a result, I joined the Hughes staff in July of 1953."

Before being allowed contact with Hughes, new staff members were required to go through at least six weeks of briefing and indoctrination. After being on board for two weeks, Whetton's first contact with Hughes was a quiet ride in a hotel elevator. This short visit made a lasting impression on Whetton as to Hughes' physical stature and his dark, piercing eyes. This very same impression was experienced and so described by every other new staff member. "He had to assume that I was one of his newly hired vassals because I exited the elevator on the floor below his then private domain."

MIAMI

Whetton's training period was cut short, lasting just over three weeks, when he and part of the staff were removed to Miami where Hughes' entourage occupied the top two floors of the Columbus Hotel. The reason for the Miami visit was to explore the possibility of moving Hughes Aircraft to the Miami area. Whetton was given the assignment to go out and record the addresses and telephone numbers of all phone booths within a five-block radius of the hotel. This was done as a security measure since Hughes did not trust communicating through hotel switchboards.

After preparing the phone list, Whetton presented it to the Boss. Hughes had him read the list of numbers and addresses that filled twenty-six lines of a legal note pad. Whetton tore off the sheet to leave it with him, but he didn't need it. He had the document memorized.

After this, Hughes would dispatch a staff member to one of the phone booths to pass a message to someone he was working with. Whetton: "We would then stand by at the booth until he called to have us pass on the message. When moving about Miami or Miami Beach, Hughes would often stop at a booth to make a call. This required us to carry dimes since Hughes seldom carried any kind of money."

He often made nighttime trips to Miami Beach. One night, Hughes had Whetton drive with him and partway across the causeway they were pulled over by two Miami police officers for exceeding the speed limit. Everyone exited the vehicles and Hughes started talking to the officers. After a short conversation, the officers were mesmerized. The entourage parted company without receiving a ticket or a warning. Hughes then remarked at how polite the officers had been, and that they had a very friendly discussion about policemen and their dangerous and difficult jobs. Hughes asked Whetton to find out their names. Whetton told Hughes he had their badge numbers and would do so.

The next day, Hughes requested that Whetton deliver a deep sea fishing outfit to one and a set of golf clubs to the other   their individual hobbies—courtesy of the Boss. Both reluctantly accepted the gifts, but Whetton convinced them that it was merely a gesture to acknowledge and reward them for their professionalism. They tried unsuccessfully to get Whetton to identify the Boss as Howard Hughes.

Hughes was aware of Whetton's Navy background so he called him to say he wanted to look at a yacht he was thinking of purchasing. "I asked if it was gas- or diesel-powered. Since it was gas-powered, I informed him not to consider it, and that he should never buy a gas-powered boat of any sort. I then told him about an Admiral's barge—gas-powered—that exploded in Japan as the Admiral and I were about to board. We replaced the barge with one that was diesel-powered."

A major part of the Miami plan was to find homes and cars to accommodate about 150 of Hughes' key employees. To furnish this need, Whetton was directed to research the purchase of a tract of 150 homes, each to have at least three bedrooms, two baths, and a screened lanai furnished with 150 new Chevrolet four-door sedans with air conditioning.

The Miami visit was cut short for reasons known only to Hughes himself, but he was harassed with the constant publicity from the *Miami Herald* speculating that he was planning to relocate the Hughes Aircraft Company to Miami. Though somewhat true, Hughes still resented their invasion into his private world.

In the middle of the night everyone packed up, leaving Miami to return to staff headquarters on Romaine Street in Hollywood. Bill Gay and Whetton were told to fly commercial, and the rest of the staff flew with Hughes. Their experiences are recorded in the chapter Flying with Hughes.

It was from this point on that Whetton ceased to work the call center desk except when specifically assigned by Hughes, and he became deeply and personally involved with the day to day dealings of Howard Hughes.

DOWN TO BUSINESS

Whetton recalls, "The first incident was a call from Hughes about 4 p.m. one afternoon. He stated that he wanted to buy a new hat to wear to Noah Dietrich's wedding. He described in detail his choice of color from charcoal gray to charcoal with a brown cast. He did not know his hat size. I stopped at a couple of men's clothing stores without success. I finally found a hat shop and told the owner that I needed to buy a new hat for my boss, but I did not know his hat size. He asked me who my boss was, and I told him I couldn't reveal his name. He then said, "Okay. You work for Howard Hughes. He wears a size seven and three-fourths." I then left with three different hats so that Hughes could make a choice, and we could pay later for the one he selected.

"Mr. Hughes was very happy with the choices and kept all three hats, but was preoccupied and never did make it to the wedding; however, he was well represented by most of the staff.

"One night we were working in Bungalow 19 at the Beverly Hills Hotel. About 11:30 p.m., Hughes told me he needed some needles and thread to darn some socks. He gave me explicit instructions as to needle sizes and darning thread colors. I left the hotel about midnight to acquire the items. I went to Walgreen's Drug Store on La Cienega and found a janitor inside the store working on the floors. I tapped on the door and tried to convince him to let me in. A twenty-dollar bill through the crack in the door secured my entry. I found what Hughes wanted and left money in an envelope to cover the cost. Needless to say, Hughes was quite pleased.

"Another time, Hughes called me at home to say that the hotel power was to be shut off from 12:30 p.m. to 3:30 a.m., and that he had work to do and needed some light to work by. I thought of the battle lanterns we had aboard ship that were battery-operated and would turn on when the power was lost to light the inboard passageways. I proceeded to Hughes Aircraft and convinced a security guard that the Boss would really appreciate borrowing a couple such lanterns for the night. The guard, somewhat reluctantly, helped me cut the chain anchoring the lanterns to the wall. Hughes had his lights ready to turn on before midnight and asked me to thank the security guard when the lanterns were returned the next day."

During the planning for purchase and development of a fleet of Boeing 707's for TWA, Hughes would go into a four-to-six week work cycle beginning at 3 p.m. and working intensely until 3 or 4 a.m., during which Whetton would report to Bungalow 19.

Whetton: "Each afternoon I would have to call Hughes' banker's (Ben Sessel) secretary at the Bank of New York to determine Mr. Sessel's location for that evening. Hughes would begin calling contacts in France regarding the purchase of Caravelle jet engines. He would then work his way west with his calls, the last one at about 2 a.m., to the chief engineer at Boeing. He had the plans for the 707 lying on his bed and would go into lengthy discussions about changes or redesign features from the 707's electrical system or cabin pressurization, to the air conditioning system."

Hughes would have Whetton retrieve his pen from his closet so that he could make notes on the plans. Foolishly, Whetton asked the Boss early on why he was calling these people at such odd hours. He replied with a smile, "You will notice we have no trouble finding them because they are always in bed sleeping."

A NUISANCE

Hughes disliked having to "fire" people. Perhaps the most extreme example of this dislike was in the case of a minor executive of what was to become Hughes Aviation. This person, because of a long and close association, had almost unlimited access to Hughes, but his constant "bugging" of Hughes got to be annoying. He wouldn't let anyone call him down or fire him, but he finally couldn't stand it any longer.

Hughes called the person up and told him he had a very important and difficult job for him overseas and that there would be first class airline ticket for him at the Pan American counter to Singapore. The flight desk also had reservations for a small suite at the Raffles Hotel in Singapore with full credit. Most importantly, of course, his salary with bonus would continue, and he was to check into the hotel and wait for detailed instructions by phone. Records show that the man had followed instructions. But to allow himself more freedom, he began having his meals in the dining room. Five weeks or so later, he started going out at night. The phone calls never came. After three months or so, the guy got the idea that no call was coming and so elected to use his ticket home. Upon arrival, he resigned so fast that Hughes did not have to fire him.

HOME SWEET HOME

Whenever Hughes needed to lease a house, the usual process of executing his detailed plan never changed. Whetton, often accompanied by Leo Wadsworth, would execute the lease and prepare the house. More often than not, Hughes would never enter or visit the premises.

The first such assignment involved a house in Palm Springs. First, all locks had to be changed and the old keys retained so that at the end of the lease the locks could be changed back to fit the original keys. Then every item in the house was carefully inventoried, including fixtures attached or unattached. For example, items such as washers, dryers, and refrigerators, were described and serial and model numbers recorded. These lists included items right down to the last knife, fork, and spoon. If alcoholic beverages were found, the bottles were marked, the items removed from the premises and stored in one of the vaults at Romaine Street to be returned to the premises upon termination of the lease. Included in the Palm Springs home inventory were the oranges and grapefruits on trees in the yard. Lastly, all windows were sealed with duct tape to prevent dust from entering. It was well known by all that Hughes was allergic to dust.

Another home in Bel Air was inventoried in a similar manner, and this process really paid off. At the termination of the lease, the owner, in an article on the front page of the *Los Angeles Times*, accused Mr. Hughes of stealing valuable art from the premises. Maheu, who had just recently been brought to Hollywood from Washington, was assigned to investigate. Within two weeks, the *Times* front page had another article, detailing that the owner had been jailed for smuggling art into the country. This charge included recovered art that Hughes had been accused of removing, as well as other art remaining in the house.

HUGHES AND CARS

Hughes had a passive interest in automobiles and was often curious about some of the newer models. On one occasion he had Whetton pick up a new Packard from the Hollywood Packard dealer. He kept the car for a couple of days, but probably never drove it.

Whetton: "While working with Hughes one evening, he asked me what kind of car I had. I told him I had just purchased a new 1955 Buick Century four-door hardtop with all the bells and whistles. He explained that people were coming in to buy RKO Studios, and he would like to trade me cars for a few days. We exchanged keys, and I left driving his black 1951 Chevrolet stick shift with a radio, but no heater. Getting possession of my car was interesting. He really did not want to give it up. I told the Boss he could keep it if he took over the payments. As he handed me the keys, he remarked that it was a jazzy car."

Hughes did have one car that was his very favorite—a 1953 Buick Roadmaster with very low mileage. This is detailed by Eric Peters at http://www.buickbombsight.org. "An unnamed bidder paid ($1.62 million) at a recent Barrett-Jackson automobile auction . . . for a low mileage 1953 Roadmaster hardtop sedan once owned by eccentric billionaire and aviation pioneer Howard Hughes. The pastel blue and sea foam green car was modified with a 24-volt electrical system powerful enough to start Hughes' personal aircraft, enabling him to drive directly onto the tarmac, jump-start the plane and flee the Paparazzi—without ever having to dash from a parking lot through a terminal. The Roadmaster 's air conditioner was converted to run on electricity, so that Hughes could keep cool even with the engine off. The interior also features a cabin air filtration system designed by Hughes himself that incorporates a dust trap and bacterial filter—features that are only just now becoming available on modern cars. Hughes used the car for transportation as well as a mobile office when he stayed in California at the Beverly Hills Hotel—where he maintained one of his many residences. It was an especially beloved possession and Hughes had it secreted away in storage, where it remained for decades after his death on April 5, 1976. According to Craig Jackson of the Barrett-Jackson Auction Company, the $1.62 million paid for the Hughes Buick is 'a phenomenal price for this one-of-a-kind piece of Americana.' It's also apparently the most money ever paid for a Buick."

This Buick had substantially more mileage on it traveling back and forth cross-country in a rail car than was recorded on the odometer. Its last noted travel by rail occurred in 1954 when Whetton was instructed to have the car shipped from Miami back to its normal storage area in Los Angeles. In processing the shipping, Whetton was given detailed instructions to be followed before the shipment could take place.

Since the rail car would be traveling through Texas in early summer, the railroad had to be contacted and a chart obtained as to what the recorded temperature would be inside a boxcar traveling through Texas at that particular time of the year. After this was determined, Whetton was instructed to contact a Buick engineer to determine what, if any, damage might occur to the car's interior but especially to the rubber insulation around the doors and windows. Fortunately, Whetton was personally acquainted with Buick's Chief Engineer who was able to verify that all of the parts in question could withstand temperatures substantially higher than those expected. With this information in hand, Hughes ordered the car to be shipped.

Aside from the Buick and his 1951 Chevrolet, Hughes was known to own personally only one other car. This was a Chrysler that was stored in Las Vegas that he used while there. While in Hollywood, in order to travel occasionally incognito, Hughes would often borrow the personal cars belonging to Wilbur Thain and Gordon Bench.

HUGHES AND THE LA TIMES

Over the years, Hughes fostered and perpetuated a warm and friendly relationship with the publishers of the *Los Angeles Times*, Norman and Dorothy Chandler. As told by Ellie Pugmire, "On several occasions I personally delivered important documents for Hughes such as cash, checks, legal documents, or letters. One such delivery was the personal check from Howard Hughes for the amount of $25,000 that I delivered to "Buffy" Chandler at the *Los Angeles Times* building downtown, who was raising funds to build the beautiful and impressive Dorothy Chandler Music Pavilion. This was the first of many contributions he made to the music center. For this, Hughes' name is carved in marble along with other contributors on the walls inside this magnificent edifice. Ironically, my husband and I had season tickets for the light opera when the Pavilion was completed, and the seats we occupied on the 7th row center were directly behind the seats with the engraved name of Howard Hughes, as donor of those seats, staring at us for the next ten years."

One night in October 1955, Whetton received a call at home from

Hughes during which Hughes stated that he had a very special assignment involving the Chandlers. He said he would discuss the details when Whetton reported to him for his normal shift at 3 p.m. at the Beverly Hills Bungalow 19.

Hughes had learned that the Chandlers were planning an extended tour of Europe. His detailed instructions followed: Whetton was to contact the Chandlers at their *LA Times* office and explain to them that Hughes had been made aware of their planned trip, and Whetton must convince them to accept Hughes' offer to fund their entire trip on TWA. When considering the Chandler's monetary and individual independence, the convincing was not easy to accomplish. When Whetton informed them of the importance to Hughes of their long and enduring friendship, and how much he would personally appreciate their accepting his token offer, they not only agreed, but also asked Whetton to relay to Hughes their heartfelt thanks.

From this point Hughes' instructions detailed as to how their trip was to be best served. Hughes wanted Whetton to personally accompany them through the entire journey. "I explained to him that I would comply with his wishes if he so desired, but the trip would cause me to miss the birth of our fourth child. He quickly said that he did not want that to happen and told me to see whom I was willing to recommend taking my place.

"I immediately contacted a friend, Robert Montgomery, who was TWA's director of sales. He then contacted his directors of TWA operations in Europe, who at the time were based in Paris and were conversant in French and Italian. They were pleased to accept the assignment. Mr. Hughes was willing to agree to the change but made it clear that I was to be responsible for directing the trip to its end.

"We contacted our Paris executive and carefully went over his assignment. He was to contact and brief us as to the Chandler's movements from one location to another. He was to take care of all expenses for their needs. At each location, Mrs. Chandler was to have available to her an English-speaking maid. He was to obtain a Leica camera and to take as many pictures as would be appreciated. In addition to making all travel arrangements, we were to purchase a new Mercedes convertible for their personal use.

"The trip lasted about six weeks and involved travel through all of Europe. Shortly after their return, we delivered a beautiful leather-bound photo album with historic pictures of their adventure. While in their offices at the *Times,* I was able to get Mr. Hughes to answer his private line at the Beverly Hills, where they were afforded the opportunity to express their heartfelt thanks personally to Hughes."

HUGHES' GENEROSITY

One night about 3 a.m., as Whetton was about to leave, Hughes informed him that there was a carton of cottage cheese in the refrigerator and a sack in the cupboard. He wanted Whetton to take the cottage cheese home and share it with his family. As Whetton approached the door to leave, Hughes told him he needed to make another call. Whetton placed the sack on the chair next to the door and Hughes said, "Don't leave it there. Put it back in the refrigerator. We don't want it to spoil." When Whetton got home, he opened the carton and the cottage cheese could not have been greener, but Hughes had been really sincere in wanting to share something personal to him with Whetton's family.

During these work cycles, Hughes would often spend weekend nights screening films at Goldwyn Studios. At almost every session he would have Whetton go to a small restaurant on La Cienega Boulevard to pick up his favorite grilled ham and cheese sandwiches and a bottle of milk for him and Miss Peters. On every occasion when picking up the sandwiches, Whetton would carefully go through the same process of watching the chef wash his hands and observe the making and wrapping of the sandwiches. One night, Whetton forgot the milk, panicked, and had to go back out and get it!

Hughes had a softer side that was expressed in poignant acts of kindness and generosity. Ellie Pugmire remembers, "When Sammy Davis, Jr. was injured and subsequently lost an eye in an automobile accident outside of Las Vegas, Mr. Hughes rushed his own physicians in to look after him. He was deeply concerned and wanted Sammy to have the best medical care possible.

"If Hughes heard of someone's child being desperately ill, he not only provided medical help, but helped the family financially as well. There was never any publicity concerning these acts of kindness, and usually the person receiving the aid never knew from where it came.

"If he heard or read of someone's plight, he saw to it that help was given. In the 1950s, during some severe blizzards, Hughes instructed his TWA cargo planes to parachute medical supplies and food to the entrapped Indians in southern Utah and northern Arizona, and tons of hay were dropped to save animal herds that would have perished without this help. He picked up the tab and this, too, was quietly kept out of the press.

"Most of Mr. Hughes' generosities have been kept secret, as he wished, but there are many incidents I heard about just because I was working for him."

One Sunday morning, the Boss called Whetton at home and asked if he had heard of a boating accident at Lake Tahoe involving a stewardess from Western Airlines. Whetton told him that he had read about it and also understood that she was going to have a leg amputated. Hughes then said to tell Lee Murrin in the morning that he wanted to take care of all of her medical bills.

Later, after Hughes' death, Whetton was having dinner with an old friend and an uncle of the stewardess. Whetton asked him if he had a niece named Bonnie. He replied, "Yes," and said the he and her family had never been able to find out who paid her medical expenses. Whetton said, "I can tell you now since he has passed on. His name is Howard Hughes."

This personal dedication for the delivery of the very best medical care for those in need extended beyond Hughes' concern for his fellow humans. One incident involving man's best friend occurred one evening while driving to a restaurant where one of his lady friends was waiting for him. Hughes ran over a dog, stopped the car, and picked up the injured animal. He drove it to a veterinarian, and with this unscheduled delay showed up two hours late for dinner.

He sat down beside his guest, his coat stained with the dog's blood, and proceeded to seemingly ignore her throughout the meal while making frequent dashes to the phone to call the animal hospital and check on the dog's recovery. The next day, a check was hand delivered to pay the bill for its care. He learned that the dog had recovered and had been turned over to its owner.

A very interesting episode that was a classic example of the very human side of Howard Hughes involved locating and rewarding the young Marine who had rescued Hughes from the wreckage of his nearly fatal crash. As the story goes, this man had just been discharged from the Marine Corp and was on the sidewalk when the plane crashed on the golf course. He scaled the chain link fence and took Hughes out of the wreckage. The only record of this man was his name. At that time Whetton was attached to a Ready Naval Reserve unit at the Chavez Ravine Naval facility. Since Whetton had contacts with the Naval Bureau of Personnel, he was able to locate him working as a parking lot attendant at a parking facility in Chicago. Whetton: "It is my understanding that he and his wife were flown to Miami where Hughes rewarded him for his act of heroism."

Another little known fact of Hughes' generosity is wonderfully displayed in his contribution for the establishment of a medical school at the University of Nevada. Hughes was so committed to advancing research and treatment that he decided to fund the development of the Nevada School of Medicine.

He worked with University President N. Edd Miller (1965 to 1973) to establish a public medical school, along with Dr. Fred Anderson and H. Edward Manville. These men, along with Dr. Rueben Zucker, worked with Hughes to make sure that the Reno school would be a bona fide degree-issuing medical school.

It was recognized by all Nevadans that specialized, and in many cases, even routine medical treatment, was sorely lacking. The great distances between cities with hospitals and the isolation of the small towns were a grave concern. For instance, Eureka residents had to travel 78 miles to Ely or 181 miles to Fallon for medical care. The hospital in Reno and the vastly improving hospitals in Clark County were always in need of trained doctors and nurses.

In 1964, the Western Interstate Commission on Higher Education requested a study on the feasibility of establishing medical schools in lesser populated western states. Their report indicated that Nevada was in dire need of a medical school and recommended one be established.

The total amount of Hughes' donations to the UN-Reno Medical School are not known but he began with $200,000 in 1969 when the Nevada State Legislature finally approved the formation of the school. Paul Laxalt, former Nevada governor, recalls, "[Hughes] called me and said he had been following the medical school fight and wanted to help, but was concerned lest his intervention would 'screw things up.' I assured him that . . . his offer would greatly help. The next day I received his telegram in which he pledged to give $200,000 to $300,000 a year for 20 years." Later Laxalt said he was surprised by Hughes' offer which was "one hell of a lot of money at that time."

With the legislature's approval, the first of twenty payments of $200,000 was made by Hughes Tool Company in Houston. On the books it was shown as an advance to Howard Hughes.

In the summer of 1971, Hughes contacted both Houston and Bill Gay and informed them that he intended to honor the $4,000,000 promise but it would be a more formal presentation than the first. Public relations chief, Perry Lieber, would set it up. Hughes designated two Nevada political figures—a former Nevada legislator, and a former District Attorney of Lincoln and Esmeralda Counties, James Leo Wadsworth, to make the actual presentation.

The University had qualified for $3,000,000 matching Federal funds but also needed $375,000 of private donations. The second installment from Hughes was increased over the $200,000 to insure the qualification.

The legal officers of HTCO, Hughes personally, and the University Regents, with the Nevada Attorney General's office had become uneasy with the informality of the twenty year agreement. Attorney General, Robert List, contacted the Nevada Operations Office and a meeting of Bob List and James Leo Wadsworth was arranged. On July 9, 1973, the third installment of $200,000 was handed to the Vice President of the University , James T. Anderson,. This occasion was also the meeting of the attorneys to formalize the rather vague promise of 1967. It was now a properly done deal. (It is of interest to note that the $4 million promised in 1967 is the equivalent of $49,662,204 today, before inflation and taxes—a formidable sum.)

The medical school donations were not all Hughes did for Las Vegas. To mention other donations, but certainly not all, the University Rebels Club received two scholarship checks of $7,500. Each check at that time was the equivalent of five full athletic scholarships. Also, in August of 1972, a new Child Haven facility received $6,537 to purchase furniture.

Most of Hughes' many acts of generosity have been kept secret, as he always wished, but there were many incidents his staff knew about because they were involved in seeing that his wishes were carried out. Wilbur Thain was personally involved with two very close-to-home occurrences; while attending medical school he was also working part time with the newly formed Operations Center staff.

MORE ON GENEROSITY

Wilbur Thain: "I do remember very well how concerned Hughes would become if something physical happened to a member of his extended family and friends, or any of his employees. I was going to medical school at USC and was rotating through the many departments at Los Angeles County Hospital where USC had their clinical activities based.

"One night, about two o'clock in the morning, I received a call from Mr. Hughes, who was very distraught. He told me that earlier in the evening, one of our drivers, while backing out of his driveway, hit his little girl with the car he was using. The driver was a young man by the name of Ben Carlisle, who at the time was driving for the future Mrs. Hughes, Jean Peters.

"Hughes was very upset—he told me in a very tremulous voice about the accident and gave me instructions to call his personal physician, Vern Mason, to say that he wanted the child transferred immediately to the Good Samaritan or another hospital he used. He instructed me to see that she was cared for by the best neurologist, and if need be a neurosurgeon, in Los Angeles. He also specified that all the bills were to come to our office for payment.

"At that particular time, I was on the neurology rotation, so I was able to catch the chief resident in neurology at the hospital. I called the County Hospital and talked to him about this child. She had been taken to the county hospital because it took care of all accidents and injuries and had an excellent trauma staff. I was told by the chief resident that the little girl was doing fine, she was sleeping, and he would not recommend moving her presently, the time being about 3:30 a.m. I discussed this with Dr. Mason, and that is what we agreed upon. The child was transferred to the Good Samaritan Hospital the next morning to be cared for by the leading Los Angeles neurologist and Dr. Mason. She made a total and uneventful recovery, and at no time did Mr. Carlisle ever receive a bill from the doctors or hospitals. Mr. Hughes paid them all.

"Previous to that time, a man identified only to me as being Mr. Hughes' valet (though I doubt Hughes ever actually had a valet) apparently suffered a heart attack and was sent to St. Vincent's Hospital to be cared for by one of the city's leading cardiologists. The valet made an uneventful recovery, and again the bills were sent to Mr. Hughes.

"On another occasion, Chuck Grindstaff, who worked with us in the office, was having a difficult problem controlling his high blood pressure. Chuck had apparently had a case of rheumatic fever as a young child, following a streptococcus infection that damaged his kidneys and left him with hypertension. Sometime in 1952, Mr. Hughes heard about this problem with Chuck and told Bill Gay that Chuck was to be taken off of all activity in the office and sent to see Dr. Vern Mason. Following Dr. Mason's recommendations, Chuck and his wife were sent to Boston to Harvard University to see one of their specialists in hypertension. Mr. Hughes paid for all of Chuck's transportation to and from Boston, his stay in Boston, his continued salary throughout the entire time, and for a nanny to take care of his children while he and his wife were there. Unfortunately, medicine had not advanced far enough at that time to permit us to do what we would do today. There were no specific anti-hypertensive medications, and the first kidney transplant was a thing of the future. Sadly, during the middle of the USC versus UCLA football game, Chuck had a massive stroke at the Los Angeles Coliseum and died.

"While in the Bahamas, one of Hughes' closest aides, Chuck Waldron, had his young daughter vacationing with him while he was on his two-week rotation. Chuck's daughter drowned while visiting. Mr. Hughes took the accident very hard, as if the young girl had been his own daughter.

"Hughes also intervened and paid for the medical care for a young actress, Marla Powers, who was suffering from a rare blood disorder. There were many other similar incidents of which we do not have first-hand knowledge, but of one thing we were always acutely aware, and that was of Mr. Hughes' dedication to the very best in medical care and research for one and all, which after years of planning, by Hughes and Hughes alone, resulted in the formation of his greatest legacy—the Howard Hughes Medical Institute."

Howard Hughes

Flying with Hughes

Hughes moved his location frequently during the 1950s and 60s and so flying with him always a unique experience. Prior to the trip to Canada, Hughes was always the only pilot flying with his select aides who were the only passengers.

As Gordon Bench documents the move from Florida in 1954, Hughes had chartered a Convair 440 from Northeast Airlines. "He hadn't flown this particular plane before, and we were not aware of this until we got to the airport and were boarded. As previously noted, he excused himself and went to a phone booth where, for the next two hours, or possibly more, he talked with the operations manager of Northeast Airlines to be briefed on flying the aircraft. This was his pre-flight check-up. Of course, there was more involved than just his being checked out to fly the plane because Hughes had previously been in discussion with Northeast as a possible feeder airline for TWA. Although we had been from home for several months and were excited to return to California, we were anxious for him to get completely zeroed in on the intricacies of flying this 'new to him' airplane.

"To all of us the waiting seemed much longer than the two hours that it took. As I recall it was about midnight when we finally left the Miami airport, headed out over Cape Canaveral and circled before heading west. As we got close to Baton Rouge, Louisiana, Hughes decided he was too tired to continue. This was probably about 3 or 4 a.m. and all we had to do, as usual, was to arrange for sleeping accommodations for a group of eight to ten people, find a cab to get us to the hotel and, as always, arrange for the plane to be refueled, tied down, and readied for the next leg of our journey.

"Fortunately we had had this experience before so we were able to accomplish these things even in the middle of the night and were looking forward to some much needed sleep in a bed, rather than in an uncomfortable chair seat in a Convair 440.

"We got everyone registered at the hotel and Hughes was secreted in his room for what we hoped would be an uninterrupted eight or ten hours. So with this, we trundled off to bed. We were physically beat and looking forward to at least a few hours of peaceful rest."

Not so for Gordon, who received a call from Hughes just after he had gotten to sleep. "He asked me to get him a couple of things to help him relax so he could get some sleep. Now this was about five a.m. The items he wanted were not what you would consider household items: a bottle of chilled Poland water and some Kadota figs that were one of his favorite nighttime snacks. Incidentally, if you have not heard of Poland water, it was, no doubt, the forerunner to today's Perrier. And doesn't everyone have Kadota figs in their cupboard? We had never been to this hotel and had made no pre-arrival arrangements for the group. But as luck would have it, I was able to get the items to Hughes and he thanked me profusely and went off to bed.

"But I must mention the all too typical cab drive from the airport to the hotel. There were six of us in the cab, including the driver. Hughes was in the middle seat next to the cabbie, and I sat next to him. Hughes was about 6' 3" and had long legs, so his knees were right under his chin. He was obviously uncomfortable as it was, and the driver didn't help the situation since he paid no attention to bumps in the road.

"As each bump caused a painful reaction, Hughes was, at this point, only interested in getting some shuteye. Each time the cab hit a bump, he would look at me and glare but with a little hint of a smile as if to say, 'Gordon, what have you got me into this time?' I just kept looking forward because if I had looked at Hughes for more than a few seconds, I might have burst into laughter.

"After we got to the hotel, all of us did have a laugh about the ride, though there was really nothing humorous about it. The reason this was thought to be humorous to us was that Hughes preferred any driver, even a cab driver, on his staff to avoid the bumps or, if unavoidable, then to slow down and just ease over the bumps to ease the pain.

"I don't recall how long we remained in Baton Rouge, but I know none of us got a whole lot of sleep. Before long we were en route to the airport and the final leg of the trip home."

NASSAU

Gordon Bench recalls: "Hughes had flown to Canada commandeering a TWA Super Constellation and its crew. Upon leaving Canada for Nassau, he had still retained the plane and crew. Soon after arriving in Nassau, the crew returned to resume their normal schedules, leaving the plane with Hughes, who in the ensuing six months of the Nassau stay would periodically fly the plane for recreation.

"Since the plane was chartered from TWA and sitting at the Nassau airport totally unproductive while TWA was actually hurting from a shortage, it was interesting to estimate the cost of this plane at about $16,000 per day for about 180 days, or roughly $2,880,000 in total revenue that one might say should have been in the TWA's treasury. But it must be recognized that Howard Hughes was TWA's treasury since, after all, he owned about 76% of TWA's stock.

"But finally it was time to pack up and return to Los Angeles. Meanwhile, anyone with a sense of humor (which fortunately the staff still had) would discover that the preparations for the trip home had to be hilarious. The crew of the super Connie had long since left, and Hughes was determined to fly alone back to Los Angeles.

"He had the plane fueled. Then he would go out, rev up the engines, and then cut them off. We then knew he had to fuel up again, and that we would be there at least another day. This was frustrating to all because we were also anxious to get home after such a long stay.

"He had us put all of our luggage aboard and then locked up the plane. Well, the humidity in the area was devastating to clothing, and when he finally got us back to LA, we had to get new items of clothing since ours had mildewed so badly they couldn't be worn. Now the hilarious part was Hughes' planning since each of us had to be given an in flight assignment on the airplane, much as if we were a regular crew.

"Roy Crawford, who had flown Piper Cubs, was chosen as copilot because of his flying experience. Quite naturally this was cause for very much concern. We would repeatedly corner him either singly or in groups and have Roy confirm to us he could land that super Connie if Hughes wasn't able to. I'll say this for Roy—he exuded confidence. However, none of us really could quite share Roy's confidence. We only appeared to because we were so anxious to get home we'd believe almost anything.

"My assignment was fireman. Now, I had no experience as a fireman, but I did know which end of the fire extinguisher to point toward a flame, so I was selected as the fireman. Others aboard all had their assignments. As flight time got closer, we all rehearsed our assignments, but the main thrust of effort was to have Roy continue to show his confidence. Actually we tried to visualize Roy behind the controls of this gigantic bird.

"Finally, when Hughes could no longer keep the troops happy, he decided to head home. And that was good news. The next thing we were told was bad news. He told us after we had taken off from Nassau that if the weather was bad in Los Angeles, and we had only reached El Paso, we would have to return to Nassau. The plane was fueled, and Hughes started the engines with each of us in position and fully instructed as to what we would do. Our thoughts tended to wander to the possibility that had there been an emergency, I'm sure there would have been no survivors. But Hughes was one of the greatest pilots, a fact that we knew. Period. We had not gone so far as to say he was an excellent pilot because we had no current frame of reference except for his past unbeatable record. We knew he was currently licensed and that was good enough for all of us.

"The engines were revving up. We looked out at the wings with all that fuel, and they were flapping like a giant bird ready to take off from a standing position. It seemed an eternity before the plane started its taxi approach to the main runway. At last we would be leaving this island paradise. I'm sure each of us entertained the thought that he would taxi just so far and think up an excuse to return and stay in Nassau. And I must admit if we had been in his shoes, it was a tempting place to stay because of its natural beauty and calm.

"Soon we were airborne, and it was a thrill to see Nassau behind us. We flew towards the mainland. With so few of us on the plane, we each had as much space as we needed. As we ascended we looked out and saw what is called the 'tongue of the Atlantic,' which was like looking into a canyon, but with millions of gallons of water. And so blue was the ocean. Our only regret was that we did not have a camera out of the suitcases. Had we done so, we would have taken a picture of Hughes, without his knowledge, as he walked from the cockpit back to where we were. But we didn't have the camera out and we would have been violating one of his most important wishes—he didn't want any pictures taken anytime.

"We winged towards California and eventually got close to El Paso. The weather report in Los Angeles was rain and clouds. We nearly swallowed our hearts. Not back to Nassau! Whatever Hughes' thoughts might have been about going back to Nassau, they were soon dispelled because we left El Paso, and the silver plane glided effortlessly on its way home. We did have to land and refuel in El Paso, which was not without another harrowing experience.

"When we approached, Hughes had detected a dust storm was taking place on the ground. We were all reminded of his past allergies to dust storms that we were quite frequent in Palm Springs. Hughes chose to stay our course as long as possible in hopes of outlasting the storm's duration. After circling for several minutes, he was finally forced to land with just enough fuel to make it off the runway and to refuel. We were soon again airborne and on our way home which was just that—being with our families again after what we now considered to be three long, tedious, uncomfortable months on the island of Nassau.

"Sure enough, it was raining when we reached the Los Angeles area, and we had to take our position in the flight pattern. All of us were so anxious to touch down that we kept giving 'body English' each time we banked for another go-around in the pattern.

"At long last, we heard the welcome news. We were to make our final approach! After three months, Los Angeles was absolutely beautiful, even in a driving rainstorm.

"We landed and taxied to the tie-down area where we were met by members of the Hughes Production transportation crew. All of the passengers de-planed and only Hughes and I were left. He wanted to instruct me as to how to close the airplane door after he got off.

"Well, there we were standing in a driving rain and both of us trying to get the door closed. He said it had to be a certain way, and he was right. Where he was wrong was he was turning the latch the wrong way and the door wouldn't engage. Of course, we finally got the door closed and took off on our merry way home—Hughes to the Beverly Hills Hotel, and the rest of us to our families.

"I arrived home at about 3 a.m. The flight had ended but current duty had not. I hadn't been home very long when the phone rang. I couldn't believe it—it was Mr. Hughes, and his words were to this effect: 'Gordon, I am deeply sorry to awaken you, but you are the only one I can trust right now. Would you please come to the Beverly Hills Hotel and when you get here, let the switchboard operator know and she will call me. I promise I'll call you immediately so we can get on with this project.'

"What could I say? I sincerely felt like asking him to call Johnny Holmes, Roy Crawford, Harris Albright, Billy Gay, or anyone else. But I told him I'd head for the hotel right away. I arrived at the hotel and checked into Bungalow 1 or 4—I don't remember which—and waited for his call. It came rather soon and I was surprised. I knew he had something urgent on his mind. And you won't believe what it was.

"He said that he recalled the argument we had in Nassau, and he was apologizing to me for the way he had treated me. Now, this is something that I will always remember—him asking me to forgive him. Naturally, I apologized and said it was my fault, but he said it was his—and back and forth. Anyway, I thanked him for his apology and assured him that was all in the past.

"Now we got down to the second reason for his asking me to come to the hotel. It was because he had been away from the Beverly Hills Hotel for so long that he wanted me to see that all of the hotel people were fully instructed as to how he wanted things to be as far as he was concerned.

"Sleepy-eyed, I started to the front office. This was about 7 a.m., I think. I met with the switchboard operator on duty, the bell captain and the chef, and the waiters who would be assigned to serve Hughes his food. I finally bedded down knowing I was in for several days of duty at the hotel so I arranged for my wife to bring the four boys to the hotel that night and we would have dinner there. Hughes, in fact, insisted that I do this, and he said to order anything for the family. He was very considerate and I took him at his word. I called Verdon and told her what the plan was, and that was fine with her. We thought the kids would like shrimp cocktails, steak and all, but being kids they all ordered hamburgers. Wouldn't you know it?"

MORE THOUGHTS ON FLYING

From the end of WWI to 1960 pilots were a breed apart. Even today there is a conceit in the minds of people who fly about their own flying expertise. Long time, high hour pilots think they should be able to fly anything they can get into. This conceit can get them, and others, killed.

Howard Hughes was a truly great pilot. And he was probably as conceited about his ability to fly anything, as was anyone; however, he never flew a plane for the first time without knowing intimately the flight characteristics of the plane. Those planes he had helped design he also, in effect, helped engineer the way they would fly. If he was getting into a strange plane, he found out the flight characteristics before he flew it.

Hughes' caution in the care for his executive officers is illustrated in Gordon Bench's Flying with Hughes account. He seldom allowed his top executives to fly on the same plane as himself. After Bill Gay had been in Operations for ten years or so, he seldom flew on a plane that Hughes piloted. Hughes would send Gay on a commercial flight, usually with an aide, who normally was an assigned executive and for whom the Boss was also concerned, such as James Whetton.

The story is told by one of Hughes' engineers who worked with Hughes on the Super Connie, and who also worked on the fabulous Hercules. As the story goes, Hughes, for years, leased a large hangar at the Burbank airport that was the beginning location for Hughes Aircraft. When the work was commenced on the Super Connie, the cement floor was thoroughly cleaned and the part of the working blueprints showing the modifications needed in the wing assembly and engine nacelles were laid out on the floor. Those prints were the actual size of the finished product. The modifications from the Connie to the Super Connie also involved major changes in width and size as well as all critical frames needed to support the weight and increased size of the Super, as well as the structural strengths needed to support the greater horsepower engines.

Hughes would go daily to the hangar and walk over the plans, studying each and every structural detail. When he did this he wore Keds kept in a locker at the hangar. That engineer who was with Hughes from the mid 1930s to the flight of the Hercules, said, "Those were the only times I ever saw the Boss in tennis shoes."

The story went around Operations that the outboard section of the wing couldn't be attached to the center section—the two just didn't fit. The call came from Odekirk, one of the few who could get to Hughes at any time. Hughes listened to Odekirk tell of the problem but didn't even answer him. He put on his hat, his coat, left his bungalow, got in his Chevrolet, and drove to the hangar. He put on the Keds and walked all over the plans as they lay on the floor. He didn't say a word to the engineers standing there observing. He threw up his hands, one of the few signs he ever gave of his being angry or disgusted, walked out to the Chevy, and drove off.

Several days passed with no word. Finally, Hughes got on the phone and told Odekirk, "Your problem is that you have European, English, and American engineers together working on the modifications. Your problem is very simple. Two sections of the wings are in inches and the outboard is metric." He didn't wait for an answer—he just hung up.

When the first Super Connie came off the line, Hughes did some of the test flying. After all, he had designed it, hadn't he?

The story by Gordon Bench of the flight from Miami to L.A. in the Convair 440 was a different matter. Although Hughes had five hundred or more pilot hours in a Convair 220, his personal plane, he had never flown or been briefed on the 440. Bench retells of the great care he exhibited in his approach to piloting. Normally a pre-flight briefing for a pilot who was getting in a strange plane would probably take close to five hours of instructed time and ten or so takeoffs and landings. But one with Hughes' proficiency rating could normally take one-half to three-quarters of an hour.

The Bench recital of Hughes seeking a pre-flight briefing before he would attempt the flight from Miami to L.A. in a plane he had never flown is a lesson in Hughes' attitude toward flying and airplanes. The Convair 440 was a very new version of transport. Hughes had ordered some for TWA. He contracted at Convair the most expert man available in knowledge of that plane. Hughes was going to have several flying for his airline. He had the opportunity and he was going to take advantage of it. He didn't want a pre-flight briefing that would enable him to fly the plane for five hours. He wanted to know the plane. It was not for him to be briefed on just what to look for in a walk-around and familiarizing himself with the cockpit and controls. He wanted more than to be told of take-off weights, take-off speeds, and altitudes. He wanted to know everything about the plane, and he had the man who could tell him. When he finished with the Convair expert he could have written the Form 5 (pilot's handbook) for the 440, a demonstration of his typical thoroughness.

Flying with Hughes would not be complete without disclosing an event that took place in the early 1930s—an eventful disclosure that clearly shows his deep sense of patriotism. It had to do with his hiring flyers for his epic film, *Hell's Angels*. Gordon Bench had many conversations with Hughes about flying experiences—memories that were precious to him.

If Hughes had known in the late 1920s what he later learned in the 1940s, his whole attitude and hiring process for his *Hell's Angels* film would have undergone a drastic change from the earlier hiring policies. The Treaty of Versailles that suspended the armistice agreement of November 1918 strictly restricted Germany's ability to train pilots. It even severely restricted flying of any kind in that country. Before Hitler's arrival on the scene, the military leaders of Germany were devising any or all possible means to keep their WWI pilots flying wherever possible in any part of the world to retain their renowned flying skills and at the same time, discover how the rest of the world was advancing in all fields of aviation. Germany allowed and encouraged hundreds of their WWI pilots with their permission to accept employment in any other nation. As a result, dozens of those pilots found work in many movies that were being produced about the Great War.

In Hollywood, the making of *Dawn Patrol, Hell's Angels,* and *Lilac Time*, among others, utilized the flying skills and knowledge of many of the German Aces. British and French studios were also making movies with the main theme of war in the air. In the early 1930s, these same expert pilots returned to Germany and became a major part of what became the nucleus of the well-trained, formidable, large German Air Force that eventually led Germany into WWII. Had Hughes been able to foresee that part of the future, being the patriot that he was, he never would have hired any Germans.

The Airwest Purchase

By 1968 Hughes realized that with the sell off of TWA, he no longer owned an airline. For many years he had mentally luxuriated in the knowledge that he owned an airline. He had spent endless hours of his time designing aircraft to be used by his airline, classic among them being Constellation, then the Super Connie, and finally the actual operation of these state-of-the-art aircraft. On occasion Hughes interfered with these operations to their detriment and the detriment of the airline by commandeering or scheduling them for his own personal use. He, after all, had designed and overseen the construction of the most beautiful, the fastest, and the longest range of any current propeller or reciprocal engine-powered commercial airline passenger plane then flying. British companies modified the WWII jets to become passenger planes.

At first, Lockheed, and especially Boeing airplanes, were, in Hughes' mind, not needed. This was probably because in the beginning Hughes had no intimate workings with these developers. As Lucky Lindy Lindberg originally told Pan American officials, the Super Connie was not only beautiful but could carry over two hundred passengers across the Atlantic at near 400 miles per hour. Who needed jets? This reluctance amounted to almost outright refusal to allow jets to be purchased by TWA and led to a minority lawsuit against Hughes. This is another story lost in the annals of TWA history. Hughes was undoubtedly first and foremost above all else an airplane addict. With the sale of TWA, Hughes knew he was out of the airline business. But he needed that business for his self-fulfillment, hence, the purchase of Airwest.

After the end of WWII, various groups with the attitude of taking advantage of gullible minds of others with their "ill-gotten war gains" formed in all corners of the United States. Because of their moneymaking schemes and the "to hell with the public" bent the railroads exhibited during the war, and the fact that so many of the veterans who had to ride in fifty-year-old passenger cars, the five day, and sometimes longer, trips across the country, vets had resolved never to ride a train again. The way was now wide open to travel by air. There were thousands of used planes that could be converted to passenger travel available as war surplus from the Federal government. The most plentiful were the DC-3, the Air Force's Curtis Commando, the Lockheed twenty-six passenger airline plane used for big shot transportation, the C-46—a faster, higher flying twin engine—and many other planes that could be converted to civilian use and which could be purchased from the government for much lower prices that airline promoters had ever dreamed.

The immediate major and long distance routes were quickly serviced by the existing airlines; but there were many short and seemingly low paying routes that were not serviced by Delta, Western, and the many other scheduled lines—flights to and from Las Vegas and Reno to name one. Bonanza Airlines, based out of Phoenix, hurriedly began this service with partially worn out DC-3 planes purchased from the Air Force. They were stripped, furnished with passenger seats, oxygen, and intercom. During the war, under very strict security measures, commercial flights had used the Las Vegas Army Air Base, later to become Nellis Field. With the help and urging of local politicians in Las Vegas, and of Senator Pat McCarran from Nevada who was Chairman of the Senate Transportation Committee, a large parcel of Federal land immediately south of the Las Vegas and east of the Los Angeles highways, was set apart and designated as a national airport.

County, State and a very small amount of Federal money went into building and improving one north-south runway sufficient to handle the DC-3 plane and a narrower, shorter east-west runway on the south end of the major runway. A small parking lot, ticket office, and waiting room, completed the development. By now Bonanza Airlines had gained a monopoly on the Las Vegas Air Service. No major airline would consider the use of such primitive facilities.

The major stockholders in Bonanza started a four-year battle to keep the field as it was originally built. Two of the more powerful and large stockholders in Clark Country were Harley Harmon and Hank Greenspun. Greenspun was a power to be dealt with as the Nevada publisher and owner (with the help of Teamster money) of the *Las Vegas Sun*. He was a carpetbagger from New York, now influential in Nevada politics, along with Harley Harmon, and State Senator Baker from Clark Country. These men, believing that as long as the Las Vegas Airfield remained as primitive as it was in 1949, no other airlines, at least a major one, would want to open a route to and from Vegas, especially to include the Reno or Phoenix routes. They really lost out by not knowing that Senator Pat McCarran had just introduced a bill, which passed with a large majority in both houses, to create and fund a Civil Aeronautics Administration. This statute had provisions to set up an office to build, operate, and maintain airports, and a separate agency, the Civil Aeronautics Board, was established that would control the airways and make them safe.

In the administration were several offices, one of which was the Office of Airports. By 1948 Federal funds were available to the States that passed bills and appropriations to contribute to the funds, mostly Federal, to upgrade or build new airports in locations where major airlines would not previously operate because of inadequate landing and passenger facilities.

The Federal government established regions throughout the U.S. and each State was given an airport engineer. The one for Nevada was one named Donaldson. In the 1940s, Nevada had no provision for contributory or matching funds to enable Federal funds to be used. Donaldson approached James Leo Wadsworth, at the time a freshman assemblyman from Lincoln County, Nevada and a WWII Air Force pilot who was still on reserve status. He proposed a bill that would tax all aviation gas sold in Nevada with the resulting revenue to go for adding Federal funds to upgrade various airports in Nevada. Of course the first two airports would be in Las Vegas and Reno. Bonanza Airlines marshaled support to kill the bill, knowing that if those airports were upgraded, major airlines could start service and Bonanza would lose its monopoly on various routes. Harley Harmon, then a member of the State Assembly and a major stockholder in Bonanza, led the fight. He was greatly aided by the State Senators from Clark County and Washoe County; however it was obvious to all the "Cow Counties" that it was a chance to get regular service to their counties, rather than once a week or less to such outposts as Ely, Winnemucca, etc. The bill passed both houses and Governor Pittman signed it almost the day it hit his desk.

As the airports became truly commercial, Bonanza Airlines lost most of its monopolies and became a losing investment. The same was true for two other airlines that depended on having a monopoly—West Coast Airlines out of Seattle and Pacific Airlines out of San Francisco.

In an attempt to salvage something out of what had become a major disaster, the three little air services started to talk about uniting. The President and CEO of Bonanza, Nick Bez of West Coast Airlines, and the legal staff of Pacific Airlines started meetings that ended up in a merger of the three nearly bankrupt airlines. These three airlines tried to band together but the effort was doomed to failure from the outset. First, stockholders were only interested in dollar signs. Nothing seemed to please the rapacious minds of some of the larger stockholders. Many of the holders in the three separate corporations ended up with blocks of stock out of proportion with their actual interest in the individual lines. As will be seen, this division of stock worked greatly in favor of Maheu at a later time.

On paper the merger was finally accomplished, but the employees of the three airlines were never satisfied. The shops and maintenance crews remained separate. The Bonanza Airlines shops in Phoenix and Las Vegas acted independently of the new airline called Airwest. The same was true of the individual offices of Pacific and West Coast. There was some concerted effort to fly the old routes and to develop new ones but they were a colossal failure. Their reservation system was laughable. Passengers' reservations were often misplaced or lost in the system. Entire scheduled flights ended up where there was no business for them. Planes were often pulled out of service because of improper maintenance or service, or mistakes in the planes' logs. Within a year, the airline was being called "Air Worst." If there was any choice, people just wouldn't fly Airwest.

By the fall of 1967 Hughes was a bit despondent as he no longer owned an airline. He had decided not to pursue a target he had envisioned several years before, Northwest Airlines. Meanwhile, the court battle was still going on over TWA. He was fairly certain that he had no chance to recover TWA or to buy one of the other major airlines. But he *had to have an airline.* So by the spring of 1968, he had found his target—Airwest.

Hughes' extensive intelligence in the entire field of avionics had revealed that Airwest was ripe for a takeover or outright purchase. He, of course, decided to purchase. At that time, Hughes made one of his biggest and personally unfortunate mistakes of his business career. He decided that he would use Robert Maheu to purchase

Airwest. He began one of his best-loved ploys. He started trying to outwit, out bargain, and out negotiate the powers that were in Airwest. He wrote memos to Maheu outlining his convoluted thinking of how he was to negotiate and ultimately buy the airline. Hughes had already outlined a plan in the purchase negotiations. He wrote a memo to Maheu that unfortunately came onto the hands of the Justice prosecuting attorneys.

Hughes: "The plan necessitates that the stock edge downward with the continuing bad news; and then we come along with a spectacular offer to pay the stockholders in liquidation at a price still substantially above the market."

As with too many other choice bits of information, Maheu, in his typical pattern, made use of the information Hughes was giving him. One of the very large stockholders in Airwest, Hank Greenspun, who was a close friend of Maheu, and, in many ways, a collaborator, took advantage of knowledge of what Hughes was planning. That stockholder and a few more who became aware of Hughes' plan, sold large blocks of stock. The "Air Worst" reputation, the great loss of revenue, and the appearance on the market of great blocks of stock had the result predicted by Hughes. Airwest had already decided that they would accept $22 per share for the sale.

The real individual power in Airwest was a multimillionaire Yugoslavian by the name of Nick Bez. He was known in financial circles as the Sultan of Salmon. He had a very large fleet of fishing boats and his own facilities to process and can that fleet's catch. It was easy for Maheu to convince Bez to sell. Bez made the offer for the $22 per share, which was relayed to Hughes. This caught Hughes by surprise. Hughes now was in one of his favorite games. Negotiations!

From July 30, 1968 to August 11, 1968, Hughes played the game. Finally he officially announced that he would pay $90 million. The offer was accepted and confirmed by Bez. The airline's President,

G. Robert Henry with Edmund Converse, Vice Chairman David R. Grace of the executive committee, and others objected strenuously, letting it be known to the media that it would be an outright giveaway looking at the airline's potential. At the time there were about 13,000 stockholders and neither Bez nor Grace really had the confidence of the majority of the stockholders.

Between Christmas and New Years of 1968 the stockholders of Airwest voted to sell their shares to Hughes for the $22 per share. But the Airwest Board was not going to give up without a further fight. They began dickering with Northwest Airlines. The disgusted stockholders, seeing their investment decreasing in value almost daily, found an attorney and filed a suit against the board. The stockholders were afraid that the Hughes deal to be announced on New Year's Eve would never be consummated.

Meanwhile, Maheu negotiated with some of the larger stockholders of Airwest and convinced them to load almost 100,000 shares on the stock market. Hank Greenspun, who was one, and perhaps the most influential, of the selling holders, was the one with whom Maheu did most of his dickering. Hank later told U.S. Prosecutors that Hughes had promised to make up any loss those stockholders may incur. Actually that promise, if made at all, was made by Maheu without consulting Hughes. At this turn of events, many other stockholders who had been watching the market, the newspapers, the board, and especially those who had an in with the workings of the powers in Airwest, had unloaded their holdings in the company. By the time the company actually changed hands, there were no longer 13,000 stockholders in the company. The agreed upon price was, nevertheless, paid.

Five years later in an indictment, part of the charges was that instead of the individual stockholders receiving $22 a share, they each received only about $8.75. Had there still been the total number of shares transferred to Hughes that had been outstanding in the spring of 1968, the cash paid would have been less than $22, but the stock received by the purchaser was much less than would have been transferred then.

The control of the airline passed to Hughes in early 1969, but the CAB did not approve the purchase until July 15, 1970. The final Federal approval was not made until July 21, 1970, thus the beginning of Hughes Airwest.

Airwest would have begun its successful reign much sooner had it not been for an overzealous, inexperienced Federal attorney who bragged to the media (mostly Hank Greenspun, owner of the *Las Vegas Sun*) that he was going to be forever known as the attorney who put Howard Hughes in jail.

The Securities and Exchange Commission (SEC) received an indictment from a Federal Grand Jury in Las Vegas on December 27, 1973. The main target was Howard Hughes; Chester Davis and Robert Maheu were named codefendants. This was to be the last major legal battle that Hughes would personally direct and participate in. Davis and Wadsworth fought the indictment after it was handed down. Meanwhile the conduct of the bragging prosecutor throughout the process could only be classified as pathetic. Wadsworth got the charges dismissed twice in Federal District Court. On November 13, 1974, a Federal judge again dismissed Hughes indictment in the Airwest case.

Hughes' Work Ethic

Of the endless articles in magazines and newspapers, and libraries full of books—literally thousands of pages about Hughes' life—a huge percentage is based on gossip and is pure fiction. Only Hughes' vassals actually were aware of his true work ethic and habits because only they worked with him, literally eyeball-to-eyeball and face-to-face for endless hours. It was at these times that he was intensely involved in the hands-on growth of his empire and in determining his ultimate destiny of becoming the first American billionaire.

Again, only his closely trusted vassals were allowed to be in the same space with him when he was working with others, primarily by phone, but occasionally in very private interviews with select people. Ellie Pugmire recorded many of these interviews. Hughes and Hughes alone, at times convenient to him, determined his working hours, day or night, and those of his vassals, namely James Leo Wadsworth, James Whetton, Ellie Pugmire, and Gordon Bench. These individuals worked with him during most of these arduous sessions, and they did so willingly and with a strong sense of loyalty to Hughes and his needs for comfort and well being.

Almost all of these sessions, for the best use of his productive time, occurred at night when the rest of the world was asleep. James Whetton was with Hughes during most of these marathon sessions, one after another, night after night. The schedule never changed—beginning at 3 p.m. and ending between 3 and 4 a.m., six days a week.

On his one day off, Hughes would call Whetton to discuss any unfinished business and to outline his plans for the coming week, usually to alert those he planned to call and to let them know to expect his call. More often than not, these were engineering professionals he was considering hiring for Hughes Aircraft.

Once such related incident happened on a Sunday. Hughes called Whetton at home and asked if he knew anyone at North American Aircraft. Whetton told him that the Director of Personnel of North American was a high school classmate of his. The candidate recommended by the Director was a highly paid engineer at North American. Hughes called later to let Whetton know that he hired the engineer to work with Ramo and Wooldridge at Hughes Aircraft.

When Hughes was involved in the financing and design of his order for thirty-three Boeing 707 jets for TWA, the nightly routine was very much the same. At 4:30 p.m. Eastern time, Whetton would call Ben Sessel's secretary at the Bank of New York to find where Mr. Sessel could be found that night. The reason for the call was that Hughes would be calling him at about 2 a.m. wherever he might be located.

The call routine seldom varied. His first call would be to Paris, France, local time about midnight. During this call he was exploring the possibility of purchasing Caravelle jet engines. His next call would usually be to General Dynamics in San Diego, from whom, on June 7, 1956, he ordered thirty Convair 880s.

One afternoon, Hughes called General Dynamics and made an appointment with them to pick him up at the San Diego airport at 4 p.m. to meet and discuss the purchase contract. Hughes flew himself from Clover Field to San Diego.

Several minutes after his scheduled arrival, a call was received from Convair saying that Hughes had not arrived in San Diego as expected. This was an immediate cause for alarm. Whetton called the U.S. Coast Guard since most of the flight was over open water. Very soon thereafter, Hughes called to report that when he took off, his windshield was dirty. He noticed a thunderstorm over Palm

Springs, so he diverted his flight pattern to fly over Palm Springs to get his windshield washed. This was not an unusual event. The staff had to learn to live with his unpredictability.

As previously noted, the routine for these nightly sessions very seldom changed, except for one thing. Hughes would sip away at his Poland Water but would never take time to eat until sometime during the following day.

There were two things that were consistent about his routine. Hughes always called Mr. Sessel wherever he might be at about 2 a.m. Sessel time; the last call of the night at about 2 a.m. Seattle time was to the chief engineer in charge of the design and production of the 707.

Spread out on his bed was a complete set of the working drawings for the 707. Before Hughes made the call, Whetton would retrieve Hughes' pen from the closet and drop it on his bed because his entire call was devoted to going over, in detail, various parts of the aircraft and penning in changes he wanted made to the plans. These changes mostly involved alteration to everything from the air handling and pressurization, to changes to parts of the electrical systems. It was already well known and accepted that Hughes had developed and designed the pressurization of passenger aircraft.

Most of the rest of the night, Hughes would have Whetton locate some of his close friends with whom he would discuss various projects, some of which he might be personally involved with. Chief among these were Cary Grant, Dick Powell, June Allison, and Kathryn Grayson (code name Mrs. Tourage), who at Christmas time every year would receive one dozen very choice long-stemmed yellow roses. Hughes had a color scheme for each of the important females in his life and most of his staff had to know them.

Ellie Pugmire assisted Hughes every Christmas with these personal projects. She recalls, "Howard Hughes was born on

Christmas Eve, and I felt sort of sorry for him because he had no family or close friends. With all his money, he was still a lonely man. The close friends he had in the past were long gone and now subordinates and an assortment of girls surrounded him, and they all had their own families to spend the holidays with.

"Hughes remembered those working for him, and he was known to have given a new car to one of his executives. When he wanted to give jewelry, he had several pieces brought out for him to choose what he wanted for a particular girl.

"He sent roses to many of the girls, either long-stemmed red or yellow roses, and these were kept on hand by his florist who knew what he wanted. They were absolutely top quality and some of the most beautiful flowers I have ever seen.

"Hughes Productions employees each received a two-week's Christmas bonus every year, or sometimes more, depending on the length of service, but I was more touched when I, too, received a beautiful bouquet of red roses on Christmas morning."

It was not universally known by even his vassals, until the four—Wadsworth, Pugmire, Bench, and Whetton—became involved working one-on-one, how meticulous Hughes was in storing at least rough notes of conversations and contacts he had with outsiders. For example, when Whetton was working the 3 p.m. to 3 a.m. shift, Hughes never left the room, even during his strictly personal calls. In his conversations with Boeing, he penned notes of his discussions on the plans. During his business calls with Sessel, et al, he had Whetton keep rough notes on his end of the conversation.

It was during this period, starting about 1953, that Hughes demonstrated a long-standing fear of germs. When Whetton reported to work at Bungalow 19 or any other designated location, he would arrive with a fresh box of Kleenex tucked under his arm. A sheet of Kleenex shielded everything that he touched from his entry to the bungalow. Before reporting to Hughes, Whetton would head for the bathroom and wash his hands three times with Physicians Formula soap. Hughes' vassals methodically followed this routine. However, it should be noted that the use of Kleenex by those few who had frequent contact while working with Hughes was a routine devised and used by his vassals upon their becoming aware of his fear of germs. It was never suggested or requested by Hughes himself.

Marriage of Inconvenience

James Leo Wadsworth recalls, "I set the receiver back in its cradle and walked out of my glass-enclosed office. A ghost-like shiver touched my arm as I thought about the woman with whom I'd again become involved. Chester Davis, the senior attorney for Hughes' affairs, had just told me I'd be representing Jean Peters in a divorce action—a former Hollywood star, a beautiful woman, and one of the gentlest souls I'd ever met. It had been fifteen years and six months since I last saw Jean. And now she wanted me to represent her in her second divorce. Her marriage to Howard Hughes was over.

"I nodded to the receptionist who was working late, as usual, and to a junior attorney who sat hunched over his desk. My two partners had left for the day, leaving the seventh floor office of the First National Bank building relatively quiet. I walked into the conference room with its large table and eight plush chairs, and bypassed the rows of bookshelves, stopping at the window. It was nearly dusk, another day's work behind me. The Vegas lights were just coming to life as the mellow sunset acted as the backdrop for the ever-flickering famous rainbow of neon.

"In that rare moment of quiet, a lifetime of memories flooded through me as I remembered the first time I met Jean. She was beautiful, of course, like all the Hollywood starlets who were featured on the big screen year after year. But Jean was not the typical Hollywood princess. She'd come from the small town of Canton, Ohio, and remained a reserved and a private woman throughout the years I'd known her. In 1946, Jean had won the Miss Ohio State Pageant while earning her teaching degree at Ohio

State University. The grand prize was a screen test with Twentieth Century Fox in Hollywood. She was able to secure a contract with Fox, and in 1947, her debut film *Captain from Castile* with Tyrone Power, was released. She went on to make nearly twenty films.

"I first met Jean when I set up the dinner at the Tail of the Cock restaurant for her and Howard Hughes. My initial impression was of a refined and quiet woman, not at all what I expected of a well-known film star. When she and Hughes became serious, he asked her go through the Operations Center for whatever she needed to have done, such as filling prescriptions for her asthma medicine, etc. But after I met her, he told her to call me personally instead of Operations. Jean and I became fairly good friends through all of our interaction and her reliance on me. She was a true gentlewoman.

"In the whirlwind of Hollywood life, Hughes had dated many stars and stars-to-be, becoming the frequent fodder of the media. In fact, Hughes sent his former lady friends bouquets of flowers on special occasions over the years, usually on Christmas morning— perhaps as his own quiet way of celebrating his date of birth, December 24, 1905. The women were not necessarily those he'd dated, but women with whom he had lifelong friendships. He had a different flower for each. I remember him asking me to deliver yellow roses to Kathryn Grayson when she opened at the Sahara in Las Vegas in 1956. When Kathryn saw me standing a bit awkwardly backstage, holding an armful of yellow roses, she knew immediately who had sent them. She pulled me out on stage and announced to the audience, 'This young man has just delivered roses to me from Howard Hughes.'

"I entered the world of Howard Hughes in 1947. When I moved to his Hollywood office in 1955, I heard the stories about him and Jean Peters and what happened when he screened the 1954 film, *Three Coins in the Fountain*. Out of the three women who starred in the film, Jean Peters was particularly showcased. Hughes became fascinated with her and from that moment, he was determined to meet her. He'd seen Peters in other films with Spencer Tracy, such as the 1954 *Broken Lance*. Hughes analyzed everything Tracy and Katharine Hepburn acted in, since she was a close friend and former girlfriend. But *Three Coins in the Fountain* caught Hughes' attention like no other. At the time, Jean was newly married to Stuart W. Cramer III, who was brother to the powerful Hollywood filmmaker, Stanley Cramer.

"As in most of his serious affairs, Hughes started showing up at various locations wherever Jean happened to be. Though he made these sensational appearances, often flying his own small plane, he was an intensely private man in his affectionate overtures. In fact, neither I, nor any of Hughes' closest aides, heard him use endearments in public. The most honeyed term I ever heard him use was 'my dear.' Of course, in the private letters between Jean and Hughes, it was a different story."

Letter from Hughes to Jean Peters:

> *Dearest Love,*
>
> *I have some really important news for you, which will wash aside all the items such as Reeve Field like so many grains of sand. I love you. The Dr. is coming. I will soon signal you as soon as I recover a little. I love you again.*
>
> *—Howard*

Not only was Hughes persuasive in his business endeavors, but his charm continued in his relationships with women. When he set his mind to something, the outcome showed up in the media and eventually the history books. Yet the relationship between Hughes and Peters was different from his other romantic escapades. Heralded as the "only woman he ever loved and probably the only woman who ever loved him," a poignant love story unfolded. The terms of endearment in this series of letters between Hughes and Peters speak for themselves.

> *My Dearest Adorable Love,*
>
> *I am sorry and embarrassed to ask a 24 hr. delay on the saw. The kind I have chosen must come from the land of the Golden Gate. However, our other project—the Platinum Circle—is moving right on schedule.*
>
> *I love you so much. Please give me your ETR (retire) and I will message you as soon as the Dr. leaves. And I still love you some more.*
>
> *—Howard*

From Jean to Hughes:

> *Dear Heart—*
>
> *It's just as well my saw didn't get here today as I am still making room for it. And when it comes, I want to be all set up.*
>
> *But, I'm so happy just to know you're going to get me one!*
>
> *I hope to be in bed trying to sleep by 12:30—so anytime before then will be fine.*
>
> *I love you—*
>
> *—EJ [Elizabeth Jean]*

Wadsworth continues, "Hughes talked Jean into filing for a preliminary divorce from Cramer. He then invited Cramer on a golf outing that gave Jean the opportunity to appear at court and file without his knowledge. Her marriage to Cramer lasted just over a year—from May 29, 1954 to the fall of 1955.

"Once Jean filed for divorce from Cramer, Hughes moved her into an apartment in Westwood to wait out the six-month separation period during which he provided security and maid service. In addition, I was moved into a plush apartment near Jean's so that I would be constantly available to her. She called me for all of her needs. She began to rely on my help more and more, and our relationship became that of a good friendship. I was asked to carry the divorce papers from Jean's attorney to Hughes, then to Jean again, and finally back to the attorney. Hughes spent hours poring over those divorce papers and making corrections."

On January 12, 1957, Jean and Howard flew on a private jet to Tonopah, Nevada, where they were married at the L & L Motel. In the constant quest for privacy, Howard and Jean registered for their marriage license under fictitious names—Howard as G.A. Johnson of Las Vegas, and Jean as Marian Evans of Los Angeles. Very little time was spent there, and two hours later they were on their way back to Los Angeles.

True to Hughes' secretive nature, even some of his closest staff members whom he saw on a regular basis didn't know of the marriage.

Ellie Pugmire, secretary to Hughes, said of the marriage, "Word leaked out in the newspapers in March 1957, that Hughes had married Jean Peters. None of us at the office believed this." Ellie suspected that Operations Chief of Staff, Bill Gay, knew but it wasn't until Ellie saw a check come into the office signed by Jean Peters Hughes that she was convinced they were legally married.

During the years of marriage, Jean never gave up her apartment in Westwood, and Hughes never gave up Bungalow 19 at the Beverly Hills Hotel. Yet evidences of Jean Peters creating a home out of the mansion in Bel Air came into the office in the form of receipts and instructions. Operations staff member, James Whetton, was in charge of inspecting the new home at the Bel Air Country Club and doing the entire inventory.

Ellie also remembered that in the new home in Bel Air, Hughes had two refrigerators installed—one for his wife and one for himself, which no one was permitted to use.

Wadsworth mentions, "Jean retired from acting while married to Hughes, although she never really became 'Hollywood-ized.' She also had severe allergies all of her adult life, including asthma, making film shooting difficult. Marrying Hughes gave her the financial support to not have to put her through any more misery. In fact, in the middle of the night on one occasion, I received a call from Jean's live-in companion that Jean was having one of her serious attacks and was out of her asthma medicine. I called for the driver, Johnny Holmes, and our Chief of Security, who met me at the pharmacy and bypassed the locks. I had been there often enough to know where the asthma medication was located, so I just went behind the counter and filled it.

"I left the prescription on the counter and took the medication. The pharmacist had no trouble deciphering who'd broken into his shop. He was not happy when I arrived during business hours that morning to explain. Fortunately he never called the police or pressed charges. (He stated to me, 'I knew it was one of you sons-of-bitches, so I haven't called the cops!') It was a fine job for a lawyer—covert in all aspects.

"Occasionally Hughes would have a very personal project that required the utmost secrecy. These rare requests were handled by one of only three staff members: James Whetton, Gordon Bench, or me. Late one evening, Hughes called Gordon Bench at home. Gordon was instructed to buy a new fur coat for Jean from an exclusive furrier in Beverly Hills, and that the Hughes name shouldn't be mentioned. Gordon turned to Al Tietelbaum, who was considered one of the most recognized experts in fur. Gordon considered himself a neophyte so he relied on Mr. Tietelbaum's expert advice and, between the two, they selected an exquisite mink coat for $10,000—a fortune at the time.

"Following normal procedure, the bill was delivered to Gordon's home in order to keep it a surprise. Gordon's wife was quite shocked when she opened the statement and saw not only the price of the coat, but that the owner of the coat was Gordon Bench. He explained the situation, but when the second statement arrived with the bill unpaid, she still remained nervous. When the bill was eventually paid, both Gordon and his wife were able to relax."

Jean went to dinner often with Hughes, frequently at the Tail of the Cock. Other haunts included Perino's and Madam Wu's. James Whetton recalled that they screened movies at the Sam Goldwyn Studio. The menu was the same every night, and Whetton's job was to bring in the food. At a nearby shop, he ordered the same thing Hughes' always requested—grilled ham and cheese sandwiches and a quart of milk. Whetton had the job of making sure the cook washed his hands with soap prior to preparation.

Hughes took his wife with him on many of his trips in his private plane to Miami, Palm Springs, etc. He was usually able to escape the gossip columns on such adventures, but he was no longer making gambling trips to Vegas or Reno due to the crash of '46.

As Hughes moved about the country, Jean followed. But by 1966, Hughes' health was deteriorating rapidly, and he moved to Boston on July 17, 1966 to the Ritz Carlton. He didn't make arrangements for Jean to live there with him, and she was furious. She went to Boston and threatened divorce, but Hughes refused to see her. He had his Chief of Staff, Bill Gay, try to work out a reconciliation. Of course this didn't soothe Jean one bit, and Hughes blamed Gay for the failure. This became a turning point in the relationship between Gay and Hughes for the worse, and Robert Maheu began his short-term rise as a right-hand man.

After the Boston fiasco, Jean was cut off from Hughes in all communication. She was ordered to go through Gay to relay any messages. Hughes traveled by train to Vegas a few months later at the end of November 1966. Again, Jean arrived in Vegas, ready to confront her husband, but Hughes refused to see her. He had sequestered himself on the ninth floor of the Desert Inn where his isolation had begun in full force. In order to travel from Boston to Vegas without publicity, Hughes elected to travel by a private rail car hooked to a regularly scheduled Union Pacific passenger train.

While parked in the Ogden, Utah rail yard, the aides traveling with Hughes contacted the local Union officials in an effort to have the train stop briefly on the outskirts of Vegas, long enough to allow Hughes to exit from his private car. He wanted to avoid exposure to the crowds at the Las Vegas terminal. The aides were quickly informed that the only stop the train was allowed to make was at the regular Las Vegas terminal.

Faced with this dilemma, Lavar Myler contacted James Whetton for assistance in solving the problem. Whetton immediately called the local general manager for Union Pacific. The manager, with the usual great care in observing all of the safeguards for security, accommodated Whetton's request to have a single locomotive haul the private car to a junction about twenty miles north of Vegas. The only catch was that it would cost $25,000 to deposit Hughes at the junction where the interstate crossed over a spur track, allowing easy access for Hughes to transfer to a waiting ambulance.

Whetton recalls, "We hired a Hughes look-alike to enter the front entrance of the Desert Inn dressed in a sports jacket, an open-collar white shirt, and the typical Hughes fedora hat while Hughes was carried up nine flights of stairs in the enclosed fire escape. Then he and his aides took over the top two floors of the building. The elevator doors were also locked to these floors, and a twenty-four-hour security guard was stationed to prevent any unauthorized access to the ninth floor. Anyone who visited had to be logged in and out by the security guard."

Unfortunately for Jean, when she arrived in Las Vegas, she was still shut out from meeting with her own husband. Hughes sent Chester Davis to find out what her demands were, but it was fruitless for her to speak through a mediator. She had been turned away again.

The ensuing years weren't any easier for Jean than they were for Hughes. And on January 15, 1970, Jean officially announced she would divorce Hughes. Still, matters dragged on, and by 1971 Jean had reached her zenith of patience. She insisted on the divorce, wanting the fastest way out possible. Now it was Davis' job to tell Hughes that Jean was going to get a divorce whether he liked it or not. In April 1971 he finally consented—for her sake.

Wadsworth: "When Jean found out that Hughes would not fight the divorce, she decided to file in Nevada since she knew how much longer a divorce took in California. Several of her friends had divorced in Nevada because there was no six-month wait or two court appearances. In no uncertain terms, Jean informed Davis that she was ready to proceed with the Nevada divorce. I advised Davis on how the divorce proceedings would work in the State of Nevada. Jean would need a Nevada attorney, and she would need to establish residency in the state for six weeks before filing a divorce action. Jean would also need to produce a witness who could go to court and testify that the she had been living in the state at a particular address during this time. The witness also had to testify that he or she had seen the Jean in the state every day for the required number of days."

When Davis told Jean that she needed a Nevada attorney, he gave her some names to choose from. Jean discovered that Davis had a new law office formed using James Leo Wadsworth as the founding partner. Immediately she decided she wanted him to be her attorney. Davis warned her that Wadsworth already represented Hughes in several lawsuits so it might not be possible. But Jean persisted, becoming adamant that she wanted Wadsworth to represent her.

Wadsworth: "How could I turn her down? She needed my help.
"And now the call had come. I turned from the darkened

window, the skylight now glittering with neon lights. I knew the weeks ahead would be a whirlwind, but I was prepared to help the woman who'd always treated me with a kind word and respect.

"First things first. Over the next week, I put together a waiver regarding the conflict of interest for Hughes to sign—which allowed me to represent his wife. I also had Jean sign a waiver since I currently represented her husband in those other projects. Chester Davis, although from California, could represent Hughes' side since the defendant's attorney had been picked by the plaintiff's attorney (me). I put the other lawsuits I was working on that involved Hughes, the Hughes Tool Company, and various licensing problems, on hold. The divorce became priority during next few weeks, and my already seventy-hour work week intensified.

"Six weeks later, I filed the divorce action on Jean's behalf, and then Hughes entered his pleadings through Davis. The divorce was underway. During the time required between filing for divorce and the final settlement, I drove from Vegas to Jean's rented bungalow on the east coast of Lake Tahoe.

"Jean had moved into the bungalow the early part of May 1971, living there for about sixty days, although the lease was good for one year. She had spent time around Lake Tahoe previously and enjoyed the area. She'd even specifically chosen the neighborhood where she'd live temporarily—in a small development about halfway between Zephyr Cove and the North Shore Casino. Rand Clark, one of Bill Gay's Mormon aides, found a real estate agent who was acquainted with Jean from previous visits. This real estate agent had also served as a resident witness for divorcees on several occasions—which was exactly what we needed.

"Right away, things became hectic. Davis started working on the separation/divorce settlement agreement with Hughes, and I prepared to brief Jean on divorce procedures in Nevada. Davis decided he'd fly in to meet me, and we'd drive together to visit Jean.

He'd seen every part of Nevada by air, but wanted to travel by car.

"So we set out on the 475-mile journey together. I sensed that Davis enjoyed getting away from the office for a few days and being able to talk to someone who knew all of the issues with Hughes. Once we hit Mercury, the headquarters of the nuclear test site, the road was open with no speed restrictions. We stopped in Beatty for a "cup," then again we stopped in Goldfield where I showed Davis the courthouse where I had an office as district attorney about ten years before. Davis was fascinated by the names on the court register that listed the attorneys who had appeared in the court—including Pitman, McNamee and Foley. Davis also wanted to meet all of the officers, and it was difficult to drag him away.

"Twenty-six miles later we arrived in Tonopah, where we slowed to get a glimpse of the L & L Motel where Hughes and Jean were married. When we passed through Hawthorne, I told Davis it would be the ideal place to get the divorce if we could get the judge's consent. Then we stopped for another "cup" at the El Capitan Casino. This location would later become an integral part of the "Mormon Will" debacle when Melvin Dumar cashed a forged payroll check. After all the side stops and satisfying Davis and his inquisitive and people-oriented personality, we drove straight through to Tahoe.

"When we finally arrived, Jean was friendly and greeted me warmly. She was still a lady in every way. She said she was very pleased that her Nevada attorney would be one that both parties could trust implicitly. Otherwise, the divorce could become a publicity nightmare.

"Spending the time in counsel with Jean, I marveled at how calm she appeared about the divorce, almost matter-of-fact. In that first meeting, we spent two-and-a-half hours in discussion. The friendship between Jean and Howard was still vibrant and amicable, but the fourteen-year marriage was no longer functioning. For the past five years, Hughes had increasingly divorced himself from the public and others, surrounding himself only with his very selective staff made up of Mormons. I don't know the last time Jean saw her husband, but I'm certain she never saw him after he left for Boston on July 17, 1966.

"At the bungalow, I interviewed her on two separate occasions and worked out the settlement between both parties—which remained sealed in a Nevada court. The information found in other books and articles about the settlement of a $70,000 yearly annuity that was adjusted for inflation was only a portion of what was agreed upon. My own personal records were eventually stolen during later lawsuits.

"Jean had lived with Hughes as husband and wife for only about a year (December 1960 to November 1961) out of their fourteen-year marriage. The decision to divorce on Jean's behalf was perhaps a necessity and definitely for her well-being. The intractable chronic pain from Hughes' plane crash in 1946 that should have killed him, had finally forced him into a solitary life. The long-term effects of using painkillers such as codeine eventually took their toll. It was easy to assume that he was embarrassed for his wife to see him in such pain and dependency.

"What began as an infatuation between a beautiful movie star and a successful, charismatic businessman, ended with sorrow for both. Jean did not realize how seriously ill the 1946 crash left Hughes. He was able to cover up his pain for many years and, at the time, even his physicians didn't have all the answers.

"After leaving Jean's home, we visited with the real estate agent who happened to be in town that day. When I asked her if she could be a resident witness for Jean, she laughed and said, 'Young man, I probably know as much about resident witnesses as you do. Don't you realize that this is always part of the deal when renting to Hollywood stars?'

"Davis said he'd had enough of seeing Nevada from the ground and I dropped him off at the Harold's Club in Reno. We had supper, and the next morning he flew back to California. On Davis' return trips, we flew to Reno, then picked up a car and drove to Tahoe.

"Because of Hughes' insistence on strict privacy, I arranged for the divorce hearing to take place in Hawthorne, Nevada, before the Fifth District Court, Judge Peter Breen, who was a personal friend of mine. I had spent four-and-a-half years as District Attorney for Esmeralda County, Nevada, which was part of the Fifth Judicial District of the State of Nevada. The other counties in the district included Nye County and Mineral County.

"I arrived at Judge Breen's offices in Tonopah, where he lived and worked. He was someone I trusted and believed could help me maintain the privacy we required. After hearing my long story and explanations about the divorce, Breen suggested the city of Hawthorne in Mineral County. Nye County was too newsworthy since that's where Jean and Hughes had married, and I was too well known in Esmeralda County. Judge Breen also agreed to accept the conflict of interest waivers signed by both parties. On my motion, he consented to allow Chester Davis to represent Hughes in the divorce, even though he was a registered attorney in California and New York.

"On the day of the divorce, June 18, 1971, Davis and I drove to Hawthorne, filed the pleadings, and had the court clerk take them to Judge Breen. The real estate agent who had now become Jean's friend had driven Jean there. The agent was also a Notary Public, and Jean signed all of the papers on the spot. We then went immediately into court for the hearing.

"The actual hearing took no more than five minutes on that hot summer day—the day I had purposely scheduled in order to appear before Judge Breen. I had extensively briefed Jean and taken her through the questions, answers, and court rigmarole. The entire proceedings were sealed by court order so that not even the clerk could get in touch with anyone until we were ready to get the word out. From start to finish, we were out of there in twenty minutes. This left no time or chance that any word could get out before Jean returned to California. We accomplished what we set out to do, and there was no media surrounding the divorce. That's how Hughes wanted it. We needed secrecy and could not risk involving court officials who would talk about the matter or go running to the press.

"The divorce was not ugly, as some might assume. Jean was clearly unhappy, but so would anyone be in her situation. Hughes wasn't able to meet the demands of a healthy marriage, and he regretted the hurt Jean experienced. In fact, he paid all of the expenses of her next marriage to Stanley Hough and sent them on their honeymoon in a private jet.

"It was no surprise to me because that's the Howard Hughes I remember—loyal and generous to the end."

"Only the young have the right

to betray their innocence."

Unknown

Betrayal

Being a man who exhibited loyalty, Hughes, in turn, expected it from his vassals. As ruthless as he may have appeared on occasion, he always believed that being loyal was an honorable attribute. It served him well throughout his life, and he trusted others to practice this behavior; however he experienced disappointment in some who proved to be absent of loyalty.

Howard Hughes had a form of gold fever, different from what the forty-niners had, or the Yukon, or even the 20,000 that rushed to Goldfield, Nevada in the early 1900s. Mr. Hughes had carefully watched the precious metal and chemical markets for years. Although it appeared to many of the various staffers that it was one more enterprise that he would get into "sometime," he was very familiar with underdeveloped and potentially valuable sources of precious metals.

The underdeveloped potential of Nevada appealed to Hughes. This was especially so when various Hollywood personalities such as Bing Crosby and Rex Bell purchased and began developing ranches in the state. Benny Binion's purchase of the Apache Hotel and Casino to develop the Horseshoe added to that interest.

Binion had been a Texas acquaintance of the Hughes family for many years. Hughes had purchased 1,800 acres of BLM forestland in northern Nevada—the more beautiful wilderness near the Idaho border—in the Jarbidge area. This was one of the results of his developing interest in Nevada. The acquisition took place some years before his residency at the Desert Inn Hotel in Las Vegas. He knew of the various fortunes that were made, even in the Depression, from reopening worked out mines and the milling of dumps from gold mines, such as Delemar.

Hughes believed you could grow grass in sand, but he did not want to mine the ground or to see it in a pan. He wanted to make money from the mistakes of others.

One of Hughes' most startling and, many times secret abilities was to see that he could make money where others had no inspiration or had given up. His insatiable self-doctrine enabled him to understand the difference between the masses and the remnant. The masses, he believed, were many times weak-minded and weak-willed, and with their frequent overt arrogance, they missed the obvious. The abandoned gold claims in the state of Nevada became a worthy object of interest. Hughes knew that he could produce gold where others had failed, and gold is gold, which equals money.

Early in Robert Maheu's career in Nevada, Howard Hughes instructed him to evaluate and purchase non-working gold prospects in the state. Maheu had absolutely no knowledge of mines and mining, so he put John Meier in charge of finding and buying mining claims in Nevada. Meier immediately formed business associations with various questionable persons. Through these associations came a $17,000,000 fraud scheme over the purchase of mining claims.

John Meier came into the Hughes organization, at first, by being hired as a computer clerk by Nadine Henley and Bill Gay in Hughes Dynamics. On the voluntary folding of that office, Meier appeared in Las Vegas and sold himself to Maheu as a close friend of Nadine Henley's and as an "insider" to the Hughes organizations. He touted his bogus accomplishments to the Junior Chamber of Commerce in Las Vegas as a PhD in atomic energy, and as a long-time expert in mining and former high-placed Hughes associate.

Meier was a super salesman and Maheu jumped at the chance

to get such a person into his organization. Meier was made vice president of Robert A. Maheu and Associates. He was put in charge of the mining purchases and fighting atomic testing. Meier never worked for Hughes or the Hughes Tool Company, and was never paid a salary by HTCO. Robert Maheu paid him. This was brought out in the mining lawsuit in Salt Lake City, Utah, and was the testimony of both Maheu and John Meier. Unfortunately, HTCO did pay expenses for him and furnished the funds for the mining claim purchases. He started out in a relatively small way—dealing with only proven production small mining claims.

John Meier did have an entry into the Atomic Energy Commission. The then chairman of that commission had a "screen struck" daughter who spent most of her time in Hollywood. Meier was able to strike up a very close, intimate relationship with her.

Meier's salaciousness toward deceit was evident in his associations. When doing research into potential mining claim purchases, he ran across some claims owned by Tony Hatsis. Meier checked Hatsis out very carefully, and what he found delighted him.

The Hatsis brothers, Tony and Duke, had the Utah liquor franchise for Schenley. This arrangement actually was licensed between the brothers and Schenley; it existed primarily to sell liquor to the Utah State Liquor Office. As has been documented, Las Vegas was seeded with mob activity in those days. The tentacles of mob activity reached far and wide. Many institutions, large or small, were pierced with underground embellishments, this being the case with the Schenley liquor; Schenley liquor was owned by the mafia. Tony Hatsis was one of the chief participants in the mining fraud and was rather notorious; his brother, Duke, was low key. They also owned a "members only" key club in a cellar at Main Street and 500 South in Salt Lake City. The "members only" club was really run on the up-and-up in order to keep its license.

Wadsworth, together with other fly boys of the USAF and Navy Reserve, had memberships from the fall of 1945 to 1983. Good food and any kind of drink listed in the bartender's guide were readily available. Wadsworth became a "friend" of Duke and a fairly close acquaintance of Tony.

Meier really had a nose for the type of person Tony Hatsis was; with Hatsis owning mining claims in Nevada, he took immediate advantage of this and Tony's reputation. Tony became one of Meier's favored "straw men" in the mining frauds. This relationship between Meier and Hatsis lay on equally dirty ground; Hatsis recognized in Meier a person he, Hatsis, could use.

It was not definitely established where the first meeting between these two lapwings took place. Intelligence from the Hughes investigators and testimony from two different trials and, interestingly enough, even interviews with Hatsis himself, left the first meeting place and negotiations between them contradictory. However, the very serious, nefarious negotiations took place in Las Vegas.

Hatsis quickly became the supplier of several claims to be sold to Hughes at inflated prices. Hatsis was later sued, and in the suit he accepted a judgment. As one would imagine, characters like Hatsis and the likes were frequent and welcome visitors to Las Vegas. People of this disposition were the seedlings of Las Vegas.

Besides Tony and Duke Hatsis, John Meier contacted a mobster through the Yellow Cab Company. The first "double escrow" fraud purchase of mining claims was with this man.

This was the first of many revelations concerning the fraudulent mining schemes of the unbroken descent toward the Hughes Tool Company. The principals in the following narrative were James Leo Wadsworth, Chester Davis and Bill Gay, each possessing an initial force, all being maneuvered following individual rules of movement.

John Meier and Robert Maheu were about to hear "checkmate." Sometimes in life the bread crumb trail is obvious enough that when you trip and fall, you land smack dab on top of a crumb with a big red arrow on which says, "This way." This was one of those times.

The exposure of mining fraud was revealed to Hughes Tool Company and Bill Gay in a series of events. After Howard Hughes arrived in Las Vegas he found he needed a person to run errands and do what he wanted to do in Vegas. Maheu was right there. He had traveled on the same train as Hughes from Boston to Vegas, but was nothing more than a security person. He had been stationed one hundred yards to the rear of the train when Hughes was being boarded. This was one of the only two times that Maheu ever saw Hughes in person. This was admitted into evidence in Nevada Court.

Hughes wrote a memo on a legal scratch pad giving Maheu various chores to accomplish, one of which was to purchase non-working gold prospects in Nevada.

James Leo Wadsworth had been a District Attorney for Esmeralda County, Nevada, where the county seat is held in Goldfield, Nevada. The sheriff of a long tenure in the county, who was then in his eighties, and Wadsworth became close and trusted friends. The sheriff's son-in-law, Don Brown, had, among other duties, the position of principal escrow officer for the Bank of Nevada. Wadsworth and Don Brown were first-name acquaintances.

The month of August in Las Vegas is a miserable one, and with temperatures hovering at 113 degrees, the continuity of dry heat in Nevada gets an insurgence of moisture along with the heat, so desert folk feel as if they have been toppled into hell. People who have been residents of Las Vegas for a while consider a shower too much moisture. One can hardly stand the twelve percent humidity when it's normally two percent.

On one late, hot August day in 1970, Wadsworth and Don Brown met on 2nd street in Las Vegas. Don had just left the bank and was headed to the Fremont street casinos to eat. Wadsworth had just finished lunch and was headed to the courthouse. The two greeted each other, asked about each other's families, and went on their way. After five paces, Don said, "Leo," and Wadsworth turned around. As they faced each other again, Wadsworth noticed a troubled look on the officer's face.

Brown said, "Leo, I know you worked in California for Howard Hughes, and I know you still do a few little jobs for him and his office. " (All of the work that Hughes had Wadsworth do came directly from Hughes.) "I want you to know that what I am about to tell you violates banking ethics, but I cannot, in good conscience, not do so.

"Today I settled an escrow for a mining transaction where Howard Hughes purchased some gold claims in Mineral County, Nevada. In the same escrow, Donaldson paid $65,000 to the patented owner and then they were sold to Hughes Tool Company for $225,000." (Bread crumbs.)

The officer then abruptly turned and left. Wadsworth, being of sound honesty and extreme loyalty, did not hesitate in his following actions. Even though Bill Gay and Wadsworth had only desultory communications over four years, Wadsworth went back to his office and called Gay. (This relationship stemmed from the fact that Bill Gay never forgave Wadsworth for resigning from Hughes Operations.)

Gay was surprised that Wadsworth would call him, alluding to the four-year strain; however, Wadsworth was still on the sacred list of those to be put right through. He recounted his conversation with Don.

Bill Gay: "Leo, are you sure?"

Wadsworth: "I'm telling you the way it was told to me."

Bill then demanded the name of the informant and Wadsworth, of course, wouldn't tell him. Bill then ordered Wadsworth to make sure of what he had reported.

A few days later, Wadsworth was called to participate in a conference call with Chester Davis and Bill Gay. Wadsworth had not personally spoken with Davis before, but he knew who he was, and of his entitlement. Davis conducted a lengthy and sometimes harsh interrogation of Wadsworth and was disinclined to take Wadsworth's word at face value. He found Wadsworth's information hard to believe. Chester Davis puckered up as if he had a mouth full of lemons, but adopted a more cooperative attitude and agreed to listen. He realized that he was handed a springboard for what was about to come. It was later revealed that the Hughes powers were eager to come up with something concrete against Maheu.

Bill Gay finally broke in and told Davis he had known Wadsworth for thirty years and if he said it was so, then it was. Gay then took over and asked Wadsworth to more fully examine and investigate the findings of the double escrow. Gay said he had checked with the HTCO, and the date and amount had checked out. He also obtained the name of the claims and the date with the county location. Davis then ordered further investigation and a full report.

After the Davis and Gay phone call, Wadsworth, still feeling that he was working for Hughes, went back to Panaca, Nevada, where he lived and held the office of District Attorney for Lincoln County. He spent a day in his office, and then with his wife, Kathleen, drove to Hawthorne and checked into the recorder's records of Mineral County. They spent the night in Hawthorne and on the way home checked with the BLM District office in Tonopah, Nevada. What they found confirmed what was recorded in Mineral County.

The deeds were, of course, recorded in Mineral County and with the Bureau of Mines in Reno, Nevada. To Wadsworth's surprise, the original owner was a woman, maiden name, Gentry, who was raised in Caliente, Nevada, which happened to be in Lincoln County where Wadsworth was sitting District Attorney. Her family and the Wadsworth family were generational friends. She was also an aunt of George Franklin, then District Attorney of Clark County, a former partner of Wadsworth and a "how are you" acquaintance of Hughes. On being asked to help, George ascertained from his aunt that she was paid for the claims and that her deed was to Meier's man.

In giving the facts to Davis, Wadsworth sent copies of the two deeds to the Davis and Company office in New York City. Davis, mostly with some help from Gay, spent hours on the phone and in a personal visit with the Hughes Tool Company people in Houston, Texas. There were also included in the findings some preliminary indications of other double-buyer mining deals to the amount of $20,000,000. Toward the end of September 1970, Davis asked Wadsworth to prepare the power of attorney sufficient in Nevada, giving full power to Nadine Henley, Bill Gay, and Chester Davis to discharge Maheu, void the contract between Hughes Tool Company and R.A. Maheu and Associates, and remove Maheu et al from all the Las Vegas offices.

Lavar Myler and Howard Eckersley started going to Hughes with tales of what was going on in Nevada, mainly Las Vegas, such as Maheu holding himself out as the alter ego of Howard Hughes, the money taken from the Silver Slipper cage by Maheu's orders, and the articles appearing that worthless mining claims were being purchased in the Hughes Tool Company name.

With Hughes' cellular belief of loyalty, this information was an assault. These two were burdened with revealing this information to Hughes and did so numerous times. Hughes said, "Maheu knows what he is doing. The cash is being used for political donations. I have always wanted direct lines into government. Look at the hotels he has bought for us. Maheu wouldn't steal from me." The problems were broached as often as Hughes would listen, but Hughes' belief in the feudalistic loyalty of those he trusted overcame anything that was pointed out to him. Maheu believed the background that Meier painted for himself; since he truly believed it, he had no trouble making Hughes accept it.

They tried time and again for six weeks to discuss this matter with Hughes, but he would say, "I don't want to talk of this now." They kept putting papers and memos from Chester Davis where he would see them but they doubted that he ever read any of them. An urgent call came in from the secretary of Hughes Tool Company, and of course, Hughes took it.

1970 was an off presidential election year, but the governor's office in Nevada was up, as well as all the county and legislative offices. Maheu had taken $50,000 out of the Silver Slipper cage for "the governor's race." There was also several thousand taken for other races. The Houston office received direct audits from the Silver Slipper. This call finally got Hughes' attention and he demanded some of the other material that had been gathered on Maheu.

Hughes asked about who had furnished the material on the mining claims. He was told it was Wadsworth. He asked, "Is Leo still working for us?"

Lavar said, "As far as I know, Leo was not on the Romaine Street payroll but it was common talk on the street that Leo still did various jobs directly for you."

Hughes then said, "It has been over five years since I asked him to check on some real estate titles, but I had been told he was still on the table of organization at Romaine Street." He then added, "If Leo did the checking on the mining claims, it will be correct." He then signed the power of attorney.

Chester Davis and Bill Gay lost no time in exercising the power of attorney. They, principally Chester, contacted an international and investigative and security corporation that had been organized by Robert Peloquin and Tom McNeal. The people of International Security moved into Las Vegas and forcibly took over all of Hughes' and Hughes Tool Company possessions and interests.

Checkmate!

> *"Defeated warriors go to war first*
> *and then seek to win."*
> *Unknown*

Howard Hughes

Betrayed Loyalty—The Maheu Ouster

From the heavens, Las Vegas looks like a dot of light rising in a straight line; from this lofty view it looks very mystical. One can only imagine the activity that goes on between the confines of the two Nevada mountain ranges.

The reign of mobsters in Las Vegas was on a constant rise from 1946 to around 1967. The desert became an oasis for some and a homeless shelter for others. Those dreamers who brought all they had with them, gambled until it was all gone, and found they had empty pockets and empty lives with no choice but to find work and try to get their homes back. The game of chance is not unlike the game of mining. The unknowns are vast and the hopes high, so it was almost kismet that gambling became the draw towards the west.

In the fall of 1966, Howard Hughes rented the entire top floor of the high-roller suites and the floor below at the Desert Inn Hotel in Las Vegas for his personnel. He planned on staying ten days. At that time, the hotel was owned by two mobsters—Moe Dalitz and Ruby Kolad. By the fall of 1970, Hughes Tool Company owned The Desert Inn, the Sands Hotel, the Castaways, the Frontier, the Landmark, the Silver Slipper, and Ten Harold's Club. Hughes decided to purchase the Desert Inn and never left until Thanksgiving eve of 1970. This is where he was living at the time of the ousting of Robert Maheu.

Accompanying Hughes to the Desert Inn were Lavar Myler and Howard Eckersley, both of whom were Notary Publics, George Francom, Roy Crawford, and John Holmes. Along with these five were other personnel who had been with Hughes for a long time but did not have his immediate attention. Maheu, in frustration at his inability to gain any influence or even socialize with the five, labeled them the "Mormon Mafia."

Maheu didn't really know how Hughes chose to work and never did understand the Hughes mind and workings of his "modern feudalism" system. From the late 1940s Hughes chose to work through a communications system he had devised; working with his five Mormons was just an extension of his Operations Center at 7000 Romaine Street in Hollywood. Maheu was simply frustrated because he couldn't talk to Hughes and had to take his final instructions on purchases from Hughes Tool Company in Houston and his instructions on Las Vegas activities by phone from the five, or occasionally by written memorandum. It was frustrating and humiliating to him.

Hughes required lengthy explanations and argument before he would sign the power of attorney as drawn by James Leo Wadsworth at the instructions of Chester Davis and Bill Gay. In addition to the things mentioned in the chapter, Betrayal, the five, but mostly Lavar Myler principally, and to a lesser extent, Howard Eckersley, explained to Hughes some of the things that had been done in his, Hughes,' name: the grand mansion on the Desert Inn golf course that Maheu built for himself, the $900,000 for "political contributions" drawn from the Silver Slipper cage, Maheu's claim that he was Howard Hughes' alter-ego, and perhaps of most immediate importance was the double escrow on the Mineral County mining claims—all of which finally convinced Hughes to sign the power of attorney.

One change in the power of attorney that was demanded was that Raymond Holliday be substituted for Nadine Henley as one of the three to take control of the Nevada interests. Hughes was still under the spell of Maheu—he still believed that Maheu wouldn't steal from him. The loyalty of Hughes to his employees, whether his own or those of HTCO, attached to his person and the trust he had in them caused a disbelief that any of them would ever steal from him.

The power of attorney was signed. Hughes then had his staff arrange for him to leave the Desert Inn and Las Vegas on Thanksgiving Eve of 1970. They secretly left the hotel and went to Nellis Air Force Base where a private plane was waiting. On December 4, 1970, Chester Davis flew to Los Angeles with a copy of the power of attorney. It had yet to been served on Maheu.

The power of attorney did not arrive in the penthouse without extensive backup. Both Chester Davis and Bill Gay talked to the five and the officers of Hughes Tool Company in Houston. HTCO called and sent written evidence of questionable actions on behalf of Maheu and his employees. Davis and Gay made this request of the Houston office of HTCO for the financial information on the Mineral County mining claim purchase and the subsequent revelation to Houston of the apparent double escrow that caused a flurry of activity in that office.

All of the audits of the Maheu expenditures in Nevada were reviewed. The information of the purchase of the Landmark and the advertised bankruptcy price as opposed to the price paid by HTCO was reviewed and discussed, as well as the over $900,000 that was withdrawn by Maheu from the Silver Slipper cage—allegedly by Hughes' authority—was revealed. This back up revealed many lies, larceny, and thievery. Chester Davis contacted a Washington, D.C. attorney who Maheu used for his personal business and revealed the contents of the power of attorney to him. He then told the attorney that Maheu could save face by resigning, and if he didn't he would be publicly fired. Maheu refused, and started a fight to void the power of attorney

As mentioned in the chapter entitled Betrayal, Davis contacted a worldwide private intelligence organization (Intertel) through its president and chief operations officer, Robert Peloquin. After some explanations and mutual advice, Peloquin and his vice president, Tom McKean, with several of their operatives who were personnel of Intertel, descended on Las Vegas.

Peloquin and McKean had spent some time in the Justice Department and in the office of the Attorney General of the United States. Those who worked with them knew them as very experienced prosecution attorneys. Their government work included investigations they conducted themselves and also work as supervisors of investigative, undercover, and law enforcement officers. Not only were there other retired attorneys from the Attorney General's office, but officers formerly of the Border Patrol and Immigration Office and former DEA gun and alcohol enforcement officers.

The Hughes officers and attorneys worked with this organization for over eight years. It was the consensus of opinion among the attorneys that not only was this the best and most efficient organization any had worked with, but the easiest and most helpful of any intelligence organization any had ever known. Intertel was an integral part of the legal work needed by Hughes from the service of the power of attorney, preservation of assets through the investigation of the forty odd phony wills, to their tracing of the funds from the mining escrows. Using the, by then recorded, power of attorney, a copy of which had been delivered to the licensing (gaming) authorities of Clark County, Nevada, and the Nevada State Gaming control board, the Intertel personnel took control of the Silver Slipper, the Maheu offices in the Last Frontier, and bank accounts, as well as all the other Hughes interests in Nevada.

Upon serving the power of attorney on the Maheu forces and officers by Intertel, it was discovered that Maheu and Associates had fabulous office space. An entire floor in the Last Frontier Hotel had been taken over. Maheu had a twelve-by-fourteen foot office with a corresponding reception room. His desk had been custom made—a hand-carved, seven-foot long by four-foot wide extravagant display of his self-proclaimed royalty. His office chair was more like a throne that he could move easily from one end of the desk to the other.

He had three phones with the "status" red one which all visitors were made to believe connected him directly to Howard Hughes. There were several other plush offices connected to his—one for his son, Peter, and another second only to Maheu's in opulence, belonged to Hooper, Maheu's chief of security. Hooper was, next to Maheu, responsible for drawing cash from the Silver Slipper cage.

Hooper also handed out thousands of dollars to various political candidates. He kept thousands of dollars in his upper right hand desk drawer in $500 and $1,000 wrapped bundles. Candidates went into the office, one at a time, and were handed cash. No receipts were given, and the only records kept were by Hooper, himself. Verification of this came from Richard Bunker, a candidate. Bunker was a friend of all three of Hughes' Las Vegas attorneys and a distant relative of Wadsworth. Again, it must be stated that Maheu & Associates was on a contract of $500,000 per year from HTCO.

Although neither would ever admit it, intelligence developed pointed out that the amount handed to any candidate was on the advice of Hank Greenspun with the concurrence of Maheu. Greenspun had made enough breaks on television and in his newspaper column to indicate this.

Maheu, with his well-developed acuity in political matters, had immediately hired an attorney by the name of Thomas Bell. Maheu introduced Bell to the gullible Las Vegas inhabitants as Howard R. Hughes' personal attorney for Nevada matters. Bell's brother was Under Sheriff of Clark County, Nevada. The brother was actually the main force in that department, and the Bell family was a political force. Also, Bell was a relative newcomer to the Nevada Bar. He was very likable, good looking, knew everyone of any importance in the state, and was a golfer. Maheu saw to it that he was accepted as a member of the Desert Inn Golf Association.

Bell immediately petitioned the 7th Judicial Court of the State of Nevada for a temporary injunction to stop the actions of the Davis and Gay people. The petition for the injunction, backed by an affidavit of Maheu and a well-drawn memo of Law, was hand-carried to Thomas O'Donnell, District Judge. O'Donnell was a frequent "comp" of Maheu's and a golfing pal of Thomas Bell at the Desert Inn course. Thomas O'Donnell had been a member of the Nevada Legal Bar since 1956. He was a very competent criminal prosecutor, an Irish Catholic with a very wining way. He jumped into Clark County politics after only six or seven years after migrating from Pittsburg. He found himself elected as a District Judge after only four years of law practice, and because of a very close friendship, Wadsworth supported him.

O'Donnell signed the injunction but failed to set an immediate hearing as required by law and court rules. Judge O'Donnell, coincidentally, and conveniently, immediately left for a stay at La Costa Spa and Golf Course in San Diego, California. To make things even more salacious, O'Donnell's vacation was "complimentary," and arranged by Maheu. This old saying seems to apply here: "If it looks, waddles, and quacks like a duck, it's a damn duck."

Since O'Donnell was out of the jurisdiction, the Chief Judge set a hearing in the Department of Judge Howard Babcock. Judge Babcock was a former United States attorney and highly rated.

Morton Galane was, for eight years at that time, one of the more competent and successful trial attorneys in Nevada. He was a migrant from New York—having been a member of the bar there; he moved to Las Vegas and passed the Nevada Bar. He became a very good trial attorney and was recognized as such. By the time of the subject hearing, he was well known to Hank Greenspun.

Greenspun, himself, was a migrant from New York, and a disbarred New York attorney for having been convicted under the federal statute of giving "aid and comfort" to an enemy of the United States. This was a hard statute to understand. The "aid" was furnishing arms and ammunition to the State of Israel. Enemy of the United States was then defined by the Courts as any nation with which the U.S. was not an ally by treaty and whose support may work against the foreign policy of the United States. Greenspun got a lot of sympathy from the community in Clark County, and especially those in the mob-controlled arenas.

Greenspun was considered by many to be the worst kind of carpetbagger. He bought the *Las Vegas Sun* newspaper with money borrowed from the Teamster-controlled Yellow Cab Company of Las Vegas, and immediately began trying to control Nevada Politics.

The Hughes attorneys had to face public opinion from some sources that had been aroused by the ever-ready pen of Herman "Hank" Greenspun. Greenspun was infuriated that Maheu was being fired. Maheu was not only a friend—if Greenspun ever had such—but in losing Maheu he was losing a ready source of easy money. In defending Maheu, attacking the Hughes attorneys, and Maheu's "Mormon Mafia," Greenspun never let facts interfere with sensationalism. As he said in discussing his intelligence on the matter, "There are some truths you come to by instinct."

An example of the Maheu money source can be illustrated with the closing of the escrow whereby Maheu purchased the Landmark Hotel for the Hughes Tool Company. The Landmark was in bankruptcy and was offered for sale by the Trustee and so advertised, for the sum of $12,500,000. Maheu told the Penthouse that if it were purchased for that amount, small businessmen in Las Vegas who were creditors of the Landmark would be ruined. He further said, "$17,500,000 was necessary to make those creditors whole." The escrow closing papers received by Hughes Tool Company in Houston disclosed that Greenspun was awarded $250,000 as a finder's fee and Greenspun's Washington D.C. attorney received an attorney's fee of $250,000. (A finder's fee for a sale that was publicly advertised and an attorney's fee for one who was not even an attorney of record—this defies reason!)

William Morse and Joseph Foley were Irish Catholics, Morse had been elected District Judge in the 8th Judicial District of Nevada (Clark County) in 1966, but found the overwork not to his liking, nor was the little income, compared to private practice, acceptable. He did not run for re-election in 1970. His father was one of the "old timers" in the Clark County Bar Association.

Joseph Foley was the 3rd of five brothers who were lawyers in Nevada. Their father was a good and well-liked federal district judge. The five brothers formed a law partnership but, as could have been expected, soon broke up in a nasty, rancorous lawsuit.

Foley and Morse had agreed to form a partnership. Foley had done some work on the Meier mining claims and Chester Davis had used him a time or two for Hughes' work. How Wadsworth was brought back into the fold exemplifies the power the Hughes name had in Nevada in 1970. It also shows that feudalism was still working, at least in Wadsworth's case.

Wadsworth was in the District Attorney's office of Douglas County, Nevada, talking to Robert List, who had just been elected Attorney General. Wadsworth had just accepted the position of Chief Deputy Attorney General. There was suddenly a loud knock on the office door. A highway patrol sergeant came into the office and asked if James Leo Wadsworth was there. On Wadsworth's admittance that he was, the patrolman then said, "I don't know who the hell you are, but every highway patrolman in the state is looking for you." When questioned further by List, the patrolman continued, "All I know is that the Major got on the statewide network and said the Howard Hughes office is trying to locate Mr. Wadsworth. Mrs. Wadsworth told them that he was on the highway someplace going to see you, Mr. List."

He then gave Wadsworth a number to call Bill Gay for Hughes. List offered his phone to make the call. Wadsworth called, and Bill Gay related that Hughes had just been made a defendant in a court action and they needed a Nevada Attorney. Wadsworth told Gay that he had no intention of getting into the Henley/Gay rigmarole again. Gay said, "It isn't for me, it is for Mr. Hughes and he needs you immediately." Wadsworth then told Gay that he would consider it but couldn't be there for three days because he was going to talk it over with his wife.

Wadsworth and his wife discussed the proposal, and Kathleen pointed out that the pickings from private practice in Lincoln County, Nevada, would be very slim, that they would have to move back to Las Vegas anyway, and that it would also be a good start to have his name on a Howard Hughes' court action. "Besides," she said, "don't you owe it to Mr. Hughes for the relationship he has had with you for the past fifteen years?"

Feudalism reared its head again.

Wadsworth arrived at the Sands Hotel on that next Friday, December 7, 1970. When he entered the 7th floor suite that the Hughes entourage had taken, he found Chester Davis, Bill Gay, Nadine Henley, Joe Foley, and the top officers of Intertel, Robert Peloquin and Tom McKean. The personnel they put together was a judicious mixture of enforcement and investigative officers from such federal and state offices as immigration, border patrol, DEA, etc.

Gay, Davis, and Henley took Wadsworth into a private room, showed him a temporary injunction signed by Judge Thomas O'Donnell enjoining all of the Hughes' people from further interfering with Maheu and the Hughes property and operations in Nevada. The Maheu papers had been drawn by Bell but a substitution of attorneys was also served, substituting Galane for

Bell. Thomas Bell was not the trial attorney—it was Morton Galane.

Wadsworth told them that he was still not interested in becoming a cog in the Gay Wheel of Fortune. Chester Davis said that there were already some problems with Hughes and pointed out that Hughes knew Wadsworth, and also that Wadsworth had drawn the original power of attorney. Chester Davis and Bill Gay had requested that Wadsworth organize a law firm to deal with the immediate Hughes' problems in Las Vegas.

Again, against his better judgment, Wadsworth agreed to become the attorney of record, but for the hearing on the injunction only. The firm that was organized to handle Hughes' Nevada legal issues was Morse, Foley & Wadsworth, Attorneys at Law.

In a court of law, two long tables sat, opposing each other as if to say, "This is where the battle is to take place." The accusers or plaintiffs sat across the aisle from the defenders or defendants. On this day in history, sitting at the plaintiff's table were Morton Galane and Robert Maheu. On the defendant's side sat Joseph Foley, William Morse (who had resigned his judgeship about two weeks earlier so he could take part), Chester Davis, and one of his junior attorneys from the Davis & Cox office in New York, and the Hughes handwriting expert, Mr. Ralph Robertson, from San Diego.

Wadsworth appeared only long enough to introduce Chester Davis. The judge told the attorneys he had read the written motion to admit Chester Davis for the hearing, and was impressed with Mr. Davis and his bar membership, and then said, "Chester Davis is admitted to the District for this hearing only but there must always be a Nevada Attorney present in court during court proceedings." This labyrinth was impressive and stood to make history.

Hughes was newsworthy his entire adult life and combined with Las Vegas and the mob connections, this led to massive coverage by local, national and some international media. All three major radio and television services sent well-known reporters and illustrators to Las Vegas for the hearing on the power of attorney. At that time cameras were not allowed in the courtroom so an accomplished artist attended every session of court. Characterization of the major actors, attorneys, court officers, and witnesses appeared on national news.

Howard Babcock, of the 8th Judicial District, Clark County, Nevada, was the judge, the Chief Judge of that District appointed to hear the matter of the validity of the power of attorney. Under Nevada Rules of Procedure, a hearing on a temporary injunction took priority over all but criminal matters. Judge Babcock was a former Deputy United States Attorney whose office for that position was in Reno but his home and family were in Las Vegas. The Clark County bar members universally held him in high esteem. He was a "no nonsense" judge. No theatrics were allowed in his court. When he made a ruling on evidence, etc, he enforced his rulings with impartiality.

Immediately after being appointed, Babcock ordered up the entire file on the injunction that consisted of the request motion for the injunction, the affidavit of Maheu to support it, the points and authorities (the originals prepared by Bell), and the order of O'Donnell finding good cause for the issuance and, separately, the temporary injunction itself. This injunction, directed to Davis, Gay, Holliday, and all acting for them or under their instructions, which included Intertel and its minions, ordered them to cease and desist in actions to replace Maheu, to return control of the Hughes holdings to Maheu, and to remove themselves from the hotels and casinos and the Maheu offices. The supporting affidavit and points and authorities attacked the signature on the power of attorney, and therefore the power would be null and void and of no effect.

Judge Babcock immediately saw the great harm that could come from having so much of the gambling establishment of the state without ultimate control of the actual owners, i.e. HTCO and in the case of the Silver Slipper, Howard Hughes. Babcock entered an order giving the Hughes people five days to answer the request for the injunction and Maheu three days to reply. Immediately upon learning that Babcock had been appointed, Foley went to Babcock's chambers and told the secretary that he would accept all services. This was the first appearance of an attorney on behalf of Hughes and HTCO.

The afternoon of the day the injunction was issued and served, Chester Davis organized a meeting of Morse, Foley, Wadsworth, Gay, Holiday, Nadine Henley, and Intertel officers on the 7th floor of the Sands Hotel, which had become the Davis and Gay headquarters for Nevada. Davis opened the meeting with a short statement that the meeting was to determine how best to answer the supporting documents for the injunction. He did not offer an opinion.

Davis' method became well known to the attorneys who worked with him over the next seven years. He asked for ideas and opinions of all persons who he thought were involved, then would issue orders as to how to proceed. Holliday immediately asked if Hughes had been informed of what was transpiring. Davis answered that whenever there was any lawsuit or court action involving Hughes, and to some extent, HTCO, Hughes very often would issue instructions on how the matter would be handled. He then stated that he had, so far, received no word from Hughes or communication from the staff about any faction of the Maheu matter. However it had been repeated several times that Hughes had sent word to Davis, Gay, and Henley to "get Maheu out of Las Vegas."

Judge Babcock invited the attorneys into his chambers and explained that because of his calendar he could not set a hearing earlier than five days, then gave a court date and stated the hearing on the injunction would start at 9:00 a.m. on a certain date. He gave the Hughes attorneys five days to answer the demand to make the temporary injunction permanent and to serve and file the answering Points and Authorities. Galane was given three days after receiving the answer to file a response to the Hughes answer. By the end of this time the battle lines were drawn.

At the onset of the hearing, Judge Babcock spent some time in delineating the scope of the hearing. He restricted the hearing to the determination of the genuineness of the power of attorney, verifying that the signature was indeed that of Howard Hughes. He instructed the attorneys to meet and determine what examples of Hughes' signature and handwriting could be used.

Galane's opening statement was in his usual bombastic style. He stated that he would prove that the signature on the power of attorney was a forgery, in fact, a tracing, that he would show that Hughes was taken from Nevada by force and without the actual knowledge of Hughes, himself. He further tried to impress on the court that it was necessary for the truth to be established that Hughes, himself, be forced to appear. He picked up and waved a handwritten memo, purportedly from Hughes to Maheu, which, he maintained, would prove that under no circumstances would Hughes ever allow Bill Gay to be in a position of authority in his, Hughes', affairs. (This memo, which was genuine, told Maheu that Gay was at fault in the breakup of his marriage to Jean Peters and not to allow Gay to take part in any part of Nevada and Las Vegas.)

Judge Babcock then ruled that the memo was not germane to the hearing, and the proof as to whether the signature on the power of attorney was actually that of Hughes, as well as the effect of the power of attorney, if genuine. He then suggested that the attorneys meet in his chambers to see if exhibits could be agreed upon so that the lengthy offers of exhibits and the usual arguments could be avoided. Galane demanded that the original of the power of attorney be produced. The Judge so ordered. He also ordered that Hughes attorneys produce genuine signatures of Hughes.

The Judge reminded Galane that the sole purpose of the hearing was to determine if the signature on the power of attorney was genuine, and it would not need the personal testimony of Howard R. Hughes. Galane took exception to this ruling, reserved his exceptions to the ruling of Babcock and said, "I will get Hughes on a witness stand sometime. I have some very special questions to ask Mr. Hughes. Yes, I have."

The Judge told him, "The Court has ruled that this is a hearing to determine if the temporary injunction should be made permanent. It is your injunction, so you will please proceed."

The first question to be determined was, "Is the signature on the Holliday, Davis, and Gay power of attorney genuine?" It was agreed among the attorneys for both parties that the original power of attorney would be produced in court and subject to examination by the court and handwriting experts. It was further agreed that the Hughes party would furnish examples of Howard R. Hughes' signature and handwriting. The genuineness of such would be subject to proof. Cancelled checks with the Hughes signature were submitted through Nadine Henley who had been secretary, then executive secretary to Hughes since 1943 and was directly responsible for the keeping and security of Mr. Hughes personal files. The Texas bank on which the checks were drawn confirmed that the checks submitted were genuine and that Hughes' signature was authentic.

The power of attorney was a notarized document. A member of the personal staff of Hughes, Lavar Myler, was put on the stand, and he testified that he was present when Hughes signed the power of attorney and saw it notarized by Howard Eckersley, a Nevada Notary Public.

Galane's strategy became apparent. He wanted to get conflict between the (what he called alleged) witnesses to the signing by Hughes and the Notary Public who notarized and witnessed Hughes' signature. Not really knowing the background of Lavar

Myler and believing in his own powers of examination, he called Myler as his first witness.

Chester Davis had used Lavar Myler at various times as his legal secretary. Myler had been with Hughes not only as a personal attendant but as a correspondent secretary since the early 1950s, perhaps even the late 1940s. Any such person could not be confused on a witness stand, even by such an expert as Galane. Myler underwent lengthy examination as a "hostile witness." Galane had carefully and thoroughly prepared his attack on Myler.

Maheu had publicly started to opine that Hughes had been taken out of Las Vegas against his will, or at least without really knowing what was going on. Hank Greenspun published Maheu's statements in his newspaper, the *Las Vegas Sun* and added rumor and suppositions to them. Galane went too far trying to extract conflicting statements from Myler and actually convinced everyone in the courtroom, including the judge, that Hughes was certainly in command of the move. Myler's testimony was so beneficial to the Hughes case that the Hughes attorneys had very few questions, being careful to not give Galane room to further examine Myler under redirect examination. (Chester Davis informed his defense team that Hughes would not like his relationship with Myler or his attendants to become too public.)

Judge Babcock, from the very start of the hearing, made it plain that the hearing was restricted to the proving of the power of attorney to be a forgery or genuine. In spite of Galane's insistence and arguments almost to the point of contempt, the judge would not rule that the personal presence of Hughes was necessary, nor was it necessary to delay the hearing for Galane to take Hughes testimony by interrogatory. Therefore, Galane had to attack the signature on the power of attorney by the use of handwriting experts.

By stipulation, certain letters from the signature on the power of attorney and the same letters from the previously entered checks were extracted and greatly enlarged. Each was entered into evidence as separate exhibits.

Since it was Maheu who was attacking the power of attorney and signature with his temporary injunction, he had the privilege and duty to present his evidence first. Further, he had to justify the injunction. To do this, he first called Myler, whom he called an "alleged" witness to the signature. As previously stated, he went rather deeply into the circumstances and attendees of the signing. He found that Myler was a very good and unflappable witness as to the events, so good, in fact, that Chester Davis did not find it fit to ask more than two or three questions,

It was now time for Galane to play his trump. He called Charles Appel, the internationally recognized handwriting expert to the stand. Mr. Appel was the handwriting expert who was principally responsible for the conviction of Hauptman in the Lindbergh kidnapping case. He studied the ransom note received by Charles Lindbergh on ransom for his son. Appel told the authorities that the man who wrote the note was a carpenter, probably of German descent, and was within a few years of the correct age of the person who wrote the note. Hauptman was arrested and investigation proved that Appel was correct in every part of his identification of the alleged kidnapper.

When Galane, who started to qualify him as an expert, called Appel, Davis stood to stipulate that Appel was a recognized expert witness as to handwriting. Galane would not accept this stipulation and told the judge that Appel's full qualifications were very important to the case. It was evident that the court was impressed to have such a noteworthy witness appearing in his court. Having Appel in his court and for this hearing was a very big media matter. Appel's appearance on behalf of Maheu did make international news. Newspapers, radio, television, and street gossip ate it up. On qualifying Appel as an expert, hundreds of his court appearances were alluded to. His most recent case was a celebrated criminal action in France.

It was evident that Appel had spent some time studying copies of the power of attorney, the submitted checks, and memos that had been sent from Hughes to Maheu. In all, the number of memos from Maheu and Greenspun amounted anywhere from 68 to 150, however, only three showed up at this hearing.

Appel was first put to answering questions about the signature on the power of attorney. He was then asked to compare the signature to the one on a particular check. Appel testified that the letter "A" is one of the letters that was the hardest to copy in an attempted forger. He also spent time on the "R's," the two letters, which according to him, were two of the most difficult to forge.

After a learned discussion on the "A's" in "Howard," Appel was shown an enlarged copy of an "A" on the power of attorney and an "A" from an admittedly genuine signature of Hughes, then asked why it was not Hughes' signature.

Holding the letter so the judge and those in the courtroom could see his explanations, Appel pointed out several "hard for the untrained eye" to see areas of that "A" which made it certain that it was not from the genuine signature, i.e., from the check, and therefore was not the genuine signature of Howard R. Hughes. He further went on quite adamantly to say that it was obviously a copy, but probably a forgery on the power of attorney. He then said it could possibly be an attempt at tracery, and that the same faults would show up in tracing as in forgery. Galane just kept insisting on opinions of Appel to a point of redundancy. Finally on an objection of "Asked and Answered," the judge told Galane that he was being repetitive. Then on a direct question from Galane, Appel stated, "It is my considered opinion that the signature on the purported power of attorney is not that of Howard Robard Hughes."

The court called a noon recess.

Wadsworth had been sent to talk to George Franklin, then District Attorney of Clark County. On returning to the courtroom he sat down with Peloquin and McKean. In a whispered conversation, Wadsworth was told by these very good prosecuting attorneys that Davis knew nothing about cross-examining handwriting experts. After listening for a few questions and answers, Wadsworth went to the Bar and let himself into the attorney closure and told Davis he would conduct the cross-examination of Appel. Galane, of course, could have objected. Galane and Wadsworth had been opponents in several important cases but were friends. Galane also knew that Babcock would not rule against him since Wadsworth was the Nevada attorney of record in the case.

During this hour and a half break, the Hughes attorneys had been briefed rather extensively on how to track Appel's testimony. In the thorough briefing and instructions from the Hughes expert, Robertson emphasized over and over that one couldn't allow Appel to hold up both the blow up of the checks and the blow up of the signature. He stated that one could recreate a word, even his signature, and do so that there would not be slight differences in letters. Galane and Appel were being very clever in showing the letter "A" from the two documents at the same time. Of course there were differences that could be pointed out.

Chester Davis knew that Wadsworth had some experience with Robertson in his service as District Attorney in Esmeralda County, Nevada, and also he had run afoul of him as a defense attorney in the U.S. District Court for the District of Southern Nevada. Chester, with no objection from any of the other Hughes attorneys, had Wadsworth contact Robertson and flew him up to Las Vegas for this trial.

Robertson was an interesting person. He had retired as a sergeant after twenty plus years as a criminal investigator for the

San Diego, California Police Department. He then took hours of instruction to amplify his already extensive experience as an active investigator. He qualified in the California trial courts in San Diego County as a handwriting expert.

He was so convincing in his qualifications and testimony in court under skilled cross-examination that he began to be used all over the state. The district attorneys of Nevada began using him rather extensively. Although he was never used in a case where Babcock was the prosecuting attorney, he was used in more than one case for the prosecution in the United States District Court for Northern Nevada when Babcock was a member of the U.S. Attorney's Office for Nevada. There was no trouble in qualifying him as an "expert" when court took up after noon. Galane was so certain that Appel would stand up to any testimony from any reputed expert that he made only perfunctory attacks on Robertson.

It was the defense's turn to argue their case.

Wadsworth, in cross-examining Appel, first reviewed the questions about the signature on the power of attorney. Appel compared that signature to the one on the check. He basically gave the same testimony as before as to why it was not Hughes' signature. He pointed out the differences for the judge and all in the courtroom to see. He said the untrained eye would miss the areas that made it certain it was forgery of Howard Hughes' signature. Wadsworth handed a blown up "A" to Appel and asked him why this was a forgery. Wadsworth, then holding the enlarged version of the "A" asked, "Mr. Appel, what if I was to tell you that is the blow-up of the "A" in the Howard on the check?" The judge asked and was told by the court clerk that it was.

Meanwhile, Appel was frantically grabbing papers of his own that he had been allowed to take to the witness stand with him. Mr. Galane demanded of the Court that he be allowed to take the witness on voir dire, or if Wadsworth was through with his cross-examination to redirect. The judge asked Mr. Galane if he was going to try to impeach his own main witness. Galane then said he had no more questions of Appel and insisted that Hughes had to personally appear in court, that until he had asked Hughes some pointed questions the matter could never be put to rest.

Judge Babcock reminded Galane that the only matter before the court was the question of the validity of the temporary injunction— that is, should it have been issued, should it be made permanent, and the answers depended on the validity of the power of attorney. When Galane stated that without personally questioning Hughes he had no more evidence to lay before the court, the judge turned the evidentiary part of the hearing to those attempting to uphold the power of attorney.

On submitting the matter to the judge for decision, the testimony of Myler and the notarized signature was argued by the Hughes attorneys. Galane argued that Appel was world famous, that Myler was one of the Mormons attached to the very people who had spirited Hughes away, and that he had no chance to question Hughes as to the actual decisions of Hughes in the move.

Judge Babcock carefully went over the evidence presented. He said that there was "no evidence that Hughes had been forced to sign the Power," and finally said, "I find the expert presented by the Hughes attorneys more compelling than that of the testimony of the expert of Mr. Maheu." He then made a decision that the power of attorney was genuine, that it contained the desires of Hughes, and that the temporary restraining order should be extinguished.

(Note: Just when you think you've seen the last of the duck . . . for most of the last day of the hearing, Judge O'Donnell was present in court wearing golf course attire and house slippers. He sat against the wall near Maheu.)

The written decision of the judge was filed with the county

clerk and numerous certified copies were made. Every entity where Maheu had taken over was served a certified copy by the Intertel Agents. In spite of heavy publicity, especially from the *Las Vegas Sun*, Hank Greenspun, editor, owner, and publisher, the changeover went rather smoothly, much more smoothly than was expected because of the nature of the major businesses, hotels and casinos.

A battle was won, but the war was not over.

Revolutionizing of Pain Treatment

Toward the end of World War II, speed in the air had become deeply imbued in the minds of the upper command of the Army Air Force. It spilled over to all of the engineers that were designing aircraft and selling it to that Force. Of course, Hughes had been designing for speed in airplanes for well over ten years.

With perhaps the P-38 (soon to be in service) lightning interceptor concept in his mind, especially since it had been partially designed by his close friend, Jack Real, Hughes took a preliminary design to the Air Force generals. He was certain he could design and make the fastest plane in the world, something he had previously accomplished many times over. Of course, jets were becoming known, but flight range, endurance, and one-pilot operation were still of primary concern. The Air Force gave Hughes a contract to furnish three of his designs for testing and acceptance. Even though the war ended in 1945, the military and Hughes continued to want the envisioned plane built and put into service.

In July of 1946, the first twin-engine Interceptor, known as the XF11, rolled off the production line. As with nearly all the planes Hughes had designed and manufactured, there could be only one pilot to test the plane. That pilot was Hughes, himself. After exhaustive ground, taxiing, and engineering tests, the plane was ready for flight. Even though the engineers suggested that perhaps the forty-one-year-old Hughes should let another pilot test fly the radically designed plane, their suggestions were answered, as always, in the same way. Hughes had designed it, had been the chief engineer, and had it built in his air service, so he was going to be the one to first fly it.

On July 7, 1946, Hughes, with Odekirk flying pursuit, took the twin-engine, twin-tailed interceptor on its first flight. The end result was a horrific accident from which no normal human could be expected to survive. The plane crashed into a home in a new housing development in Beverly Hills, and in spite of the injuries described below, and without being able to tell how he escaped from the demolished plane, Hughes, the consummate pilot, was later able to help ascertain the cause of the failure of the plane. When Hughes was testing single engine flight characteristics of the plane, and subsequently hit the feathering control for the one engine he had shut down to test fly with a single engine, the Hamilton-Beach prop actually went into reverse pitch. This made the plane uncontrollable, since one engine was pulling the plane and the other was in reverse.

Fortunately for Hughes, a Marine sergeant had witnessed the accident and rushed to his rescue, pulling him out of the wreckage. Hughes spent five weeks in Good Samaritan Hospital in downtown Los Angeles. His numerous injuries have been widely written about and detailed, including being read into the record of a trial in Ogden, Utah.

Hughes injuries included multiple burns—third degree in various areas—to the left ear, a large one that extended from his head, over his left shoulder, down his left side to his buttocks, and took in the little finger of his left hand. (Dr. Vern Mason informed the authors that these horrible burns probably contributed to Hughes' later kidney problems.)

Hughes also sustained fractures of his chin and jaw, his left knee and elbow, thirteen ribs, and serious fractures of the fifth, sixth, and seventh cervical vertebrae. The impact was so forceful that it displaced his heart to the right side of his chest.

Within about two hours after the plan crash, Hughes asked Dr. Mason, "How am I doing?" Mason replied, "I'm not going to lie to you, Howard, you might not live." Hughes reportedly stated, "Do what you can. I'm prepared."

Perhaps the foremost medical authority on practical pain management thirty years after Hughes' death, Forest Tennant, MD, PhD, studied pain and its management. Dr. Tennant was the authority called as a prosecution witness in the trial of Wilbur Thain, MD. Tennant left that rather long and complicated trial with, if not admiration, at least with conviction that Hughes' doctors managed their patient's pain with sympathy, skill, and knowledge beyond the usual treatment of the time. He further left the trial with the opinion that, in certain areas of pain relief, Thain was a physician well ahead of his time.

The revelations and so many media stories about the high dosages of Valium taken by Hughes led to his being mistakenly labeled as an addict. A memo written by Hughes in 1958 giving explicit instructions to his aides as to how to obtain the Valium and opiates that he was taking added to the belief that Hughes gave instructions of how to obtain forbidden drugs for the purpose of abuse. Later information and evidence at the trial revealed that it was simply the detailed instructions he gave to whomever was to accomplish a chore for him. The drugs he named in the memo were those that had been prescribed by his physicians.

Typically, Hughes wrote memos to detail how a person was to go about certain purchase, for example buying Kadota figs, which he ate every day during the latter 1940s and 1950s. The fig memo was given to each new vassal immediately on being hired with explicit instructions for their purchase.

This memo was not at all surprising to the aides or to anyone who had worked on the staff at Romaine Street. If Hughes ran out of Kadota figs, and had someone in the office been sent out to buy more, he would be given the same detailed instructions on how to buy the figs or whatever his needs dictated. The revelation of this memo was greeted with great glee by the ousted Maheu and by too many of the gossip sheets. The *Las Vegas Sun* published stories of it over and over. When the full explanations for the memo and for the drug use were revealed, there was never an admission of fault or apology from any of the formerly gleeful gossip mongers.

Today, a whole new science has developed on the use of drugs for the relief of severe, long-term, and multi-caused pain as a result of the intense and precise study of Hughes and the thirty years that he lived with pain that would have killed a lesser man. There is now a whole new set of terms used in the treatment of intractable pain, now defined as "incurable, severe, and constant." As a result of Tennant's study, new drugs were developed and are being used for long-term treatment. It is generally accepted that the fame and widespread interest in Howard Robard Hughes, together with the volumes of publicity involving Hughes, were instrumental in requiring a revisit to the long-overdue study of pain and the future of its treatment.

At the time Hughes' death and the trial of the doctor who was primarily responsible for the prescriptions of the Valium and opiates taken by Hughes for most of the thirty years of his life after the accident, anyone who took drugs above the prescribed amount was considered an addict. It didn't matter whether those unusual amounts were by prescription or illegally obtained. After the thirty-year revisiting of the study of pain and its treatment, an addict is now a person who compulsively uses drugs for non-pain related reasons.

As a result of the study of Hughes' pain, a new term was added to the medical dictionary: pseudo addiction. This is now given to persons who have pain that is uncontrollable, which cannot be cured, and who seek opiates and other drugs for relief of pain. That is not the only new term added to medical use—also included are "intractable pain," and "breakthrough pain." Other words and terms have been added, some due to the long-held misunderstanding of how and why drug serum levels have such a serious effect on renal failure, or on the other hand, why renal failure or problems affect the serum levels of drugs.

Outsiders, such as room waiters, bellhops, and phony self-proclaimed insiders, but mostly the garbage collectors and profiteers such as certain news reporters and book authors who claimed to be knowledgeable of Hughes' problems with pain, used their imaginations—fueled by their faulty knowledge—to speculate as to the effects of the use of drugs on Hughes. Wilbur Thain states, "Those of us who have learned the factual truth and understand the differences as now defined between addiction and Hughes' pseudo addiction look upon such persons with utter disgust and disdain."

It is a fitting final victory for Hughes that most of this remarkable man's amazing achievements and contributions to the benefit of mankind worldwide took place during the thirty years of his seventy-one years of life that found him suffering twenty-four hours a day from severe, intractable pain.

As his physician in the last years of his life, Wilbur Thain described Hughes' skin as "extremely sensitive to touch," and that cutting his fingernails and toenails "hurt like hell." As Hughes aged, he developed degenerative arthritis in several joints that further aggravated his pain. After his fractured left hip was pinned in 1973, he did not walk again. Thain offered Hughes a walker, a wheel chair, and even am attractive physical therapist to help him walk again. Hughes replied humorously to the latter, "No Wilbur, I'm too old for that."

Tennant's short summary of Hughes (as follows), and his study of the man describes the Hughes that most of those who knew him best have felt for many years. Yes, Howard Hughes was different in some ways, but what else should you expect of a pure and total genius?

Tennant: "Hughes was a flamboyant personality who pushed the envelope in several industries, and it is difficult to name a person in the last century who has accomplished more. Many of his contributions occurred after 1946 when his plane crashed, after which he developed intractable pain and required opiods. Even in his death, Hughes is an inspiration and teacher on how to survive with severe pain and injury. His self-designed, directed, and administered therapeutic regimen should be studied by pain practitioners and patients."

Howard Hughes (signature)

Final Days

Wilbur Thain: "I pronounced Howard Hughes dead on April 5, 1976, at 1:27 p.m. CST. In those last few moments of the billionaire's life, I knew that my life had changed forever, and the world would never be the same again. I had lost a dear friend . . . a friend who had called me by my first name . . . a friend who I had called Howard.

"The legendary aviator, industrialist, and philanthropist had always chosen his own destiny and lived life the way he wanted. But now, at the age of seventy he left behind an unforgettable legacy intermingled with shrouded mystery, half-told truths, and unquenchable gossip.

"Howard was gone, sooner than I or any of my constituents could have ever guessed. But I believe Howard had died the way he wanted—in an airplane, traveling fast through clear blue skies. His only regret? That he wasn't flying the plane himself.

"Family did not surround Howard at the moment of his death. In fact, he had no family. The final beat of his heart and last labored breath occurred while racing across the Texan skies in a Lear jet, headed toward a hospital where we hoped his life could be saved.

"After Howard took his last breath and all heart and respiratory activity stopped, I asked one of the pilots of the Lear where we were. He pointed to the port side. 'We're over Brownsville, Texas—thirty-eight miles behind and to the west of our present position on the way to Houston.

"A month before, at the beginning of March, Hughes had refused to eat and drink appropriately. Although it was not unusual for him to go on fasts, this one was more prolonged. In the past, whenever I questioned him about fasting, he simply said, "It brightens my thoughts and surroundings.

"Since this particular fast worried his aides more than usual, I received a call at my home in Utah from Lavar Myler. Howard was lethargic and refusing any medical attention. Norman Crane was there that week working as on-site physician. Norman, Homer Clark, and I all rotated duties so that one of us would always be there. For them to contact me and insist that I fly to Acapulco meant that they were seriously concerned and needed my support. I spent the day arranging transportation and finally arrived in Acapulco the next day on March 7th.

"Upon my arrival, I went immediately to the Acapulco Princess Hotel where Howard was staying. The balmy weather and surroundings belied the mission that I was on. The hotel stood on the edge of the Pacific Ocean, just south of the main city. Hughes stayed on the top floor with beautiful views of the ocean and hillsides east of the hotel. The rooms were very deluxe. The doctors' room was on the floor below and equally nice. The downstairs had a variety of restaurants off the lobby as well several swimming pools. Guards were placed at the elevators to keep the press and strangers from entering the Hughes area.

"Norman Crane and Lavar Myler met with me and told me that during the time it had taken me to reach Acapulco, Howard had started eating and drinking again. Lavar had me look into Howard's room from the doorway, where I couldn't be seen, and listen to their conversation. The room was darkened as the drapes were drawn, but not taped. It was uncluttered, his memos and papers stacked on a table on the right side of the bed. His usual projector and screen were down by the foot of his bed. The other furniture, including a television set, was pushed to the side to accommodate his medical equipment.

"When Lavar told Howard that I was there to see him, Howard said, 'Tell Wilbur that I want to see him, but I am going to sleep now as I am very sleepy. Tell him to get some dinner and go to bed early because I will probably call him in the middle of the night.'

"Howard was procrastinating our visit as usual. He typically slept at least eight hours, sometimes up to sixteen. So I waited. I also overheard them discussing some business problems, and Hughes appeared to be his usual self. His mental state sounded as sharp as ever. Later, after he fell asleep, Lavar had me come into his room and examine him. 'Look," Lavar whispered, 'but don't touch, you might awaken him.'

"I looked at Hughes, noting that he was sleeping peacefully in his hospital bed, resting comfortably and breathing normally, showing the skeletal defects noted in more detail in the medical portion of this book. He appeared to have lost some weight which he couldn't tolerate as he was always skinny. But he appeared thinner than usual and was probably down to about 110 to 115 pounds. His left shoulder showed some bruising from his recent fall where he sustained injuries to his scalp and shoulder. The lesion on his scalp was healing well.

"The week before, he fell while trying to go to the bathroom without help. He hit the side of the bed, knocking a lesion off his head. This turned out to be a cylindroma of low malignancy, a rare tumor of the connective tissue, which is the tissue that holds the cells together. He also sustained a separation of the acromioclavicular joint (the front of the shoulder).

"Dr. Homer Clark was still in Acapulco at the time of his fall, and so he had been able to take the scalp lesion home to his pathology laboratory to confirm the diagnosis. He also checked a fresh urine sample and reported this to be negative for chemicals (albumin and sugar) and microscopy. Hughes refused to permit his doctors to draw any blood for lab work.

"With my visual exam finished, I left the room, leaving him to sleep. I had some lengthy discussions about Howard's health with Lavar Myler and another aide, as well as Dr. Crane, before retiring.

"I waited again to be summoned, but Hughes never called. The following morning, after checking his room to find him still sleeping, I left with a group to travel to Managua, Nicaragua so Jack Real could visit with General Somoza on business matters concerning airplanes purchased from Hughes. My job was to evaluate the medical situation since the earthquake there, and to evaluate, for the second time, the possible purchase and rebuilding of the Roche Laboratories that were badly damaged by the earthquake. We spent three days in Managua, and then I headed back to Utah.

"The apparent crisis with Howard was over, although I kept in close contact with Dr. Crane while in Utah.

"A couple of weeks passed with continual monitoring. Then on March 30, Norman Crane called me at 1:00 a.m. Hughes was in pain, demanding more codeine, as he didn't think it was handling the extent of his pain. Crane called several more times that night.

"Howard had reached a nadir in his drug quantity. He'd received his usual weekly delivery on March 27th, so I refused to increase his supply for the current week. With back and forth communication, Norman as the middleman, Howard ultimately agreed to wait for a review of his medical needs until I returned for my regular rotation on April 10th.

"Norman also reported that Howard had become very lethargic, refusing to eat or drink adequate quantities of food or liquid. When we suggested that we should draw a blood sample to test, Howard refused. We wanted a full CBC and chemistry panel, but without his cooperation, we could do nothing to further diagnose his current ailments. He also refused Norman's request to examine him. Howard just wanted the pain to be gone.

"Two days later, on April 1st, I spoke to Norman. I was on my way to the Bahamas to attend a fund raiser for the Exception Children's School in Freeport. This was a school for the mentally and physically handicapped children of Freeport, Grand Bahamas, which I helped them to develop while we were in Freeport. Norman reported Hughes was status quo, perhaps eating a little better.

"I was relieved and continued with my plans in Freeport. After the fund raiser, I tried to call Norman, but was unable to secure a line. I returned to Miami on Sunday, April 4th. I checked in with Operations, but couldn't reach Acapulco. That evening, about ten or eleven, I received a call from Norman telling me that Hughes was very bad. He'd had an episode about 5:00 p.m. of a 'shock-like' state with decreased blood pressure, elevated pulse, and sweating. I told Norman I would come to Acapulco the next morning on the first available airplane and to plan to move him out of Acapulco as soon as possible.

"At 1:00 a.m. on April 5th, I received another call from Jack Real. He said that Dr. Crane had told him that Hughes was starting to have multifocal seizures; they thought he was going to die. I was shocked. 'You've got to be kidding,' I told Jack.

"He told me they'd arranged for a plane to fly me from Miami to Acapulco, and he was trying to get transportation to fly Hughes to the United States. My flight was set for a 3:30 a.m. departure. I left immediately for the airport, and we finally departed at 4:30 a.m. in a Lear jet, stopping in Key West to get fuel. We arrived in Acapulco around 8:00 a.m. and went directly to the hotel. Dr. Crane and Dr. Larry Chaffin were both in attendance when I arrived.

"It's hard to explain what I saw when I entered Howard's room. Hughes had deteriorated rapidly in the single short month since I had last seen him. Howard was comatose, his pupils fixed and non-responsive. His reflexes were present, and there was no localized paralysis. His temperature was 99.6, and he was hooked up to oxygen by nasal catheter, but he was totally unresponsive to speech or touch. An IV previously started had infiltrated—the needle had slipped out of the vein and fluid was swelling the skin around the needle—so a new one was started using an intra-cath. The intra-cath is a unit that permitted me to insert a needle into a vein and push a small plastic catheter into the vein. This allowed movement without pulling out the needle.

"Hughes symptoms mirrored that of a possible stroke, so we administered two ampoules of intravenous cortisone through the IV. We waited about an hour, but there was no change in his condition.

"Dr. Crane told me they'd called a local physician, Dr. Montmayer, to come in and see Hughes the night before. Montmayer had recommended getting Hughes to the best and closest medical facility in the United States. The closest one was in Houston, Texas, and Crane had already made the arrangements to go there. At the same time, Jack Real was trying to secure another airplane for the transport since Jack felt that the Lear jet that brought me to Acapulco would not handle a stretcher.

"When Howard's blood pressure and pulse stabilized, Norman Crane and I went down to the hotel restaurant to get a bite to eat. While we were there, I met the two Lear pilots who had brought me to Acapulco, Roger Sutton and Jeff Abraham, and discussed our problems of securing a larger airplane. They assured me that by rearranging the seats we could fit in the Lear with the oxygen. I told them to go get the plane ready, and we would be there as soon as possible.

"I hurried back upstairs and arrangements were made to transport Hughes to Houston. Jack Real had no success in locating another aircraft, so the Lear was our only option. I grabbed the medical file on Hughes' table and put it in my briefcase. Dr. Crane was watching Hughes and the aides were busy shredding a lot of their papers. These papers were primarily Hughes business papers, memos to and from his business partners, many containing information that should not fall into the hands of newsmen. Nothing secret, but taken out of context, they could very well make for bad, inaccurate press. This concern proved to be real, since information later confiscated by the police, was released, inappropriately, to the news media.

"Dr. Crane and I secured Howard's arm so as to not interfere with the IV flow, and when the local ambulance arrived, Hughes was transported to the airfield.

"Two of the aides accompanied me to the airfield to make sure there would be no problems. We tipped the Mexican guards substantially and waited for the ambulance. When it arrived, with the help of Gordon Margulis and Chuck Waldron, Hughes was placed aboard the aircraft. We lifted off about noon—four hours after I'd arrived in Acapulco.

"I monitored Hughes' respiration which remained labored and shallow, with occasional episodes of Cheyne-Stokes respirations— labored, deep rapid breathing followed by a pause. Hughes remained comatose and non-responsive throughout this time. The only conversation occurring was between Dr. Chaffin, John Holmes, and myself on the flight.

"At liftoff, I listened to his pulse with my stethoscope. His apical pulse was 92, and became more rapid on ascent, then decreased after the jet leveled off.

"During the next hour, Hughes' breathing gradually slowed, stopping completely about 1:20 p.m. His apical pulse slowed until I could no longer hear it.

"At 1:27 p.m. CST, I pronounced Howard Robard Hughes, Jr. dead."

Howard Hughes

The Lost Will

Great controversy surrounded the death of Howard Hughes. Everyone was asking, "Did he, or did he not leave a will?" A fight ensued among hundreds for all or any piece of the two billions Hughes left behind. It was a very serious matter, but at times it was downright comical. Many of those who had worked closely with Hughes, sometimes sorrowfully and sometimes with humor, felt that the man still existed somewhere. And those who believed that crossing the great divide to death was the end of everything enjoyed this comedy of greed during his final days, watching the fight over his wealth.

There seems to be no doubt that Hughes had three wills. He left evidence of these wills, which were prepared and signed from the late 1920s to at least 1949 or 1950. In the summer and fall of 1949 there was frequent exchange between Hughes and Raymond Cook from his Houston law firm and his main Los Angeles attorney.

As with so much of his private life where he chose to involve his Operations staff, he did not use the same messenger for the entire matter. The initial messenger was replaced by another after two or three months and that replacement was taken off the job and another chosen in early October of 1949. This procedure was not uncommon for Hughes. Hughes felt that if one of the messengers became too familiar with the contents of what he was carrying, he would certainly never became familiar with the entire matter since multiple messengers and messages were involved. And Hughes knew, as well, that not all of his vassals would keep to the "no peeking" order.

The result of all the back-and-forth messages between Hughes and the Los Angeles attorney was an actual will that became famous in the fight over the Hughes Estate and was known as the "Blue Line Will." The attorney merged all of the messages into a formal will. Contrary to the usual practice of attorneys in putting formal wills on heavy bond paper, this will was typed on regular legal stationary used for court documents—the margins were designated by blue lines on the stationary, hence it's name. There seems to be no doubt that Hughes signed the will. Dr. Jack Pettitt, PhD testified that he had seen the will, and it was duly signed and witnessed. Neither the will nor the witnesses were ever produced in court. The original will mysteriously was lost.

There was definite proof that Hughes had signed a will sometime in the early 1940s, and it was sent to his attorneys in Houston. It was supposedly placed in Hughes' safe deposit box in a state bank. That bank was taken over by the Bank of America, and the safe deposit boxes were moved from the small bank to the larger one. However, when the box was later opened, no will was found. Nadine Henley, who said she found documentation in one of her shorthand books that supposedly explained this in a letter dictated by Hughes telling the Houston attorneys to destroy that will. Henley had a four-drawer filing cabinet filled with nothing but her shorthand tablets containing Hughes' dictations. It was more than frustrating to those trying to prove a legitimate will that no one ever got to examine that tablet.

There was an early 1950s will prepared that was known to Bill Gay and the other members of the 7000 Romaine Street staff. The contents of that will were freely discussed among certain people. It was given to Henley to have Hughes sign it, but she and her husband left for a trip around the world, and it was never presented to Hughes.

One of the real mysteries in the Estate-Will controversy occurred after the death of Hughes. Within two weeks of his death, some of his family appeared in Las Vegas. His closest relative was a very wealthy aunt. She transferred all of her rights and interest in the estate to her son.

It was in the interests of Hughes' relatives that Hughes had died intestate, without a will. But it was in the interest of Hughes' attorneys and his closest aides to be able to prove a will as they knew that Hughes had directed what he wanted to be done with his estate. Both sides were equally adamant in the search for a will, or to prove that one did not exist.

To the great unease of the long-time Romaine Street staff, a thorough search was made of the Hughes apartment at that location. Even the pockets of his many jackets, sport coats, and trousers were examined. The offices and filing cabinets at that location were searched in their entirety. His lockers at Burbank Airport and at the Hughes Aircraft field were also checked. The search revealed memos of phone calls and letters from Hughes to various attorneys, and those attorneys were interviewed. It is interesting to note that even Bill Gay and Nadine Henley did not know that Hughes was communicating with attorneys without their knowledge. No valid will was ever found.

Six phony wills were filed or presented to the attorneys for the estate. Another thirty-six claims of one kind or another were presented. The end result was that Hughes died without a will. With one exception, the relatives got it all. The one exception was a woman who claimed she was a surviving widow. To avoid a lawsuit, she was bought off for a low six-figure amount.

Texas, California, and Nevada all claimed to be Hughes' state of residence. By the time it was all settled there were so many claimants that the estate had to be broken down into 169 portions. Some got one portion, some got more, while a first cousin, Will

Lummus, received roughly sixty percent since he got his mother's and his own. His mother was Hughes' closest living relative. Hughes Aircraft was not included since it had already been given to the Howard Hughes Medical Institute in 1953. During the trials, the so-called heirs tried to have that cancelled, claiming that Hughes was incompetent at the time the Institute was founded.

In a later trial filed in Federal court in Los Angeles, they failed in an attempt to nullify the lifetime contracts given by Hughes to the close aides who lived with Hughes from 1970 on. However, the authors do feel it necessary to disclose our experiences in a search for his original will.

One day while in conference at Romaine Street, Mr. Cook had Dr. Pettitt read the entire will that Hughes had just signed. The content of this same will had been disclosed in detail by Hughes to Jean Peters. It was a copy of this will that was finally surrendered by Hughes' Houston law firm for which an attempt to probate was filed in Las Vegas court. (*Note: Scans of the original court document of David B. Tinnin's Affidavit in the Eight Judicial District Court of the State of Nevada, Clark County can be found in the Appendix and make very interesting reading.)

The one thread that was common knowledge to many of Hughes' staff because Hughes had often expressed it, was that it was his intent that his entire estate was to be left for medical research. He continued to express this long after he had formed the Howard Hughes Medical Institute in 1953.

The lost will trial is a matter of public record in so far as what occurred at the trial and what was reported in the press. The real inside story, most of which has never been disclosed, is only known to a small handful of his closest aides who were involved in various stages of the will's production. His trusted attorney from the Houston law firm, Raymond Cook had shared the original will with Dr. Jack Pettitt, who had read it. The only other person who had been told of its contents was Jean Peters Hughes. Both of them testified that it was Hughes' intent to leave his entire estate to the Howard Hughes Medical Institute and to fund medical research.

Immediately following Hughes' death, James Leo Wadsworth and James Whetton were summoned to join Bill Gay and Nadine Henley in a search of the Romaine headquarters for any record of a will's existence. Also present was a lawyer from Andrews-Kurth.

In the search, no will was found; however, found among Hughes files was the original of a letter from the head of the Houston firm and addressed to Hughes personally which read, "Dear Howard, Enclosed is a copy of your will, the original of which we have on file." This was presented to the Houston lawyer and then strangely disappeared from sight. Shortly after this letter was found, the Houston firm produced a copy of Hughes' will. Meanwhile, the whereabouts of the original up to this time remain elusive. Efforts to trace it through Houston bank vaults were unsuccessful. It strangely, if not purposely, had disappeared. In Nevada a copy of a will can only be probated if two people can testify that they had seen and read the original. Dr. Pettitt was the only one who had done just that. Mrs. Hughes had only secondhand knowledge of its contents, having been told of the will's detail by her husband.

Howard Hughes (signature)

Howard Hughes Medical Institute

Wilbur Thain: "In Hughes' early years, he had serious thoughts about creating a medical institute. Prior to his first marriage to Ella Rice in 1925, he spent a lot of time creating his first will. In that will he set aside considerable money, which was available from the Hughes Tool Company. He planned for the development of a Howard Hughes Medical Laboratory to be established in Houston, Texas. The laboratory would be charged with the development of specific products that would aid in the protection against many of the diseases which existed in Houston at the time. The world had not yet developed significant antitoxins and vaccines to treat the many extremely serious diseases that existed throughout the world at that time. Hughes directed that scientists would be hired to develop treatment modalities for these diseases. He also directed that only the best scientists would be hired to run these laboratories.

"One thing Hughes constantly told many of us is that he would like the Institute to find a "new penicillin" or something similar to it. On one occasion we talked for more than two hours about an indefinite concept he had in his mind concerning a reward that would be given to an outstanding researcher, something akin to a Nobel Prize."

"I had the good fortune of spending two periods of my life working for Hughes: from 1948 to 1952 I worked in his Operations office handling telephone calls at night while I was attending medical school at USC. Again in 1972 until the time of his death in 1976, I participated in a rotation with two other doctors in providing what little medical care he would permit. During this second period of time, Hughes and I discussed extensively his thoughts about what he would like the Medical Institute to accomplish both during his lifetime and after his death.

"I know that as early as 1952, Hughes was discussing the formation of a medical institute with his tax accountant, Tom Slack, and with his main attorney, Raymond Cook. The efforts of these two lawyers came to fruition in 1953 with the separation of the Aircraft Division from the Hughes Tool Company. This created Hughes Aircraft Company (HAC). The Howard Hughes Medical Institute was created in December of that year, and later that month, Hughes gave one hundred percent of the Hughes Aircraft stock to HHMI as an endowment."

GROWTH & DEVELOPMENT OF HHMI

Hughes' physician in Beverly Hills was Vern Mason. Hughes met Mason around 1928 during his stay in California. They talked about a medical laboratory to be built in Houston, not the present HHMI.

In the 1946 crash of his XF11, Hughes was so terribly injured that Mason did not feel he would live. During the course of his recovery, Hughes had many discussions with Mason about the medical lab and future research. This discussion was the basis for what was to transpire with Hughes' dream of the Howard Hughes Medical Institute.

When plans for HHMI were instituted, Hughes decided that all researchers, even though they might be working at a major university, they would actually be working for and be paid by HHMI. Their laboratories, building, and the university might be updated or rebuilt by HHMI, but the actual payment to the researcher would be completely covered by HHMI. Secondly, the researchers would be permitted to develop their own programs and were not held to or stymied by a previously submitted proposal.

If something new came up, they were permitted to proceed in a different direction if necessary. The important thing was freedom of scientific thought and direction that might occur to the research scientist. This idea was very new and unique and is still so today, as most grants given to researchers still require a comprehensive program of research to be established prior to the time the grant is awarded.

Wilbur Thain: "Dr. Mason became the first medical director of HHMI, establishing the original program in Miami, Florida. Why he chose Miami is unknown except that Hughes had interests in Miami, and Dr. Mason had planned on retiring to that area when he completed his internal medicine practice. The first researchers were chosen by Mason and permitted to progress with their own research. I recall having read in some of the journals published by the Institute that some of the early work done on the use of intravenous catheters by the cardiologists was researched by the early investigators."

Ellie Pugmire: " . . . the Medical Institute (was initially) headquartered in Miami, Florida, with Dr. George W. Thorne as Director for Medical Research. The finances for the Medical Institute came from Hughes Aircraft Company, the major stockholder, with Howard Hughes as the sole trustee. Bill Gay and Chester Davis were on the Executive Committee.

"I believe that Mr. Hughes' final goal in life was to see that HHMI would be taken care of financially to carry on medical research so that everyone in the world would benefit from it. Therefore I believe that he made a will that provided for this. I hope his personal wishes are carried out, and that he will also be remembered for his contribution to medical research."

James Whetton: "Throughout the intensely active daily involvement of his business life, which began at the age of nineteen when he assumed ownership of his father's Hughes Tool Company, this same degree of intensity continued with little change in his work ethic up to within a day or two of his passing. The concept of HHMI was that it be a major institute for medical research and eventually for genetic research. Hughes wanted to find ways to explain many of the problems of human health, just as he sought to satisfy his questions about some of his own health issues during his life."

Wilbur Thain: "The secure environment that Hughes preferred to operate within has, in all probability, never been duplicated or known to so effectively exist in the business world. For example, without a doubt, his plans for the future of what was to become the greatest of his legacies, the Howard Hughes Medical Institute, was kept strictly confidential until he and his attorney, Raymond Cook, publicly announced it. With this disclosure, the Institute was incorporated in Delaware on November 17, 1953."

Because of its huge monetary value, the filing was followed by a series of lawsuits involving the IRS, eventually reaching the United States Supreme Court. Again, before the public announcement, not even his closest aides were aware of his plan, which also called for the Institute to be the only recipient of the Hughes Aircraft stock, and also eventually his entire estate.

The process was started when the legal documents for forming and incorporating HHMI were prepared by Raymond Cook, a key partner in Hughes' Houston law firm, Andrews-Kurth. Mr. Cook had also prepared a condition to Hughes' will, transferring the ownership of Hughes Aircraft stock to the newly created HHMI.

The IRS was quick to recognize that the transfer of the stock to a not-for-profit institute would result in a huge loss of tax revenue to the U.S. Department of the Treasury, thus, the legal battle over the acceptance of the process began.

Andrews-Kurth Associates was one of the premier law firms in Houston, Texas. Howard Hughes, Sr. and Hughes Tool Company had used it since the 1920s. A partner, Raymond Cook, who knew both of the Hughes, was a senior partner who had opened offices in Washington D.C. and had moved to live in Virginia by the middle 1950s.

Hughes continued to use Raymond Cook for major issues, excepting TWA, until he left the Los Angeles area for Boston on July 17, 1966. The Operations Center at Romaine Street issued instructions and requests to Cook even after Cook had retired to Virginia.

The filing of the papers forming HHMI was immediately followed by a request to the IRS for a ruling that the corporation forming HHMI be designated a non-profit corporation. The IRS minions, following instructions and long-established custom, immediately turned the request down. The financial security and wherewithal to accomplish the result Hughes envisioned was established by transferring the stock of Hughes Aircraft to the Institute. Hughes Aircraft was one of the major contractor/suppliers of defense materials to the United States. The IRS would not consider the thought of losing the multimillion yearly gross from the tax rolls.

Noah Dietrich immediately employed the law firm of Hogan and Harston, and senior partner Seymour Mintz, who had once been a special attorney with the IRS. Mintz filed a suit in U.S. District Court in Washington D.C. in an effort to overturn the IRS ruling. The trial court sided with the Institute, and the IRS immediately appealed to the Circuit Court. This court ruled that the Internal Revenue Service must conduct more hearings and issue a new ruling in the matter.

The problems with the non-profit status were considerably complicated by Hughes' request that he be allowed to draw one million dollars from the Aircraft Company for living expenses, because he was giving up a major source of personal income to

HHMI. The final order of the Supreme Court in transferring the matter back to the lower courts implied that the request was not out of line, seeing the eventual loss of administrative decision allowed the living expense.

As a matter of course, the Hughes interests, including Hughes himself, now brought politics into the picture. The IRS had not given up in the courts and appealed the Circuit Court decision to the United States Supreme Court, who, without a formal hearing, dismissed the appeal and returned the matter to the Circuit Court.

Meanwhile, Robert F. Bennett, who later became a U. S. Senator from Utah, was brought into the picture as a representative for Hughes in Washington. At this time, Bennett's father, Wallace Bennett, was a senior-ranking senator from Utah and Chairman of the Senate Banking Committee. At that time, the not-for-profit status had not been resolved.

Following is Robert F. Bennett's letter to James Whetton detailing his personal involvement in resolving this most important issue.

> To: James Whetton from United States Senator Bob Bennett(Utah)
> Re: HHMI
> In either late 1971 or early 1972, the Nixon Treasury Department announced that they considered HHMI to be a foundation, subject to all of the regulations that applied to foundations. They said that HHMI was in violation of several requirements that must be met for a foundation to keep its tax-free status, specifically: A foundation's portfolio must be diversified; no single asset can be more than, say, ten percent of the total. (I cannot now recall the exact number.) HHMI's only asset, Hughes Aircraft, was 100% of its portfolio.

The foundation must pay out a certain percentage of its earning every year. (Again, I am not certain, but I think the number was six percent.) HHMI's annual payout was around one percent.

The consequences of this ruling would have been the sale of Hughes Aircraft, which, at the time, was valued at approximately $125 million. The proceeds would then have had to be invested in a diverse portfolio of stocks, with an annual payout of roughly $7 million.

Hogan and Harston lawyers went to the Treasury officials and pointed out that HHMI was set up under a specific legislative definition of a medical institute, going back about twenty years, and that it had never been structured along traditional foundation lines. They said that the law was clear and that they would take Treasury to court on the matter.

I was not present at these discussions, but I was told that the Treasury lawyers' response was, "Go ahead and sue us. The issue won't be settled for years, and, in the meantime, you will have to divest yourselves of Hughes Aircraft and make the necessary disbursements. Even if you win, all it will mean is that you will be able to go back to your present structure, and Hughes Aircraft will have long since been sold."

I was representing Summa Corporation in Washington at the time, but I was asked if I could assist HHMI and Hughes Aircraft in this matter, even though they were not my clients. I agreed to do so, and took Hogan and Hartson lawyers to see Charles Walker, the undersecretary of the Treasury. We made our case, to see if he would intervene on HHMI's behalf. He was cordial but refused to act to change the decision.

I then took a Hogan and Hartson lawyer with me to call on Rep. Wilbur Mills (D-AR), who was chairman of both the House Ways and Means Committee and the Joint Committee on Taxation. I had worked with Chairman Mills while I headed the Congressional Relations office at the Department of Transportation during the first two years of the Nixon administration.

He, too, was cordial. I explained that the Treasury Department was acting in a way that we believed was in conflict with the laws that Congress had passed years ago, and that we were unable to get them to relent. He called in his top aide and told him to draw up a letter to the Secretary of the Treasury for his signature, in which he would tell the Secretary that, when the Secretary next appeared before either of Rep. Mills' Committees, he would be asked to explain why he was not complying with the intent of Congress with respect to the law governing the structure of medical institutions engaged in research.

I never saw the contents of such a letter and cannot guarantee that it was ever sent, but, soon after our visit to Rep. Mills, Treasury issued a statement that the matter of HHMI would be delayed for further study. Nothing was ever said about it again. HHMI was never required to sell Hughes Aircraft until it did so at a time of its own choosing, for billions more than it would have fetched in 1972.

Wilbur Thain: "The Institute has continued to grow and expand into other facilities, the latest of which is at the Janella Farm in Virginia. This is a large development of research laboratories and, more recently, administrative space to house a number of the Hughes research fellows. It is unique in that all of the labs and rooms have glass walls making it easy to communicate between researchers.

"In 1984, because Hughes did not name a board of trustees, but simply left it in the hands of his attorney, Chester Davis, and Bill Gay, the CEO of his residual company called Summa Corporation, the Delaware courts established a very distinguished Board of Directors, eight people, to be trustees of HHMI. Hughes Aircraft was later sold to General Motors and the financial resources of this sale established the Institute as a driving force in biomedical research and science education.

"While Vern Mason was the original medical director during HHMI's early years, George Thorne, MD from Harvard University took over the position upon Mason's retirement. Since that time there have been many learned researchers holding the position of authority at HHMI.

"The annual report of 2010 for HHMI shows endowments of $14,765,000 and disbursements of $889 million during 2011—all of this money coming from an endowment that is now approximately $14.8 billion. This endowment is now held in stocks, bonds, and many other equities.

"Though Hughes wanted a new penicillin, developments within the past few years at the Institute include complex structures working as antibiotics to shut down bacterial ribosome's. Two of the newest have the potential to treat drug-resistant infections like tuberculosis.

"At the present time there are about 330 Howard Hughes Medical Institute investigators who continue to push to the extreme edge of knowledge in many important areas of biomedical research. Widely known for their creativity and ability to take risks and explore the boundaries of science, these researchers include thirteen Nobel laureates and 147 members of the National Academy of Science. All of these people are searching desperately to try to understand the mission of the Institute searching for the "Genesis of life."

Appendix

Ellie Pugmire 1976

Note from James Leo Wadsworth: Ellie Pugmire's job was necessary to replace Bill Gay's secretary who was leaving. She was exposed to a different type of interview than usual. Besides an examination of her experience and credentials, she was lectured on how the Romaine staff was organized. She also heard of the plans for the future of Hughes' personal staff. Needless to say, she was excited and could see the pot of gold and the curve of the rainbow. She was promised a good salary, at that time, of $80 per week with more to come as she proved herself. Ellie Pugmire's memoirs have been left in their entirety.

This story is gratefully dedicated to John and Ramona Bernhard, for their devoted friendship.

A SECRETARY REMEMBERS

Howard Hughes's vast empire was like a giant spider web, and Hughes was the spider. It went in so many directions and the web crisscrossed endlessly. He spent many long years spinning the web and many of us were caught up in that web, while others are still there. The spider is dead, but the web remains, and what happens to the web is no longer any concern of the spider. He did his job the best way he knew.

Unlike the allegory above, the story I'm going to tell is real. Howard Hughes and the people who worked with him are real. The manner in which Hughes chose to live was his privilege. We make our own destiny, whether we attain fame or anonymity.

Having had the opportunity to work with Mr. Hughes on his personal staff for more than six years, I believe I gained a first-hand knowledge of him that would be of interest to many. He was a genius in his knowledge of things; he lived alone and lonely most of his life; he strived relentlessly to attain his goals; his working habits were uniquely unconventional; he manipulated people and made many demands of them; but I found him to be a most fascinating and capable man who lived surrounded by luxury, yet he cared nothing about the everyday luxuries most of us are so eager to attain.

I never saw him wear a new or even decent pair of pants or shoes, and he never wore socks. He never had a wristwatch on, and he usually borrowed a jacket from someone when he needed one. He never wore a necktie and wore only white shirts that we delivered to him from the office. The way he lived his life, in his own private world, these things were unimportant to him, and labeled him an eccentric.

Yet, I felt it was a privilege to have worked with Howard Hughes. I met many wonderful, talented people as a result of that association, and I'll be grateful forever for that and the unique experiences I had during those years which I will now relate just as they happened to me.

THE FIRST TELEPHONE CALL

It all started in the early spring of 1952 with a telephone call from Hollywood, California, and the voice at the other of the phone identified himself as Don Alder, who was in charge of personnel for Howard Hughes. I was sitting in my private office in the penthouse of the Bank of America Branch on the corner of Market and Montgomery Streets in San Francisco where I served as Media Director for the Charles Stuart Advertising Agency when the call came in. He stated that he had heard reports of my exceptional skills and abilities and that they were putting together a personal staff for Howard Hughes and he would like to interview me.

MY APPLICATION

A few days later I received an employment questionnaire, on the Hughes Aircraft Company letterhead, which I promptly filled out. A condensed version of that four-page document is as follows: Date: March 29, 1952; Name: Ellie Pugmire; Age: 29; Color of Hair: Blonde; Color of Eyes: Blue; Height: 5'3"; Weight: 122 lbs.; Husband: Richard Pugmire; Daughter: Joan Marie (Age 6); Education: Utah State Agricultural College; Qualifications: Rapid, accurate typist, 90-100 W.P.M., Dictation (Gregg Shorthand): 150-160 WPM; Employment Record: 3 years Media Director for Charles Stuart Advertising; 2 years Secretary to Advertising and Promotion Manager of Radio Station KLX, Oakland, CA; 4 years Civil Service positions with Department of Internal Revenue, War Department, and War Food Administration.

The application was promptly mailed to Hughes Productions in Hollywood.

THE INTERVIEW

My application was impressive enough that my husband and I were flown to Los Angeles where I would be interviewed by Bill Gay, the man responsible for forming a personal staff for Howard Hughes.

We were guests of the Hughes organization and stayed in a posh hotel on Wilshire Boulevard for a few days. We were taken to dinner with several members of the staff and their wives and the "red carpet" was rolled out for us. An interview was set up for my husband, Rich, with North American Aviation (presently called Rockwell International) as he was an engineer by profession, and we both went to our appointed interviews.

I was taken to Hughes Productions, 7000 Romaine Street in Hollywood, where I first entered an old, dungeon-like building that had been built in the 20s, formerly Multi-Color, Inc., a movie film-manufacturing establishment, which Hughes had acquired at one time. The long, narrow halls were a dismal grey color, and most of the offices were dingy and dilapidated, the carpeting showing worn spots. The offices were later redecorated and the building painted.

At the east end of the building on the second floor we entered Bill Gay's office and were seated in front of his desk. He was a tall, youthful-looking man about two years my senior, and he was very pleasant, yet formal. His assistant, Francis Fillerup, was also present when the interview took place.

My job was to be Bill's secretary to replace his present one who was a Phi Beta Kappa honor graduate of USC. The organization of the staff was outlined, and the plans for the future talked about. I could almost see the pot of gold at the end of the rainbow. But it would have to wait for now, as I was told that I would start at $80 per week, which supposedly was more than any of the other girls started at, with promises of much more to come.

Another of my duties would be to take dictation from Howard Hughes personally, and I was warned that Mr. Hughes was a fanatic perfectionist and that no erasures or corrections of any kind would be permitted on any typing I did for him. I had been well trained in both shorthand and typing, and, although I hadn't used my shorthand a great deal, I wasn't concerned that I couldn't do the job. I knew I was qualified.

So we sold our home in San Francisco and left our interesting jobs there for a much more exciting future in Southern California.

7000 ROMAINE STREET

About 8:00 a.m., dressed in my prettiest business-like dress with white collar, gloves, and hat (abandoning the gloves and hat very shortly as this was not San Francisco), I drove my grey Plymouth coupe into the parking lot behind the building and entered through the back door and up the stairs which ended at the office I was to occupy, located just outside of Operations, the large room where all the telephone messages to and from Hughes were processed, and about fifteen feet down the narrow hall from Bill Gay's large office. There was always plenty of work to do, and I don't ever remember being bored from that day on.

Down the hall, in about the center of the building, were a couple of offices occupied by Nadine Henley, Executive Secretary to the President (Hughes), and her three girls. They handled the fan mail, Mr. Hughes' airplane log, and other matters.

There were offices for Noah Dietrich and his secretary—the Controller of the Company and his secretary; Tom Slack, Hughes' personal attorney, and his secretary; the Bookkeeping Department; the Switchboard; and some other offices for the members of the personal staff.

In the basement, Mr. Hughes' personal collection of films was stored, as well as many scrapbooks pertaining to Hughes. The drivers had a room on the roof of the building, and the fleet of Chevrolets was parked in the lot where I had parked that morning.

STAFF MEETINGS

Board Meetings for the personal staff were held on Monday mornings, being presided over by Bill Gay and Nadine Henley, and I took the minutes of the meetings. Some of the original staff members were Dr. John T. Bernhard, Dr. Jack Pettitt, Dr. Ernest Wilkins, Francis Fillerup, Glen Brewer, Hank DiRoma, Howard Lundeen, Marty Cook, Don Alder, Leon Frazier, and Kay Glen who was in charge of Operations and the drivers. There were others who joined the staff later on.

THE MORMONS

I would like to mention at this time that the myth that Howard Hughes hired only Mormons (members of the Church of Jesus Christ of Latter-day Saints) is untrue. Members of the staff who were not Mormons included Nadine Henley and Hank DiRoma. Bill Gay hired all of the members of the LDS Church who were working for Hughes personally.

It is true that Hughes would not allow anyone working in the same room with him to smoke, and so only non-smokers and non-drinkers were hired —and they were the "cream of the crop," well-educated and tops in their various fields of Political Science, Education, Stock Market, Business, Science, and Law. Hughes had many companies at that time, including the Hughes Tool Company, Hughes Aircraft Company, RKO Motion Picture Studios, Gulf Brewing Company, and TWA Airlines, and Bill wanted top-flight bright young men who would be qualified to assist in matters pertaining to these companies as Hughes was personally running and making all major decisions. He was in full charge of his empire.

Nadine Henley, who was the same age as Hughes, formerly worked at Hughes Aircraft Company, and I believe her father had worked for Hughes, also. She moved to the Romaine Street offices and was the person who hired Bill Gay to work for her during his summer vacation from Brigham Young University—and he never went back there.

Bill dreamed of the many opportunities available for a personal staff to assist this giant industrialist in his overwhelming task, and one by one, members were sought out and hired, with the sanction of Hughes himself.

MY FIRST MEETING WITH MR. HUGHES

I had been diligently practicing my shorthand, whenever I found the time, with the aid of the Professor, Robert W. Messer, a sixty-five-year-old retired New Englander school teacher, who had been hired to teach shorthand to the girls in Miss Henley's office and to the boys in Operations, so that we could all become more proficient in our jobs. My speed had improved, and I was ready when the call came.

Just before 5 p.m. the call came in, and Bill Gay announced to me that we were going out to the Beverly Hills Hotel to work with Hughes. This time I took my shorthand notebook and pencils. We arrived at the hotel about 5:30 p.m. and waited in the lobby for the summons to his suite. We were both a little nervous, and I had no idea what to expect. I was beginning to get hungry and thirsty and really wanted to go to the ladies room, but Bill said that we had to wait right there. And we waited there until about 9:30 p.m. when we finally heard from the east side of the building. He answered the door immediately and stammered an apology for keeping us waiting. Then I was introduced to him and asked to sit in a certain chair.

Hughes told me not to take any notes unless he specifically asked me to. I noticed he was a tall, lean, about 6 ft. 4 in., clean-shaven and neat appearing handsome man in his mid-forties, with brown hair combed straight back. His personal barber, Eddie Alexander, was cutting his hair regularly at this time. His fingers were long and thin and the nails about a quarter of an inch long. He wore a white shirt, open at the neck, the cuffs rolled, back, and had on a nondescript pair of old trousers and brown shoes, with no socks. The living room of his suite appeared quite neat and clean except for the stacks of magazines and newspapers around the room and large manila envelopes placed in neat piles on the couch. From the first, I was awed by his dynamic personality and his brilliance.

Among the items discussed with Hughes was the matter of a new building for the staff. Bill mentioned a specific location and explained how it met our requirements, etc., however, when Hughes wanted to know the answer to a specific question regarding the property, Bill didn't have the answer, and that closed the subject. We never did get a new building.

That same evening, about 10:30 p.m., a knock on the door brought one of Hughes' waiters from the hotel kitchen with a table filled with food for Hughes' supper. There was a chafing dish with hot bubbling gravy, which the waiter kept stirring, and then he placed the roast beef, peas, and potatoes just right on the plate. Some of the gravy was put on the beef and the rest set-aside for Hughes to spoon out as he wished.

By that time, not having had a bite to eat since noon and smelling that heavenly aroma, my stomach was really beginning to growl. Hughes asked me if I had eaten and I said, "No." "Well, then, you'll just have to wait until we are finished," was all he said. I was taking notes, and he dictated between bites, and the loud noises my stomach was making were embarrassing me terribly, but Hughes was hard of hearing and apparently didn't notice.

I have been in the room with him many times while he has been dining, and because he was who he was he could slurp and make all the noises he wanted to while he was eating. That didn't concern him at all.

After Hughes finished his meal, we continued working until after midnight. I noticed that he placed himself so he could watch very carefully all of my shorthand notes. When he wanted me to read something back to him he would point with his finger to a specific place on the page, and I could have sworn that he could read shorthand himself. He was easy to take dictation from as he knew exactly what he wanted to say, but I felt he was testing me to see just how fast I could take dictation, and he would deliberately speed up, still watching my note taking.

Having a very soft voice, I had to really shout so that he could hear me. He hated wearing a hearing aid, and I soon learned how loud I had to speak so I wouldn't have to repeat myself. All of his telephones were equipped with amplifiers so a normal conversation could be carried on with him.

After all the letters and instructions had been dictated and read back to Hughes, I felt that he was satisfied that I knew what I was doing.

The first encounter was over and I went to my home very tired and hungry. The next morning, at the office bright and early, I began transcribing the words Howard Hughes had dictated to me.

MY FIRST ASSIGNMENT FROM MR. HUGHES

Shortly after I started to work, Hughes was appearing and testifying in the downtown Los Angeles Federal Court regarding the Communists in the motion picture industry. He didn't completely trust the accuracy of the court reporters, and my assignment was to take my shorthand notebook with me and sit unobtrusively in the courtroom and take down every bit of Hughes' testimony.

I arrived all alone and found where the proceedings were taking place. The halls were filled with reporters, and the room jammed with spectators. I went over and spoke to the bailiff and told him that I worked for Mr. Hughes, and I had to be in there. A couple of the reporters heard the name Hughes and started to question me, however I disappeared into the courtroom where the bailiff found a place for me to sit. I felt almost like an idiot writing shorthand in my lap as fast as I could, but I suppose people thought I was a news reporter. As it turned out, Hughes never asked for my transcription.

THE GROUND RULES

The first and foremost rules for all employees of Hughes were loyalty and secrecy. We were not to discuss anything we were doing with any other employee or even the members of our families, and, above all, not to friends or outsiders.

Every scrap of paper thrown into the waste baskets, plus all of our shorthand notes and books, were burned each day in the furnace located in the building. I realize, at this late date, that I was pretty naïve, and I did as I was told. How I wish I had kept some of those valuable notes taken during that era.

I understand the transcribed notes have all been put on computer cards and are guarded in a special office set up by Bill Gay in Encino, in the San Fernando Valley, for his future use. Dr. Jack Pettitt, a scientist, who had also been sent to Harvard for business training by Gay, was in charge of this office.

MY DUTIES AT ROMAINE STREET

I performed all of the usual secretarial duties for Bill Gay: screened his telephone calls, made appointments, dusted his office, took dictation for both business and personal use, ordered his lunch, ran errands, planned staff parties, helped select office equipment and furnishings, and worked overtime willingly.

WEDDING GIFTS

Hughes received many invitations and wedding announcements, and I was the one who went to Bullock's Wilshire to purchase a lovely piece of Steuben glass, have it gift-wrapped with Hughes' personal card placed inside, and then have one of the drivers deliver it to the appropriate destination. When I left the organization years later, what did I receive? Steuben glass, of course!

TAKING TURNS

Hughes promised to cooperate and make use of his personal staff set up for him. The plan was to have Bill Bay and Nadine Henley take turns going out to the hotel with their respective secretaries to take dictation from Hughes. I went out with Bill on the first occasion and the next time Nadine took her secretary with her. After that, Hughes always requested from Operations that "Ellie" be sent out, and this caused a great animosity from Nadine during all the subsequent years I worked for Hughes. I believe she may have resented the fact that I got along so well with him, plus the fact that she did not hire me or meet me until after I started working at Romaine Street. I was *not* one of her girls. She is the only person in the business world I have associated with who treated me this way.

This resentment showed up when it came time for raises and other considerations; however it did not affect my relationship with Howard Hughes. He still ran the show, and when he asked for me to do some work for him, the request was granted.

THE SEATS MR. HUGHES BOUGHT

On several occasions I personally delivered important documents for Mr. Hughes which weren't trusted to the drivers, such as cash, checks, legal documents, or letters. One such delivery was the personal check from Howard Hughes, to the Times Building downtown, where funds were being raised to build the beautiful and impressive Dorothy Chandler Music Pavilion. This was the first of many contributions he made to that Music Center, and his name is carved in marble, along with other contributors, on the walls inside this magnificent edifice.

Ironically, my husband and I had season tickets for the light opera when the Pavilion was completed, and the seats we occupied on the seventh row center were directly behind the seats with the engraved name of Howard Hughes, as donor of those seats, which we gazed upon for the next ten years.

ONLY EIGHT HOURS FOR WOMEN

I kept employment records of all members of the staff, including the drivers and Operations, in my office. The yellow slips were the "start" slips, the blue were the raises and promotions, and the pink ones were the termination slips. Once a year, usually in October, lists of all employees were typed showing a record of their employment with a space provided for the new increase, if any. The drivers were all paid on an hourly basis, the rest of us on a weekly basis, and the checks were disbursed through Hughes Productions.

Almost everyone kept timecards that were filled out daily and submitted on a weekly basis. The drivers were paid overtime for all of the hours they worked in excess of forty, and they made fantastic salaries.

Most of the time I worked between seventy and ninety hours a week, but I was only paid for eight hours of overtime because, at that time, the State of California Labor Board would not permit women to work more than eight hours a day, six days a week, and the office didn't want to get into trouble with the State government if our paychecks for women showed more than forty-eight hours. My salary never was adjusted to compensate for the long hours I worked.

I always used my own car when I worked away from the office, and when I used it for errands, and I was never compensated for the gasoline I used, only the parking fee. I shouldn't have been so timid.

MR. HUGHES AT ROMAINE STREET

Mr. Hughes never set foot in the Romaine Street offices during the years I was there, so the myth that he dictated to the girls at the office is completely untrue. Whether he ever did so in the past has never been confirmed by anyone I talked with.

LIPSTICK, PERFUME AND NAIL POLISH

I have read so many books and articles written stating that the girls who worked with Mr. Hughes were not allowed to wear lipstick, perfume, or nail polish, and furthermore, that they had to wear white or rubber gloves when typing. During all the time I worked for Mr. Hughes I always wore lipstick, perfume, and nail polish and never once did he ever object to or even mention the subject, and I never wore any kind of gloves when typing for him. But he always inspected each page that I typed to make sure there were no erasures or corrections and that the margins were even on both sides of the sheet. Even if there were just a flaw in the good bond paper we used, he would have me type it over again. I really enjoyed the challenge and took pride in all the work I did for him. And he noticed.

THE BEVERLY HILLS HOTEL

Mr. Hughes lived at the fashionable and expensive Beverly Hills Hotel that is located on Sunset Boulevard in Beverly Hills. When we worked there it was usually on the third floor in the east wing of the main building. He always rented a suite on either side of his to insure maximum security. When he lived in the bungalows behind the hotel, he always had guards close by to see that no one approached his bungalow. It was even off-limits to the maids and any cleaning or laundry needed was taken care of by his own employees.

The management of the hotel knew the eccentricities of this man and they went along with his wishes. After all, he paid many thousands of dollars every month for many years to the hotel, and I doubt that the money he spent there was ever equaled by any other resident. Hernando Courtright was the manager then before he moved to the Beverly Wilshire Hotel. Hughes saw to it that everyone connected with the hotel received lavish tips to insure top service, and this was done on a regular basis.

HAVE TYPEWRITER, WILL TRAVEL

Mr. Hughes always told me whether or not to bring my typewriter, and if I needed it, I would have one of the drivers deliver it along with the metal typing stand, boxes of good bond paper and onion skin paper, carbon paper, pencils, paper clips, etc. I always used a heavy IBM Executive electric typewriter that had marginators on it. His personal letters all had to be marginated—perfectly even right margins, but other instructions and legal documents didn't have to be marginated; however, I always made sure they were as even as possible.

Remembering my first experience with Mr. Hughes, I always tried to eat something before I went out on an assignment because I knew I would probably be tied up for hours, and I usually was. Of course if I was in a conference with other people and food was ordered, I always ate with them.

When I worked in Las Vegas, I didn't take my typewriter with me and used a rented one instead, but I had to make sure that I brought along plenty of supplies to work with as I might be there two days or two weeks, depending on the project I was working on. If we knew where we going to be working for a long time, we had the drivers transport my typewriter and stand.

LEARNING MY LEGAL

My experience in taking legal notes up until this time had been very limited, but Mr. Hughes wanted me to go to Las Vegas to work with Tom Slack, his attorney at Romaine Street, and his secretary, Frances Magisano. A number of the Houston attorneys were also there at the Last Frontier Hotel—Raymond Holliday and Raymond Cook among them.

Frances and I would take turns taking dictation, and while one took dictation, the other would transcribe. The pressure was really on, and we worked from 8:30 a.m. until after 7:00 p.m. every night for a week. Frances was a fabulous secretary and wrote perfect shorthand notes, so I told her that it would be faster if she would take all the dictation, and I would transcribe all the notes. That arrangement worked out beautifully.

It wasn't long before I was at ease with the legal terminology, and this was a great learning experience for me, and worth more than any legal secretary course I could have taken.

Mr. Slack left the organization after a while and retired to his farm in Virginia. Mr. Hughes missed him very much and telephoned him many times to persuade him to come back and help him again, but he never did. Frances was hired as Lawrence Hyland's secretary when he was made president of Hughes Aircraft Company in Culver City.

So much of my work after that was involved in typing legal documents of all kinds, and I really enjoyed doing it. I worked with many of Mr. Hughes' attorneys, but I believe I worked more with Raymond Holliday than any of the others. He is truly a magnificent person to work with, and my association with him and others I worked with, as a result of my position with the Hughes organization, was very rewarding to me.

LAS VEGAS AND SHOW GIRLS

After working with the attorneys and Mr. Hughes as many hours as were required each day, we were free to go to dinner and attend any of the shows we wanted to. Jimmy Vernon made reservations for us, and Hughes was the magic name in Las Vegas that got us the best tables, either the first row of raised booths or ringside, if we wanted to sit there. We ordered whatever we wanted and just signed for it. All tips and gratuities were taken care of so we could relax and enjoy our dinner and a fabulous show after working hard all day.

Mr. Hughes was actively signing up "starlets," putting them under contract to Hughes Productions, and some of these were discovered in the chorus line. I was usually sitting toward the middle of the showroom and, as soon as the lights were darkened and the show began, in came Mr. Hughes with Walter Kane, who acted as his talent scout, or another of his male employees, and they sat down at his ringside table to watch the show. Perhaps one or more of the girls would be pointed out by Mr. Hughes and, after the show, the aide would go backstage and contact the girls.

Mr. Hughes never personally approached the girls. That would come later, if, after his photographers at Christy-Shepherd Studios had photographed them. After Mr. Hughes had studied the 8 by 10 black and white glossies, he would meet them. The photographers had instructions to photograph the girls standing, fully clothed, with little or no makeup on, with full front and side views, plus close-up views from every angle. The sets of finished photos were placed in individual tan envelops with the girl's name written on the outside, and these were picked up at the studio and later delivered to Mr. Hughes. Very few of those photographed were put under contract.

SNEAKING HOME AT 5:30

Mr. Hughes had very peculiar working habits, and it was good that I was young then and could work all night, if necessary. He didn't go to bed in the evening, get up in the morning, eat regular meals, or work during the day, as normal people would do. He would sometimes be awake for three days and nights and then would call the boys in Operations and tell them he was going to sleep now and would call them again when he awoke. Everyone could breathe easier while he slept and spend the time catching up on other things, knowing that they would not be disturbed for at least twelve to fifteen hours.

One day I was called out to the Beverly Hills Hotel in the early afternoon and went up to his suite. By this time Bill Gay did not accompany me when I worked with Mr. Hughes, so I was completely on my own.

We worked on some serious problems regarding Hughes

Aircraft Company, and Mr. Hughes wanted me to take certain notes covering this meeting. In this manner, he always had a record of his instructions, and there could never be any question as to what the instructions were if the question came up at a later date. There were two or three others present during this particular conference.

About 8:00 p.m., Mr. Hughes excused us and told us we could go and get something to eat, but he wanted us back no later than 10:00 p.m. We had dinner in the Polo Lounge of the hotel. He had some telephone calls to make, and I'm sure he didn't have anything to eat.

After the dinner break we were refreshed and ready to get back to work. The discussions seemed to go on interminably, and I could see the men catch a glance at their watches occasionally, but Mr. Hughes would be the one to tell us when the meeting would end. His mind was fresh and alert, and he never showed any fatigue no matter what the hour was. Well, it was after 5:00 a.m. when he ended the meeting and I had to drive home to Westwood.

The sky was getting light in the east, and it looked like a beautiful morning. The birds were beginning to chirp, and I'm sure alarm clocks were beginning to ring. I drove into the driveway as quietly as possible. I thought, "I hope the neighbors don't see me coming in at this hour. What would they think?" I have a dear, understanding husband, and he always knew where I was, and he knew what unconventional hours I had to work, and that was all that was important. Without his help at home I never could have worked those late hours.

NO OVERTIME

After a very brief rest I was at the office by 9 a.m. I had to go into Operations to answer the phones for a few minutes when Kay Glenn had to go on an errand down the hall. The phone on Mr.

Hughes' personal line rang, and I had to talk with him for a few minutes and explain where Kay was and when he would return.

A few minutes later Bill Gay received a call from Mr. Hughes asking why I was at the office as I had just left him after 5 a.m. that morning. "I don't want her working overtime," was what he told Bill. He must have thought that I was paid for all the time I worked, and that I was getting a big salary. I wished at some point that I would have the opportunity to tell him what I was paid, but he never asked.

MR. HUGHES, THE MAN

We had a very good working relationship, and I think he could relate to the fact that I was a quiet, shy person by nature. He was comfortable working with me, and I believe this was important to Mr. Hughes.

He was never unpleasant with me although his serious face usually looked like he was scowling. At times, when he smiled and "poured on the charm," he could melt any girl's heart, I'm sure. He was a very handsome, virile looking man, and everyone felt his rather shy, boyish charm.

In a room filled with people, his dynamic personality would dominate the completely, and I don't know anyone who wasn't affected by his presence. I observed this time and time again.

MR. HUGHES AT SAN SIMEON

Mr. Hughes was a close friend of the late William Randolph Hearst, and he was invited many times to lavish parties at the Hearst Castle in San Simeon. Hearst and Marion Davies were always together at these affairs, and I have seen many pictures of Mr. Hughes that were taken at San Simeon with Hearst and various movie stars. I hope that some of these pictures will eventually be published because in later years he was seldom seen in public and photographed.

MR. HUGHES MAKING A PASS?

Mr. Hughes was actively dating girls during this period, and his name was linked with dozens of actresses. It is true that he had a whole string of starlets and others vying for his attention.

I was still fairly young and attractive then and people knew I was working with Mr. Hughes regularly, and I'm sure many wondered if there was ever anything personal in our relationship. One friend came right out and asked, "But did he ever make a pass at you?" The answer is emphatically, "No."

For one thing, he was too much of a businessman to mix business with pleasure, and for another thing, he was never known to look at or date a girl who was over twenty-five years of age. I was already thirty years old, and in his eyes, I was a mature and valuable employee who could take his orders and perform my duties with skill. I appreciated the good relationship we had, and the thought that he would ever attempt to make a pass never entered my mind.

CORNFLAKES AND FIGS

What did Mr. Hughes eat for breakfast? The few times I was present while he was having breakfast in his room he ate only cornflakes with milk and a large bowl of figs. Breakfast might be in the morning or late afternoon, depending entirely on when he wanted to have breakfast.

He never drank coffee, and I never saw him drink anything alcoholic. He only drank bottled water and we kept a supply of it for him at the office. I had the impression at that time that he was very careful of what he ate and seemed to take care of himself health-wise.

I remember reading his instructions regarding the girls who were under contract, and he stated that they should not drink coffee as it was bad for the complexion, and that alcohol would cause premature wrinkles in their faces. He didn't smoke, and he seemed to be very aware of the hazards of smoking. I imagine he preferred that the girls he dated didn't smoke either.

He never wore glasses, and his eyes seemed to be good although he squinted some. I know that he did a tremendous amount of reading, and I was always amazed at the vast knowledge he had about a lot of subjects.

LAS VEGAS

Mr. Hughes' legal residence then was Las Vegas, Nevada, and the only big hotels on the strip were the Flamingo, the Sands, the Desert Inn, and the Last Frontier. We usually stayed at the Flamingo Hotel when working in Las Vegas, and the accommodations were quite elegant.

Las Vegas then was like a small town compared with the present Las Vegas, and with $5 you could play the slot machines for hours. Also for $5 you could see a great show and dinner was included. Again, the palms of the maitre d's were well-greased with that green stuff, as well as the waiters and hotel personnel, and the Hughes people were welcomed everywhere.

McCarran Field was just a small airport on the strip and Mr. Hughes had a hangar for his plane there. The Convair was guarded day and night wherever it was parked, whether it was Clover Field in Santa Monica, Palm Springs, or Las Vegas.

An apartment had been fixed up for Mr. Hughes to live in when he was in Las Vegas, and special air conditioning was installed that would purify the air and keep the dust out—making it like a laboratory clean room. A lot of time, money, and effort had been put into this place but Mr. Hughes only stayed there a few times.

He was secretly buying up land around Las Vegas, through an employee named "Mac", and had around 19,000 acres at that time. Even back then he envisioned building a supersonic jet landing field which could service the entire world. These supersonic planes from everywhere would be able to land without the restrictions a large metropolitan area would have, and he had plans in his mind to construct a whole new city there. He was always years ahead in his thinking and planning.

ON CALL

I could never attend a function or be away from my home without first calling Operations and giving them a number where I could be reached. I was "on call" twenty-four hours a day, and the office knew where they could reach me at all times. When Mr. Hughes wanted to contact you, they had to be able to get in touch with you immediately; therefore you sometimes felt you had no privacy at all. This was required by a man whose number one aim was to have this privacy at all times and at any expense. It was just part of the job.

On a Sunday, one such call came to me while I was attending church. I was told to listen to Walter Winchell's radio broadcast that evening and take down in shorthand everything that Winchell said about the Chinese Communists' prolonged artillery bombardment of the Nationalist-held offshore islands of Matsu and Quemoy.

My typewriter was brought out to my home, and when Winchell started his rapid-fire report, I frantically took down the report, got it typed, and the driver rushed it back to the office where, presumably, it was sent to Mr. Hughes.

I never could figure out why that particular part of the broadcast was so important to him, or why he couldn't have just had it recorded, but my job was finished for the evening, and who knows what my next assignment might be?

NOAH DIETRICH'S HOUSE

When Noah Dietrich married his second wife, Mary, he gave a big party at his home in Beverly Hills and invited all of the employees at Romaine Street, as well as others who were working for Mr. Hughes at that time. He wanted us to meet his bride.

My husband, Rich, was also invited and most of us met at Romaine Street where we bundled into the fleet cars and took off for the affair. His private drive was off Coldwater Canyon, I believe, and wound around the hill until we arrived in a large parking lot in front of his mansion. It was like the homes you saw in the old Hollywood movies, complete with an Olympic-sized swimming pool, with life-sized statues at the far end. He had purchased the home from Charles Boyer who built it in the 30's.

He showed us the dining room where, by pushing a button, the whole ceiling would slide to one side and you would be dining under the stars. It was a very romantic home, and I could just picture the debonair Boyer in this setting. The library had an interesting narrow spiral staircase that went up through the ceiling and ended in a private circular study. It was a unique house in every detail.

The evening was very joyful and small groups gathered here and there swapping tales about Mr. Hughes. Perry Lieber, who was the public relations man at RKO at that time, related a humorous incident that happened to him. He was warned by Mr. Hughes to never telephone him from a private telephone; he must always use a pay telephone. He was at a party high up in the hills above Beverly Hills, with no public telephone within miles, when he saw that it was time to telephone the Boss. It was late and raining, and he didn't want to get into the car and drive to another phone, so he took the phone inside a large closet and called Mr. Hughes. The first thing Mr. Hughes asked was, "Are you in a phone booth?" Perry said, "Yes." Mr. Hughes said, "Give me the number and I'll call you right back." When the phone rang, after quite a few minutes had passed, Mr. Hughes said, "You're not in a phone booth. You're at so-and-so's place. You get your blankety-blank self down to a phone booth right now, and don't you ever try that again." Perry said he never tried to fool the Boss again.

In later years Perry was still in public relations and took care of VIP's who came to Las Vegas, providing them with wonderful accommodations and entertainment. All I had to do was to call him, and I was also treated like a VIP.

THE ACADEMY AWARDS

Every year Mr. Hughes gave away his personal invitation to the Academy Awards, and I had the opportunity to use one of his tickets a couple of times.

I went with Lucile Turner, Nadine Henley's personal secretary one time, and Neita Bond, who also worked in Nadine's office, and Neita's husband, Lew. Lucile is a very bright and personable administrator and became office manager for Chester Davis' law firm in Beverly Hills, after spending seven years as manager of his New York City office.

We arrived at the Pantages Theater on Hollywood Boulevard, in Hollywood, where the Awards were held that year, in Lew's beautiful Cadillac, all dressed in our finest formal wear, and we pulled up in front of the theatre where all of the limousines lined up to let off the stars and celebrities attending the affair. As we got out of the car, people shoved and craned their necks to see what movie stars were in that group, and I heard a young voice say, "Oh, they aren't anybody!"

Inside the theatre we were taken to seats located in the center toward the front. Famous familiar faces surrounded us, and you could just feel the excitement and electricity in the air.

The seating capacity of this theatre was limited and the Academy Awards were later moved to the Santa Monica Civic Auditorium and finally to the Music Pavilion in Los Angeles.

It was just about one of the most thrilling experiences I remember and one of the side benefits of working for Howard Hughes. He had no desire to appear at these affairs, and I was glad to be able to use one of his personal tickets.

After the Awards we also went to the Beverly Hills Hotel, in Beverly Hills, and attended the gala dinner party there. I remember we were following behind John Wayne's car, and it was quite a procession from Hollywood Boulevard to Beverly Hills.

I couldn't wait for the next time I would be able to attend this grand affair, and that night, anyway, I felt like I was "somebody."

THE TEN CENT REFUND

Mr. Hughes was known to be a penny-pincher, and this showed up in various ways. I know that he made his telephone calls at night because of the cheaper rates, and more than once was known to have advised people who were calling him to call after the rates went down.

On many occasions a small envelope addressed to Howard Hughes at Romaine Street appeared and inside was a dime refund from the phone company reimbursing him for the dime that wasn't properly released from the pay phone he was using.

Others were busy spending his millions, and he was making sure that he wasn't cheated out of his dime.

THE BUNGALOW PORCH

Mr. Hughes had moved into a bungalow behind the Beverly Hills Hotel, and I was again summoned to be there with my typewriter. It was shortly after lunch, so I had eaten, and I hurried out to the hotel.

He had me set up the typewriter and its stand in his living room, and we proceeded to work. He seemed to be a little irritated that day as the problems seemed to be building, and he was under constant pressure to make decisions concerning many things at this time. He was on and off the phone most of the afternoon.

At times he seemed to forget that I was there, and I knew he had a reputation for some pretty strong language, but I was a little embarrassed and surprised when I heard those shocking words for the first time. Many of his early years were spent around oil fields in Texas and rough language was just a part of his life.

Once, after a really blistering tongue-lashing at someone, he turned around and saw that I was sitting there. He apologized for his language, and then said he thought it would be better if I moved my typewriter out on the front porch as he had some private calls to make, and he would let me know when he was finished.

He helped me set up the typewriter and placed it on the far side of the cement porch, which was next to a walkway that went around the bungalows. The porch was just a large square, flat cement slab about 15 feet by 15 feet with no rails or bushes around it for privacy.

I felt a bit foolish sitting there typing and received some inquiring glances from people as they passed by. I finished my typing around 5:30 p.m. and waited for the Boss to call me. I didn't dare knock on the door, so I just waited and waited. The evening was beginning to cool off, and it was getting darker and darker, and I still didn't hear from him. There was nothing I could do except wait.

By this time it was evening and people were walking by on their way to dinner. I'm sure they thought I was out of my mind sitting there in front of a typewriter in the dark. I was finally fed up and about to call the office or do something when the front door opened and Mr. Hughes said, "Oh, you're still here. I guess you better go home now."

I gave him the papers I had typed and was on my way home, feeling pretty much like an idiot.

THE LOOK MAGAZINE INTERVIEW

In 1954, Mr. Hughes agreed to give a personal interview to Stephen White, who wanted to write a series of articles about him for *Look* magazine. Mr. Hughes said he would give the interview but with the condition that he could approve the copy before it was published. The conditions were agreed upon, and the appointment was finally set up. Mr. Hughes also wanted me to be there taking shorthand notes.

The meetings were at Walter Kane's apartment, 8484 Sunset Boulevard, Hollywood, and we met there around 8 p.m. one evening. Greg Bautzer, who was another of Hughes' attorneys from Beverly Hills, Stephen White, Mr. Hughes, and I were the only ones present.

Both parties made concessions and trade-offs. Mr. Hughes hated anything said about his private life and was very candid about his empire, too, but he could also be very persuasive when he wanted something. Bautzer acted as an advisor for Hughes. We spent several very late evenings working on this until the final approved copy was typed.

Mr. White was an excellent writer, and I believed Mr. Hughes was satisfied with the series when it came out in the magazine.

BUT KEEP YOUR CLOTHES ON

On one occasion after working in Mr. Hughes' suite on the third floor of the Beverly Hills Hotel all afternoon and evening with some businessmen from out of town, the negotiations seemed to go on and on, and it was soon 1:30 in the morning.

The meeting wasn't over, but Mr. Hughes was finished with me for a while; however he didn't want me to go home. He took me next door to one of the rooms he kept vacant on both sides of his suite and said, "I'll call you when I need you again. You can go to sleep in the bed and can take your shoes off, but keep your clothes on."

I complied with his wishes and about 3:00 in the morning, just as I began to doze off to sleep, there was a knock on the door. Mr. Hughes and another man walked in and he said, "You can go home now. I need the bed for so-and-so, and I'll let you know when I'll need you again."

Oh well, I couldn't sleep with my clothes on anyway and another good night's sleep was shot.

THE RED ZONE

When I worked at the hotel, I always drove into the hotel garage, and the parking attendant parked my car and then returned it to me when I left, but not so with Mr. Hughes. He wanted to leave and return in secrecy so he had the Beverly Hills Police Department paint a section of the curb in the middle of the block on Crescent Drive a bright red so that no one could park there, and he would be assured of a parking place for his Chevrolet. No one ever put a parking ticket on his car parked in the red zone.

THE HOLLYWOOD SCENE

Mr. Hughes appeared in Hollywood in about 1929, and he immediately became a part of the motion picture industry. I have heard many of the stories of his escapades with actresses from the men who worked directly with him during this fabulous era when he was dating Billie Dove, Jean Harlow, and Katharine Hepburn. He appeared at many parties, and this wealthy, handsome young man was flooded with invitations. He met Hollywood's famous actresses and had no trouble getting dates.

Others he dated were Olivia de Havilland, Ginger Rogers, and Lana Turner. I don't know how true the story is about Miss Turner having her linens monogrammed "HH," and when Mr. Hughes wouldn't marry her she was told that she could always marry Huntington Hartford.

Linda Darnell, Yvonne De Carlo, Ida Lupino, Mitzi Gaynor, and Faith Domergue were others. Ava Gardner and Terry Moore came later, as did Jean Peters.

Terry Moore lived in Westwood, a suburb of Los Angeles, with her parents at the time she was dating Mr. Hughes. I have personally known Terry and her parents, the Kofords, for many years. In my opinion Terry and Mr. Hughes were never married in spite of her claims, and I know that Mr. Hughes got a job for her father at Hughes Aircraft Company.

Still others he dated were Kathryn Grayson, Mona Freeman, Anita Eckberg, and Susan Hayward. Miss Hayward's twin sons called him "Uncle Howard." I know that he used to take them for airplane rides in his private plane.

The girls Mr. Hughes dated never divulged any secrets or discussed their relationship with him, and I don't know whether it was because of a fierce loyalty or fear. I know that he never divulged any of the details of his relationships with them either.

PALM SPRINGS

For a while Mr. Hughes lived in Palm Springs, California, and I made a few trips there when my assistance was needed. It is just a couple of hours' drive from Los Angeles. Some of the drivers moved their families to Palm Springs and were assigned to guard duty and to chauffeur some of the starlets around as well as take them shopping and to dinner, and see that they were kept busy.

We provided places there for Anita Eckberg and Ava Gardner to live in. Joyce Taylor was another starlet who was around for quite a while and she, too, spent some time in Palm Springs. Glen Brewer was squiring these girls around most of the time, especially Ava Gardner, in Las Vegas and the Bahamas as well as Palm Springs and Lake Tahoe.

Mr. Hughes was very good to the women he was involved with and saw to it that they had everything they wanted. I don't recall that he was unkind or ever "got rid" of them. They just left when they got tired of the setup.

TALENT SCOUT

Walter Kane worked for Mr. Hughes for many years and lived in a lavish apartment on Sunset Strip in Hollywood. Mr. Hughes would borrow his apartment for conferences when he didn't want his hotel used for such meetings, and I was there on several occasions.

Kane's name was linked with the girls or starlets, and he was designated as a talent scout. When Mr. Hughes wanted to meet someone whose picture he may have seen in a magazine, Kane was called and his job was to contact the girl. He lived on a grand scale and was well paid for his services.

THE VASECTOMY

Mr. Hughes was a cautious man, and there were never any big scandals concerning him with girls. He made sure that he would have no paternity lawsuits, and in his early life he had a vasectomy performed by his personal physician. I can only suppose that some of the girls knew about this. A reliable employee told me about it who had been with Mr. Hughes for a number of years and who used to be an escort for the girls.

JANE RUSSELL PUBLICITY

Mr. Elliston Vinson, of Foote, Cone, and Belding Advertising, handled all of the advertising for Mr. Hughes. Mr. Hughes valued his ability and when a film at RKO was ready for distribution, he called Mr. Vinson in to discuss with him some new and unique ways to advertise the picture.

The approach was usually geared toward sex, and Mr. Hughes went as far as the law would permit in his copy. Today it wouldn't even attract attention. One line he wanted to use for a Jane Russell picture was, "She'll knock your eyes out," which doesn't seem at all that clever today, but the only thing showing in the ad was the bosom for which she was famous. I worked with Mr. Vinson during these sessions with Mr. Hughes, and we would do the ads over and over until he made the final decision as to what would be used.

Jane Russell became famous after making *The Outlaw* for Mr. Hughes. At RKO she made *The French Line,* and there were censorship problems concerning the movie. Both Jane Russell and Marilyn Monroe worked together at RKO in *Gentlemen Prefer Blondes.* I was invited over to the studio where I watched some of the filming of these movies on the sound stages. I was much more impressed seeing these stars in person, and naturally I went to see both movies when they were released. Both stars were "hot" properties at RKO and made quite a few movies there.

Mr. Hughes tried to personally handle all the publicity until it was just too much for him to handle, and he eventually gave up and turned it over to Mr. Vinson or Perry Lieber to work out.

Miss Russell's relationship with Mr. Hughes was strictly a business relationship. Everyone knows of her lifetime contract with him, and I won't go into that. I felt that she got the best of the deal.

HRH

In all memos and notes concerning Mr. Hughes, we always referred to him as "HRH." The initials, of course, stand for Howard Robard Hughes, but most of us knew it really stood for "His Royal Highness," and, among ourselves, referred to him in that manner. Somehow it seemed to suit him.

He was actually Howard Robard Hughes, Jr., the only son and child of his father who made his fortune by inventing a rock drill bit for his company, the Hughes Tool Company in Houston, Texas. It was originally called Sharp-Hughes Tool.

Hughes took over this company when he was nineteen years of age. He had lost his mother, Allene, and his father. His mother reportedly was responsible for his obsession with germs, and they seem to idolize each other.

FOLLOWING INSTRUCTIONS

When Mr. Hughes issued an instruction he would specifically state how he wanted it carried out, in minute detail, and it better be carried out just as he wished or you'd suffer the consequences. Those who worked for him learned early that you didn't deviate from his instructions; you just did the job he set forth and in the manner he prescribed. You also learned not to be concerned with his motives.

One such example was when Darryl Zanuck notified Mr. Hughes that he wanted the red carpet rolled out for his lady friend, a well-known actress, who was traveling on TWA to Paris. The lady didn't receive the kind of treatment that was expected and word got back to Mr. Hughes promptly. There was an investigation, and the TWA man responsible was immediately fired.

THE ATOMIC BOMB TESTS

Business transactions and important documents had to be signed in Las Vegas so we spent a great deal of time working there until the government started testing atomic bombs in Nevada— and then everything stopped.

Mr. Hughes did everything in his power to put a stop to these tests in Nevada, but he didn't succeed.

After the first test in the mid-50s, he put out a directive to all employees and their families that they were not allowed to visit Las Vegas or drive through Nevada, and he didn't even want us to fly over that area. He wouldn't even touch a piece of mail that came from there. He was extremely concerned about the fall-out, and it was many years later before he returned there.

The entire fleet of Chevrolets that were used by employees in

Las Vegas was just abandoned, and no one was allowed to bring them back to Los Angeles under orders from Mr. Hughes. They just sat there for several years. I don't know what eventually became of them.

DIETRICH EXITS

When we arrived at the office one morning we found the building locked. No one was permitted to enter, and a note on the door told us to go home. The next day the mystery was cleared up.

Mr. Hughes had decided he no longer wanted Noah Dietrich around, and he had all the outside locks changed as well as those to Mr. Dietrich's office. Eventually Mr. Dietrich was permitted to pick up his desk and personal belongings. He had worked for Mr. Hughes for thirty-two years, and this was a real shock to him. This caused a feud, which eventually led to a long, involved legal battle.

Dietrich's office was next to mine at Romaine Street, and I saw him almost every day. One day, prior to the above event, he called me into his office and closed the door. He asked me if I would come to work for him as his private secretary to replace Helen Blankenhorn who had been with him for many years. This was during the period when Bill Gay was spending most of his time out in the Valley and Mr. Hughes wasn't personally meeting with people as he had previously done. I suppose Mr. Dietrich thought Mr. Hughes wouldn't need me anymore, but I was still Bill Gay's secretary. I thanked him for his offer and told him I didn't want to make any changes. He was no longer there very soon after that.

POLITICAL CONTRIBUTIONS AND WATERGATE

Many requests for contributions from Mr. Hughes were received in the office and were usually handled by Nadine Henley and Bill Gay. No one was ever turned down unless he had Mr. Hughes' disfavor for some reason or other. Generous donations to candidates were given regardless of the party affiliation, because at some time or other Mr. Hughes might need a favor of them or might need their cooperation on a problem he might have. In Nevada everyone seemed to be on the Mr. Hughes' dole because favors would always be needed.

During the Nixon era, Mr. Hughes made a $100,000 cash contribution for his campaign, on top of money given to his brother, which all came out as a result of Watergate. Robert F. Bennett had a public relations firm in Washington, D.C. and was on the Hughes payroll to handle political situations for him. Bennett was the one who gave the $100,000 to Nixon, and Nixon was concerned that the Democrats might know about this and use it against him in his Presidential campaign; hence the break-in at the Watergate Hotel and the eventual resignation of President Nixon.

Mr. Hughes caused another incident with his $100,000 contribution to Hubert Humphrey that was delivered to him in cash at the Century Plaza Hotel in Los Angeles.

Incidentally, Bennett moved back to Salt Lake and won a seat in the Senate against his opponent, Joe Cannon. Cannon knew of Bennett's Watergate connection but didn't use it in his campaign so the public was not aware of his connection with Mr. Hughes in the past. Cannon was a young boy living in California during the 50s and I knew his father, Adrian Cannon, who was a friend of Bill Gay's.

Large political contributions were constantly given in Las Vegas, and Mr. Hughes was able to benefit from these when he needed a gaming license for his hotels, a zoning change for his businesses, or when the atomic bomb testing was going on in Nevada to make some changes, and I know he was able to work out special tax problems as needed.

PETERS MARRIES CRAMER

Jean Peters went to Rome in 1956 to make the film, *Three Coins in a Fountain*. She met Stuart Cramer III, a young, good-looking man from North Carolina, and he immediately proposed to her. She had given up hopes of Mr. Hughes marrying her, so she married Stuart in Washington, D.C. very soon after meeting him.

She hadn't been married very long when Mr. Hughes' interest in her came to light, once again. A reconciliation with Mr. Hughes was arranged, and the divorce from her husband was finalized in December, 1956.

ENTER MAHEU

While Jean was married to Stuart, Mr. Hughes hired Robert Maheu to do a complete investigation of Cramer. Maheu was doing private investigative work in Washington at that time and had been with the FBI and CIA previously.

Mr. Hughes had Maheu call our Romaine Street office, and his reports were dictated to me on the private telephone in Bill Gay's office. I was sworn to absolute secrecy, and I typed the daily reports every evening after other employees had gone home. These reports then went out to Mr. Hughes.

The reports on Cramer were very, very complimentary, indeed. There was not even a hint of scandal in his past, and he came from a very wealthy family that made their money in the textile mills.

Mr. Maheu was an expert in his field and Mr. Hughes was impressed with this man. It wasn't long before Maheu appeared in Hollywood.

Mr. Hughes rented or purchased a home for Maheu in Brentwood, a fashionable residential area located just a few miles inland from the Santa Monica Beach, and soon his family and possessions were moved into his beautiful home. His arrival in California was kept secret and very few people in the organization heard his name mentioned.

My first meeting with Robert Maheu was when I was given a thick, tan, unmarked, long envelope which I was to deliver to him personally at a rendezvous spot several blocks from the Romaine Street office. The package contained an undisclosed amount of money, in cash. This was probably the first of many such transactions to take place.

I saw Mr. Maheu on many occasions and he was so dynamic and personable that he stood out above many others. He seemed like a very capable executive to me. He showed that he was prepared when the time came, and he was given the responsibility for the Nevada Operations, and he lived and ran his operations like you would expect a millionaire to.

Maheu admitted that in the seventeen years he worked for Mr. Hughes that he had only seen him twice from a distance.

RENDEZVOUS AT TAHOE

The office was buzzing behind closed doors. Certain personnel were sent to Lake Tahoe and Reno. Secret arrangements were made to transport Jean Peters from Washington to Nevada, where her reconciliation with Mr. Hughes took place.

It wasn't long before Mr. Hughes had his attorneys make arrangements for the divorce, and all of the proceedings were kept very quiet. The divorce was finalized in December 1956, and that ended Jean's marriage to Stuart Cramer.

JEAN PETERS HUGHES

Word leaked out in the newspapers in March 1957 that Mr. Hughes had married Jean Peters. None of us at the office believed this. If Bill Gay knew, he was not talking, and we were never told about any of the details of the marriage—where or when it took place—but Jean was busy setting up housekeeping in a guarded mansion in Bel Air.

By now the starlets and former girlfriends of Mr. Hughes were a thing of the past. No longer did we have a stream of photos of girls coming through the office. He seldom, if ever, left the confines of his home, and only the guards and drivers were permitted there to make deliveries and assist them whenever needed.

I was convinced that they were legally married when I saw a check in the office that was signed by "Jean Peters Hughes."

LAMPS FOR THE LIVING ROOM

Jean wanted a pair of lamps for the end tables in her living room, and I was asked to personally go out and select a pair for her. I was told to get something not too expensive, but nice, but no other instructions as to color or style. The only thing I knew about the furnishings was that some end tables and a cocktail table, covered with smoky glass, had been made for them.

At Cannell & Chaffin I found a lovely pair of lamps that were about $110 each, which was not a lot of money for lamps, and I knew they would go with the end tables. I purchased them with my own money on condition that they could be returned. However, they weren't what Jean wanted, and I had to return them.

Next time I went to Sloanes in Beverly Hills and selected another pair and put them on my personally account. I was told that these were *too* nice and to just buy something really simple, so I ended up at the May Company where I purchased a pair of nice looking lamps that cost $30 each, and Jean loved them. Mrs. Hughes was not spending a lot of money on her home, I decided.

TWO REFRIGERATORS

In their home in Bel Air, Mr. Hughes became fanatical on the subject of germs, and he had two refrigerators installed, one for Jean and one for himself, and no one was permitted to use his.

STUART AND TERRY GET MARRIED

Stuart Cramer, after his divorce from Jean Peters, and her subsequent marriage to Mr. Hughes, met and started dating Terry Moore in 1957. Their romance got serious and it wasn't long before Terry was bringing Stuart to church with her.

Stuart became interested in the Mormon Church and had many meetings with John Bernhard, the bishop of the Westwood Ward that was located behind the Mormon Temple in West Lost Angeles, to learn more about the teachings of the Church. John was still a member of Mr. Hughes' personal staff at Romaine Street.

I was the choir organist of Westwood Ward and attended the services every Sunday I was in town. Some of the members who attended there were actress Laraine Day and her husband, Mike Grilikis, Rhonda Fleming, Mae Murray, and Patty Peterson, who starred in the *Land of the Giants* TV series. Bob Brunner, a talented musician and composer-director for the Walt Disney Studios, Ivy Baker Priest, and State Senator Robert S. Stevens were also ward members. Later, Donny and Marie Osmond and their family attended the ward also. There was a lot of great talent among the members and everyone participated and gave of their talents.

Stuart Cramer sincerely wanted to join the Mormon Church (The Church of Jesus Christ of Latter-day Saints) and was baptized before long. They were an extremely happy couple and came to Bishop Bernhard and asked him if he would perform the ceremony, which he did.

They were married in a little wedding chapel at the Forest Lawn Cemetery in Glendale, California, where about one hundred guests attended the ceremony. A reception was held at Terry's parent's home in Beverly Hills, where they were now residing.

The Cramer's built a beautiful home in the Trousdale Estates, above Beverly Hills, and they had two adorable little sons. The boys were brought to Sunday school, and it seemed that Terry had everything she would ever want.

I visited their home on several occasions and thought their beautiful relationship would last forever. I was really saddened when they broke up.

OUT OF BUSINESS

After Mr. Hughes married Jean, his personal contacts with girls ended. One by one they dropped out of the picture. The Christy-Sheppard photography studio slowed down; the voice and drama coaches had lots of free time; the Beverly Hills Hotel lost a lucrative resident; Mike Conrad, the private eye, could look for other clients; his barber, Eddie Alexander, didn't have to remain available; Walter Kane could relax for a while; and TWA would have to get along without him.

The only ones interested now were members of the press who constantly speculated on Howard Hughes—where was he, what did he look like, was he dead or alive, and when would he come out of hiding back into civilization again? When he gave his famous telephone interview, many thought he would come out of seclusion, but I knew that he would never be seen in public again.

LONDON AND NICARAGUA

The stories about Mr. Hughes wandering around the streets of London in various disguises are a lot of bologna. In March of 1973, I was in London for ten days with my dearest and closest friend, Ramona Bernhard, the wife of Dr. John T. Bernhard, the president of Western Illinois University and later the president of Western Michigan University. John is a former member of Mr. Hughes' staff.

We had heard that Howard Hughes was living at the Inn-On-The-Park Hotel in London, so we made contact with Allen Stroud and Jim Rickard, whom I had known at the Hughes offices since the 50s, who were with Mr. Hughes in London at that time. They said they would like to see us and we made a date for the next evening.

They picked us up at the Park Plaza Hotel in Lancaster Gate, where we were staying, and took us in style in a Rolls Royce with a chauffeur to the Carlton Towers Hotel where we had a delightful dinner and conversation.

We were told that just two days earlier, Mr. Hughes had met with Governor O'Callaghan of Nevada in his London suite. The only way Mr. Hughes could keep from losing his gaming licenses for his hotels in Las Vegas was to meet with the governor to prove that he was still alive. He put on his best appearance with his long hair and beard, and the governor gave him his license.

Allen and Jim told us that Mr. Hughes sat in his bare feet so that his visitor would see that his toenails weren't six inches long, as had been reported in the press. I don't know whether the governor noticed or not.

Two days before we left London, we were told that Mr. Hughes was in the hospital being operated on for a sinus infection. We doubted that this was true and believed it was another story that he wanted everyone to be told. We learned later that he had fallen and broken his hip.

Allen and Jim told us the story of their experience in Nicaragua. They were in Managua with Mr. Hughes and had their wives and families flown down to be with them during the Christmas holidays. Then the big earthquake hit the middle of the night, and more than 20,000 people were killed in it. It was a terrifying experience for them to be in the midst of it. They were stranded and there were no telephones to call for help.

They had to locate a ham radio operator to get word to Bill Gay in Los Angeles that they were okay and to send a specific kind of jet aircraft to pick up Mr. Hughes and the people with him. Fortunately, the hotel they stayed in wasn't damaged a great deal, and they were thankful to finally get out of there. It was a holiday they will long remember.

It was right after the earthquake that they flew to London and got settled in the Inn-On-The-Park Hotel, and we had our visit with them.

CHANGES TAKE PLACE

When Howard Hughes completely withdrew from the public view, many of his trusted staff members felt that there was not a great future in store for them. One by one they were lured away to challenging jobs where they were free to expand in the fields they had been trained for.

One great loss to the organization was when Dr. John T. Bernhard left and went to the Brigham Young University as president Ernest Wilkinson's administrative assistant. He also served as state senator in the Utah legislature. From the BYU he went to Western Illinois University as president for five years, and then was president of Western Michigan University in Kalamazoo until his retirement. To this day, John and his wife, Ramona, have remained our dearest friends. They, too, remember the experience of working for Mr. Hughes to be a fascinating chapter in their lives.

Francis Fillerup left to become an assistant to the Chancellor of USC, Dr. Rufus B. von KleinSmid. Francis rejoined the organization in about 1974 and moved to Las Vegas to handle Mr. Hughes' properties there.

Leon Frazier returned to Provo, Utah, where he practiced law until his sudden death. Dr. Ernest Wilkins also moved to Provo where he taught languages at BYU and had some language books published. Hank DiRoma left and Don Alder accepted a responsible position with Savon Drugs in Los Angeles where he remained until he retired.

After Marty Cook got his California law degree, he went to work as counsel for a railroad firm. During the same period, Chester Davis and Cox found a need to open a law firm in California. For this he would need an attorney licensed in California to head up his new offices. Because of Marty's long staff association with Mr. Hughes, Bill Gay recommended Marty to Chester Davis to head up the newly established firm.

Many others left and other were hired. The empire had not dwindled, but had grown to be a gigantic conglomerate.

LIBERATED WOMAN

After all this time, I was still making less than $200 a week, while others with less responsibility, were making twice that much. In those days if you were a married woman working you might receive less salary than a single woman doing the same job. The attitude was that you had a husband to support you.

I'm not a woman's libber but I have always been a "liberated" woman. I'm a strong supporter of equal pay for women after my past experience with the Hughes organization. I never blamed Howard Hughes for this, as Bill Gay and Nadine Henley were solely responsible for the salary I made.

The situation I was in would never exist today. Thank heaven.

MY EXIT AND RETURN

More than six years had passed since I entered the building on Romaine Street, and many changes had taken place. Some employees had gone to Florida to work on the Howard Hughes Medical Institute, and Mr. Hughes had departed Los Angeles to live in the Bahamas for a while. My active days of working with him were over. He was meeting with no one at this time, and he had only those aides who traveled with him to take care of his needs.

Bill Gay had absented himself from the office on Romaine Street, and I felt that it was time to go home to my family once again. My dear daughter, Joan, was now thirteen, and she needed a mother at home more than ever. And Rich was going to have a full-time wife again. I had stayed much longer than I had ever expected to stay, and I felt that my work was finished.

I notified Bill that I wanted to quit my job, and when I left I was given a lovely farewell luncheon at Scandia Restaurant in Hollywood. Many members of the staff were present, including Bill and Nadine and others. I was presented with a lovely Steuben glass vase and said my good-byes to those I had worked with for so many years.

Just a short while after I left the organization the office contacted me and asked if I would work with Raymond Holliday and Raymond Cook, together with some other attorneys, on a special project for Mr. Hughes. It would only last for a few weeks so I accepted the offer—besides I was very fond of working with the two Raymond's, both wonderful men. We had a large suite at the Beverly Wilshire Hotel where the old typewriter was set up once again and work was begun on negotiations for the sale of Hughes Aircraft Company.

The work went on endlessly for many weeks, and after the negotiations fell through, I once again returned to my home.

"DID YOU EVER MEET HIM?"

To this day I still get asked this same question even by people who knew that I worked for Howard Hughes personally. "But did you ever meet him?" I think the answer is obvious.

Howard Hughes (signature)

Court

A copy of the document from a court proceeding dated April 19, 1979, Case No. 8225, Dept. No. I, the Eight Judicial District Court of the State of Nevada, Clark County follows. It has been digitally compiled from six Xeroxed pages which, unfortunately dropped out the bottom lines of the odd pages and the top line on the even pages. They are presented as much in their entirety as possible.

APK 19 1979 D & C · LA

1 CASE NO. 8225

2 DEPT. NO. I

3

4

5 IN THE EIGHTH JUDICIAL DISTRICT COURT OF THE STATE

6 OF NEVADA IN AND FOR THE COUNTY OF CLARK

7

8 In the Matter of the Estate)

9 of)

10 HOWARD ROBARD HUGHES, JR.,)   Affidavit of

11 Deceased.)   David B. Tinnin

12)

13

14 State of New York)

15 County of New York)   ss.

16

17 I, David B. Tinnin, being first put on oath do

18 depose and state that the following is true and correct of my

19 own personal knowledge:

20 1. I am currently living and working in Zurich,

21 Switzerland, employed as a staff correspondent for Fortune

22 Magazine. Prior to my employment by Fortune Magazine, I was

23 employed by Time Magazine as a reporter. During the years

24 1960 through 1967, my duties encompassed the reporting of

25 business news, including a specialization in aircraft trans-

26 portation. As a part of that work I reported for Time

27 Magazine on matters pertaining to Howard R. Hughes and Trans

29 Mr. Hughes which commenced in 1961. From 1968 until 1973, in

30 addition to my job as a reporter, I researched and wrote a

31 book (published by Doubleday in 1973), on the subject of the

32 litigation between T.W.A. and Mr. Hughes entitled "Just About

-2-

1 Everybody vs. Howard Hughes".

2   2. In the course of my duties as a reporter, and
3 in researching for my book, I became well acquainted with Mr.
4 Raymond A. Cook, an attorney and, until his death, a member of
5 the Houston, Texas law firm of Andrews, Kurth, Campbell & Jones.
6 I met and spoke with Mr. Cook at length on subjects involving
7 Mr. Hughes on numerous occasions commencing in late 1960 or
8 early 1961 and continuing until late 1972.

9   3. Mr. Cook, as an attorney for Mr. Hughes and his
10 companies, was intimately involved in the affairs of Mr. Hughes,
11 and Mr. Cook often would provide me with background information
12 and explanations to enable me to understand events and place
13 them in their proper context in my reporting and writing.

14   4. In late 1960 or early 1961 Mr. Cook and I had
15 a conversation on the subject of the ability of Mr. Hughes to
16 obtain financing for the purchase of jet aircraft for T.W.A.
17 In this context I asked Mr. Cook why Mr. Hughes could not use
18 the assets of Hughes Aircraft Company as a source of such
19 financing. Mr. Cook responded by telling me that those assets
20 were no longer available for the use of Mr. Hughes because
21 Hughes Aircraft Company (or HAC as it was referred to) had been
22 given to the Howard Hughes Medical Institute. Cook then said
23 that Mr. Hughes had a Will and that the Will substantially gave
24 everything to the Howard Hughes Medical Institute.

25   5. During the course of the foregoing conversation
26 between Mr. Cook and me, Mr. Cook also told me that he had
27 drafted a Will for Mr. Hughes; that Mr. Cook had handed his

29 received the Will back from Mr. Hughes in envelopes. Mr. Cook
30 said that the outer envelope stated something like "Open
31 Immediately After Death", and contained instructions that the
32 inner envelope was not to be opened until approximately three

335

-3-

1   or five years after the death of Mr. Hughes. Mr. Cook said that

2   he had placed the envelopes in a safety deposit box at a bank,

3   the name and location of which I do not recall.

4   6. On several later occasions Mr. Cook spoke to me

5   on the subject of Mr. Hughes' Will. Over all the years, Mr.

6   Cook's statements to me were consistently the same: Mr. Cook

7   had drafted a Will for Mr. Hughes; Mr. Cook had given that Will

8   to Mr. Hughes; and Mr. Hughes had returned the Will to Mr. Cook

9   a short time later in a sealed envelope.

10   7. The last conversation I had with Mr. Cook on the

11 subject of a Will of Mr. Hughes occurred in December, 1972. We

12 were discussing possible courses of action by Mr. Hughes in the

13 event he prevailed in the T.W.A. litigation. The conversation

14 then turned to what arrangements had been made with respect to

15 Mr. Hughes' affairs following his death. Mr. Cook stated, and

16 in doing so he was repeating what he had previously said to me,

17 that there was indeed a Howard Hughes Will; that it was a binding

18 Will; that it was in existence at that time; and that Mr. Cook

19 had full confidence that the Will would be produced and be of

20 binding effect after the death of Mr. Hughes.

21   8. Immediately following the death of Mr. Hughes in

22 April, 1976 (Mr. Cook having died earlier), and acting in my

23 capacity as a newsman, I traveled to Houston and telephoned

24 several Houston banks and asked them if they had any information

25 concerning any safety deposit boxes containing sealed envelopes

26 . . . . the death of Mr. Hughes. I received no

27 positive responses. My reason for making such telephone calls

28 was my recollection of what had been told me by Mr. Cook as

29 related above, and my surmise that Mr. Cook had been referring to

30 a Houston bank as the location of the bank where he had placed

31 the envelopes of Mr. Hughes containing his Will.

32

Howard Hughes [signature]

The Aviation Hall of Fame Award

Awarded December 14, 1973 at Dayton, Ohio

"Developing an intense interest in aviation, Hughes took flying lessons while in his teens. In 1925 he began a career as a movie producer and in 1930 premiered his movie *Hell's Angels*, which generated a worldwide interest in aviation.

"Setting a straightaway speed record of 212 mph in 1933, Hughes later won the Sportsman Pilot event of the All American Meet. In 1934 he built his H-1 Racer that gave birth to the Hughes Aircraft Company and in which he set a world's speed record of 352 mph. In 1935 he set a transcontinental record of 9 hours and 27 minutes in his Northrup "Gamma," for which he received the Harmon Trophy. In 1937 he set a new transcontinental record of 7 hours 28 minutes in his modified H-1; and he acquired control of Transcontinental and Western Airlines (TWA). In 1938 he and a crew of four completed a flight around the world in 3 days 19 hours for which he received the Harmon and Collier Trophies and the Congressional Medal. He began the development of the XF-11 warplane in 1938. He initiated the design of the Lockhead "Constellation," and during World War II flew the first model from coast to coast in 7 hours. During the war he built the "Hercules," a huge flying boat that he successfully flew in 1947. After the war, he was seriously injured in a crash of the XF-11. After recovering, he converted Hughes Aircraft Company into a successful electronics firm. He continued to expand TWA, converting it into one of the world's leading international airlines. Later he formed the Hughes Airwest Airline.

"To Howard Robard Hughes, for outstanding contributions to aviation by his development of advanced design aircraft, by setting aerial records that demonstrated the capabilities of aircraft, and by development of domestic and international commercial aviation, this award is most solemnly and respectfully dedicated."